Retiring in Costa Rica
Or Doctors, Dogs and Pura Vida

By Helen Dunn Frame

Cover Photos show a beautiful Costa Rican sunset, a Cattleya maxima orchid sold here, a part German Sheppard rescued from abuse, one of doggi divinos's clients and my two black girls born in the same liter to a rescued former street dog.

"True Happiness of a retired nature, and an enemy to pomp and noise; it arises, in the first place, from the enjoyment of one's self; and, in the next, from the friendship and conversation of a few select companions." The Spectator, No. 15, March 17, 1711

Time is too slow for those who wait, too swift for those who fear, too long for those who rejoice, but for those who love, time is eternity. Quote from Henry Van Dyke from inscription written in 1852 for Katrina's Sun Dial in her Garden of Yaddo. She was born on my birthday, November 10th.

"The time is always right to do what is right," said Martin Luther King, Jr.

"A donde fueres, has lo que vieres, sino váyase a Roma, or Al pueblo que fueres, haz lo que vieres". These translate roughly that when in Costa Rica do as the Ticos.

"Si no se adapta, vallase al carajo (al infierno)" Loosely translated, If you don't adapt, you burn in hot water.

4

DEDICATION

To all the Baby Boomers seeking Paradise for Retirement

TABLE OF CONTENTS

ACKNOWLEGMENTS

Please extend my thanks to Ryan Piercy, General Manager, Association of Residents in Costa Rica (ARCR), for reviewing the manuscript, to Rowdy Rhodes, editor, writer, and friend, for editing and advice, and to Laurie Sklar, doggi divino, for sharing photos of dogs. As third party input always lends credibility, gratefully Jo Stuart and George Lundquist gave me permission to quote them. A special thanks to Celia Coleman who shared her experiences in publishing on Kindle and with Create Space as well as providing information about movers. To friends, including Margaret Hegboum, who provided input and those who told me stories anonymously, thank you.

INTRODUCTION

Including my Credentials

Living in Costa Rica, or in any foreign country, definitely does not suit everyone. It may be more suitable for a dream vacation home or an outstanding investment.

That is correct! Before you determine if it rates as a desired adventure for you, read about Costa Rica from various viewpoints and investigate the country with the Pura Vida mentality. Here's how Wikipedia defines the term.

"Pura Vida literally means "pure life", but the meaning is closer to "full of life", "purified life", "is living!", "going great", or "cool!" It can be used as a greeting, as a word of farewell, to express satisfaction, or to politely express indifference when describing something. The phrase used by many Costa Ricans (and expatriates) since 1956 has become widely known as an expression of a leisurely lifestyle, of disregard for time, and of wanton friendliness. However, Costa Ricans use the phrase to express a philosophy of strong community, perseverance, resilience in overcoming difficulties with good spirits, enjoying life slowly, and celebrating good fortune of magnitudes small and large alike."

The first time I responded with the phrase "Pura Vida", the Tico's face lit up with a huge smile. The story about the phrase alleges that Costa Ricans adopted it from some surfing pioneers in the 1950s. Ticos (non-pejorative name they call themselves) often incorporate words they fancy into their language, a Spanish that varies a bit from that spoken in other countries. They seem tickled when foreigners use their expressions.

Please note that much of the anecdotal content in this book provides positive and negative information based on my personal adventure as well as others' experiences. Like the game of telephone, third person reports often lack authenticity. It is for you to judge. A few chapters will contain letters or epistles I wrote to friends and family members over the years that I've lived in Costa Rica. Especially detailed, they offer some insights because I wrote them at the time I lived and felt them and not from fading memories.

Some stories relate tales told by others; some I adapted from articles I have read, and third party reports. Some friends have given me permission to use their input and I credited those stories to the sources. However, not everyone wanted to fess up in print. As a result, some true sagas defaulted to a *Nome de plume*. Sobriquets don't matter. Some of the experiences related may assist you in realizing your destiny to live comfortably abroad. My positive adventure included relatively few frustrating experiences as I learned to live in yet another different culture. If you disagree with me based on your personal adventure, controversy remains the spice of life's experiences.

Originally, I titled the book: "Don't Leave Your Intelligence at the Border" because so many people who come to Costa Rica tend to leave common sense behind. Someone else suggested adding "With the Lost Luggage" to emphasize the phenomenon.

Bottom line: Why should you value what I have to say?

Consider me a conduit. In addition to being an experienced author, writer, and editor, as well as having lived the life, I have researched extensively. I collected data, information, and, in essence, performed due diligence. I have traveled at least once in 50 countries and lived in two other countries, England and Germany, besides Costa Rica and the United States. In North America, I lived on the East and West coasts and in the Mid-west: New York City, San Francisco, and Dallas. Furthermore, I have journeyed to every state in the union at least once.

Many people have called me courageous because I packed up and moved to Costa Rica by myself. Knowing dreams have no deadlines, I decided to follow mine and live abroad. The details of how I made my decision to migrate and subsequently accomplished it divulge what may have gone through my mind as I determined that I would regret not going to Costa Rica for the rest of my life.

Feeling I should maximize my potential, I could hear my deceased son who I consider "my Guardian angel" saying, "Go for it Mom!"

For more information about me, to view a slide show, and to click on any links in the book, go to: **www.helendunnframe.com**

Among the myriad of topics addressed in this guide to loving life in Costa Rica, include doctors and dogs. As we age, having a four-legged companion seems to aid in sustaining a longer life. We have more time to explore the most prevalent topics of conversation: grandkids, ailments, medications, medical personnel, and health facilities. My book also offers value for tire kickers assessing Costa Rica as a vacation paradise or for medical procedures.

The information contained here puts you hours ahead of finding out stuff on your own. If nothing more, you may enjoy reading *Doctors, Dogs, and Pura Vida in Intriguing Costa Rica.* Never mind that I repeat a few things in order to emphasize their importance. To begin your search, you can get a promotional overview of Costa Rica by watching a video: **http://www.youtube.com/watch?v=V5hA-i-1Ssg&feature=related** (If you are reading online, slide the cursor over this link and it will tell you what to do to access it from here.)

While you enjoy the stories herein, think about what images you conjure up in your mind about Costa Rica. Great beaches, lush reserves, glorious birds, fantastic flowers and friendly people probably come to mind.

Costa Rica may stretch your creative problem solving skills but if you determinedly plan to make it work, like a marriage, you may come to love the country. Jumping the hurdles of life in the tropics inevitably makes you stronger and maybe wiser. If you later realize life in Central America isn't for you, moving on is an option.

Perhaps you could add to your images of Costa Rica life in the big but not beautiful city of San Jose. It bustles with hordes of people most days of the week making it best to walk with determination even if you do not know your destination. The Chinese added a stadium to Sabana Park's landscape rating raves and criticisms. In many people's views, it creates noise, extra traffic, and takes away from the park. For those who enjoy sports and concerts there, the Chinese receive kudos for building it.

Some performers have boycotted performing in it due to allegedly high fees charged by the management. In contrast, here and there in the city the homeless sleep off what they may have imbibed or perhaps to mask hunger. Street vendors lay their wares on black plastic sheets or bags on the uneven sidewalks, ready to fold up camp at a moment's notice if a gendarme appears or it starts to rain.

Taxis line up waiting for fares. As the first in the queue gets a fare, the drivers move forward, often by pushing their cars rather than wasting gasoline by starting them up. Sometimes drivers use the time to polish their vehicles or to visit with other chauffeurs.

Garbage once stacked high soon lies scattered because many street dogs rummaged through the bags and boxes.

Photographers hang around the Teatro Naciónal ready to snap a visitor's photo with hopes of selling it to him or her. Others offer the defunct five colones bill that sports a famous painting found in the Teatro Nacional for a mere ¢1000 or about $2. A silver colored coin replaced the bill.

A man may determinedly walk with a rusty folded bike resting on his shoulder. Guys try to collect money from drivers or sell fruits, cell covers, or sunglasses. A woman with or without a child or two may approach with a paper written in Spanish and English asking for money. Beware of pulling out your wallet no matter how much empathy you have. You might carry coins or a small bill in your pocket if you feel generous. Many parks offer respite for lovers and contain interesting statuary. In summary, San Jose provides a different kind of candy for the eyes, even if it sometimes feels like someone previously chewed it a bit.

It's a given that you will spend time and energy on choosing a place to live and your mode of transportation. You will agonize over what to bring, if anything. However, does your special "To Do List" include adapting to the culture?

Have you considered the real life and the day-to-day events of existence? These may make the difference between a mediocre experience and a wonderful adventure.

Keep in mind that Costa Rica topped the list of "happiest" nations in the world out of 142 countries surveyed (the United States ranked 114th) according to an independent research group in Great Britain. The New Economics Foundation also stated that Ticos have the second highest average life expectancy. La Nación, a daily Spanish language newspaper, reported in 2009 that 937 Ticos lived over 100 years. In 2000, only 231 had celebrated that many birthdays.

Update: Revista Dominical, La Nación's Sunday Magazine, reported on January 6, 2013 that according to the 2011 census 509 people 100 or more years old had registered. However, the article suggested that the actual number is nearly 1200 because the number registered in 2007 was 331.

In addition, according to a 2009 poll by Latinobaró Melio, a Chilean Governmental Organization that handles opinion polls around Latin America, 84% of the Costa Rican respondents had a high opinion of the U.S. Some 92% felt relations between the two countries (U.S. and C.R.) appeared good. In the then current political climate, the poll also found Costa Ricans optimistic about their families' future.

This tome aims to enable you to make an informed decision about retiring or part-time living in Costa Rica. Make it your goal to experience a life as positive as mine. Throughout the book, you will find questions and sources to help you get current answers that should result in making a wise choice. The resources checked at the time of publication appeared accurate but are subject to change. Over the time it has taken to compile this book, I found myself adding more and more information as life in Costa Rica evolved. I finally had to decide this is it. Fin!

One more point. Years ago when I worked in real estate I would state emphatically that every architect should have to live in his or her creation for three months to learn what not to do next time. Now I am convinced that readers who are annoyed by typos or even presumed errors of content due to different experiences, need to try to write a book and be their own editors. I recall reading a friend's book after publication and finding one typo. He was upset about it because he had paid an editor to review the manuscript. Therefore, I plan to write a blog on my website as well as contribute to other blogs to update information in an effort to keep the book a valuable resource. So please be my extra pair of eyes. If you learn about anything you feel would be interesting to readers, or question something, please email me at helen@helendunnframe.com. NOTE: Links in this book are also on the website.

For those readers who think they recognize themselves in the book, consider it purely coincidental unless you gave permission to relate the tales. Perhaps some of these real life stories fall into the same category as the myths, fantasies, and legends permeating intriguing Costa Rica.

BONUS: A *Moving Guide* is available *free of charge* to purchasers of this book. It includes tips about packing, work sheets and pages for notes. Email me at helen@helendunnframe.com for the password so you may download it from my website: www.helendunnframe.com. Life in Costa Rica kept changing as I wrote this book. Not only will I update information in future editions, you may find new data on my website. Therefore, you might want to log on from time to time if you are planning a move to Costa Rica.

CHAPTER One

Why Move to Costa Rica?

You Decide. . .

Question: "Why did you choose Costa Rica for retirement?"

Sometimes the answer to this frequently broached question reflects the ability to live better on less money although with the change in the financial climate, some people feel the assumption less valid. Those whose income primarily stems from Social Security may feel reluctant to admit they need to continue working beyond the age of 65. Suze Orman, known for financial acumen, encourages folk to wait until 67 or 70 to retire now in order to have a bigger fund. People with means suspect they can continue to live the high life much easier in Costa Rica than at home. (If you watch HGTV programs, many people seeking homes overseas have very large budgets and pinpoint Costa Rica often as a destination.)

Others leave their countries for the oldest democracy in Central America because the laws and politics drive them crazy, or perhaps to escape the law or creditors. Feeling unwanted by society, many believe they can fit in better with Expats who undoubtedly appear a bit eccentric in order to make the transition. Some realize that Costa Rica in August 2010 placed 35th in Newsweek's top 100 nations ranked by economy, education, politics, health and quality of life and second in the Latin American and Caribbean group.

Still other people may feel Big Brother drives them to the brink. On the other hand, the current political situation requires exiting. Some come to work or join communities, others to build them. Maybe a horrendous divorce motivated a person to flee. An unusual reason if still valid reflects a Canadian law that makes it unlawful for elderly parents to live independently in the home with adult children and their families even if they co-own it. Apparently, parents can live in a separate apartment if they own the house jointly (per Property Virgins).

Some eschew shoveling snow and freezing weather. Some men fantasize that marrying young women about their daughters' ages will keep them young. (Then they discover they married her entire family and not just the primary members. Sometimes the only way to escape the dilemma means fleeing Costa Rica.)

On the other side of the coin, due diligence reveals low property taxes, a great variety of restaurants, the lack of an army and terrorism threats, and the ability to watch familiar TV programs on cable except when transmission stammers. The fact the large Expat community enables a good quality of life also attracts settlers. Check out Costa Rica's ranking in the Global Peace Index: **http://www.visionofhumanity.org/gpi-data/#/2010/scor**. Canada scored higher but the United States far lower when I checked.

When I first visited Costa Rica in the 1990s in Puntarenas, I fell in love with the country. While there, I had an opportunity to tour the area with a man who spent six months a year in the city and owned businesses, land, a small rental house, and was building motel like suites. In the early 1990s, while benefits had decreased from years before they were far better than in recent years. (For example, one could import a car duty free.) However, I had no way to support myself in Costa Rica.

Fast forward to 2004! The son of a dear friend from childhood was investigating investing in a hotel property in Costa Rica. I watched his video about the place and fell in love with the country again. I started researching it, its lifestyle, people, culture and laws. Friends urged me to visit the country for as long as possible. This is when I decided to take a tour of the Central Valley and live for a few weeks in a casita with only essentials outside of Santiago de Puriscal.

When I wrote a friend about the experience and that I was considering moving here, he wrote back, "You already have decided to go. You just haven't told yourself that."

Bottom line: be honest with yourself about your motivations. If the real answer reveals trying to escape dealing with ghosts of years past, it won't work. Use your money to deal with your baggage first because you can't leave psychological problems at the border. Stamping your passport doesn't eliminate the necessity of living with and feeling content about yourself.

CHAPTER Two

Where to Stay While Exploring

Short Term Rentals, Hostels, Bed and Breakfast
Facilities and Hotels -- Have you heard about Motels?

Until a discussion appeared on Costa Rica Living (an online chat group) I hadn't even considered motels as a place to consider staying along with hostels, Bed & Breakfast facilities, hotels and resorts. Which type of accommodation chosen depended on the traveler's budget and how native a person yearned to live. After reading the posts, it occurred to me some people who drove through Mexico chose motels because they had secured garages, usually patrolled by armed guards, for their vehicles stuffed with belongings.

Motels in Costa Rica seem to remind people of those in the States in the 60s, places where one could rent by the hour for sex. In Costa Rica guests rent for 12 hours, but if they leave, apparently the maid prepares the room immediately for the next occupants. So eat before renting or bring food and beverages if the place doesn't offer room service. Ice machines apparently dot every other floor.

Then the discussion in the group turned to hiring a prostitute. Some said illegal but tolerated but like many discussions no definitive answer was provided. Another participant suggested consulting articles 167 through 172 of the Codigo Penal that covers variations of pimping, underage prostitution, and more.

Mimicking the days of old in the United States, motels vary from sleazy to some very nice accommodations, some even featuring Jacuzzi tubs. When I rented a casita in a rural area near Santiago de Puriscal in 2004, a one room house with a bath and kitchenette, it cost ¢10,000 a day (now $20 but more then). As I recall the exchange rate fluctuated in the low ¢400s. Depending on the location, B&B prices seem very reasonable; hotels run the gamut, and resorts, pricey.

To decide where you want to sleep, research "hotels in Costa Rica" or start with these websites:

http://www.costaricapages.com/listings/hotels.htm,

http://www.anywherecostarica.com/hotels ,

http://www.costaricanhotels.com/ ,

http://www.discoveringcostarica.com/hotels costa rica.htm and

http://www.therealcostarica.com/travel costa rica/hotels accomodatio ns costa rica.html. Check this link for more hostel information:

http://www.hostelz.com/hostels/Costa-Rica/San-Jos%C3%A9-Province/San-Jos%C3%A9

CHAPTER Three

That Ugly Word "Expat"

Can we Coin another Term?

An expatriate (or expat for short) temporarily or permanently resides in a country and culture other than that of his or her origin. The word comes from the Latin term expatriātus that means ex ("out of") and patria ("country, fatherland"). At one time, it included exiled folks but it evidently has lost that connotation.

When a Tico asks me where I'm from, I either answer with the long version or with the most recent location (Dallas, Texas). I usually add, "I'm a Tica now because I have a cédula." It always rates a chuckle because I am pale with red hair faded by sun and age to strawberry blond!

I haven't heard the word Gringo (Gringa) said in a pejorative manner here. Personally, I'm not offended by the word although some people feel it originated in Mexico as a way of telling U.S. workers who wore green shirts to go home. Some expats from other countries resent people lumping them together with Americans but locals often find it difficult to tell if someone hails from Canada or Europe. Haven't you heard the phrase, "All people of some race look alike?" It's really not true if you observe carefully.

Many people believe the term Gringo means "stranger" and use the name to include anyone other than a Costa Rican. Check out: **http://etimologias.dechile.net/?gringo**. I equate the use of the name with that of Tico and Tica, just words that denote certain groups of people in this case Costa Ricans. Even Nicaraguans refer to themselves as Nicos or Nicas.

Question: "Why do we call ethnic groups in Africa and other countries "tribes' while we call tribes in Europe 'ethnic groups"?" Also we brand areas where people of the same nationality congregate as "ghettos". Should we call the expensive compounds developed in Costa /Rica where foreigners that are more affluent congregate by the same word? Often in the States we refer to immigrants as "aliens" or more often "illegal aliens" when they entered illegally. Should those foreigners living in Costa Rica without proper documentation, often referred to as proverbial tourists, be termed "illegal aliens"?

For five years, I had a pensionada status; now I have permanent residency but I'm still an immigrant. I consider myself a New Yorker (my city of birth) and very much an American citizen even though residing permanently in the States remains too costly for me. I hear the word "expat" more among foreigners in Costa Rica but I don't recall calling immigrants to the States by that term. When I lived in Europe for five years, I didn't use either word. In my opinion, someone needs to invent a more pleasant term to signify foreigners from any country and drop "expat" from the dictionary.

CHAPTER Four

Names by Any Other

Learning to Live with How Natives Pronounce and Interpret your Name

"Señora Dune" took me a while to respond to in Costa Rica. I finally gave up trying to explain Dunn is my maiden name and Frame my married family name that I had to keep in Texas when I divorced my son's father because our child was only seven years old. According to my attorney, in 1973 the law demanded it. In Costa Rica, spouses have different names unless they happen to have the same surname because a limited number of family names exist. At least my legal documents contain the correct version because they followed the name in my United States passport.

Children in Costa Rica take their father's first last name as their first last name and their mother's first last name as their second last name. To clarify it more, a man named Jose Urrutia Mora marries Lourdes Sanchez Charpentier. Their children's last name combines the two: Urrutia Sanchez.

Hence, natives think Dunn is my first last name, sometimes spelled Dun (thus the pronunciation sounds like "Dune," something found on a beach). Sometimes they spell Helen as "Hellen". Often I find my name tags filled under D instead of F. Helen sometimes sounds like Ellen because the H often is silent in Spanish.

If you find a significant other, assuming you didn't come with one, and choose to live together even without marriage, having different names facilitates the arrangement. After a while friends consider these couples married. Sometimes having different names complicates matters. A CAJA (socialized medicine) account in the man's name can cover the woman. She needs to have a valid Carne Asegurado Familiar and at least a copy of the receipt showing an up-to-date payment to the CCSS made by the husband (Asegurado directo).

As an aside that I find amusing, the first time I heard a boyfriend call his Tica girlfriend Gordita happened when my smiling plump Tica friend proudly showed me a text message from her novio. Later I learned other endearments of affection: Gordillo (fat man), Ballenita (little whale), Negrito (little black man), Flaco (skinny), Moreno (brown man), all names we find offensive in English. Perhaps they equate to Mon Petite Chou in French (my little cabbage)? I lovingly sometimes call my chunky dog Leda Gordita and her tail wags.

As the pronunciation of words varies from English when speaking Costa Rican Spanish, even my dogs' names sound different. One responds to Davida (David plus "a") and the other Leda (from Leda and the Swan).

Locals pronounce the first name with the accent on the last a, so it sounds like Da-vi-da. Ticos pronounce the second name lay – da. These native girls respond to commands in both languages. Incidentally, as I recall Dog Whisperer Cesar Milan believes dogs don't really know the words but respond to the tone of voice. I like to think they are bilingual.

Foreigners don't always make the effort to learn a native's name especially when it's totally new to their ears. Even names we know sound different to us. For example, Eli sounds like A-lee.

One American introduced a native woman to me as Lydia. When we exchanged phone numbers, she told me, "My name is Ligia (Li-he-a)." Knowing that one's name is profoundly important to the person, I try my best to pronounce it correctly and to use it often in conversation and emails.

Sometimes foreigners find it difficult to put their tongues around Costa Rican names just as they struggle to pronounce our names. If you make the effort to learn, however, you will have a start on La Forma and acceptance by locals.

CHAPTER Five

Understanding the culture

A Road Map to Happiness in Costa Rica

Put right at the top of your "To Do List" of things to consider before you move, "Learn about Costa Rican culture". It will pay dividends in a more successful adventure. Never mind focusing intently on whether to live in the city, at the beach or in the mountains, what type of house to buy or rent, and what belongings to ship, if you can't live within the culture, you'll soon hightail it back to whence you came.

Increasingly important for all expats ranks an acute awareness of the implications of our international interpersonal encounters, even more than "The Ugly American" of the sixties. Our contemporary world remains polluted by cross-cultural misunderstandings, historical ethnic disdain, and various faux pas just as many rivers in Costa Rica reek of garbage. Today even casual travel requires personal and geopolitical responsibility.

It harkens back to my days in college when we learned in Sociology and Anthropology the definition of a culture encompassed shared values, practices, and rituals that permeate a society. While traditions pervade, occasionally different and unique individuals may contradict in some fashion dominant cultural traits or values thereby confusing the stranger trying to understand a group.

For Ticos, decorum ranks of the utmost importance. Most natives will do everything possible to avoid confrontation. Appearances include personal hygiene. A speaker at a woman's group told everyone to wet their hair before meeting with a Tico even if s/he preferred to shower in the evening.

Speaking candidly often creates a problem because Costa Ricans generally avoid conflict in all interpersonal encounters. People eagerly say untrue things because they feel the listener wants to hear a certain response. (Don't forget expats lie too.) For example, a Tico will attempt to give directions without a clue about a destination's location. A worker may agree to arrive at 8 a.m. because you wanted him there at that time although he had another job and couldn't come until noon. I call it Tico Time and try practicing patience. A Tico may accept an invitation and then not show up without explanation or a phone call. To cause a scandal, a public commotion, and even raising one's voice in public definitely are unacceptable behaviour.

At its most practical level, the appearance principle means that you should warmly greet all Tico friends and acquaintances you happen to meet. Everyone should ask permission to enter a Tico home. If invited to a Tico function, inquire about the proper attire. "Tico time", the tendency of many Costa Ricans to show up late or not at all to meetings, appointments and other commitments often causes expats frustrations. However, it's a generalization. Not all Ticos arrive late or don't call if they can't come. Perhaps time has not yet equalled "money" in the Tico society. Costa Ricans experience time in abundance, like a delightful climate, beautiful children, and a spectacular countryside. It results in a moment becoming an end rather than a means.

Don't forget the theory of event versus appointment. When you invite a Tico to dinner, he may show up two hours late because he thinks of it as an event, not a time specific invitation. More and more I find that Costa Ricans that deal regularly with foreigners have adapted themselves. I have service people who come when they say they will and arrive promptly ... or call.

By European or North American standards Costa Rica often ranks as a third world country although it has graduated to an emerging country. While the cost of living climbs, lower income citizens permeate the society. Yet you only have to go to one of the modern malls like Multiplaza oeste to realize a solid Costa Rican middle class exists and many Costa Ricans claim considerable assets if they don't boast about them. Many locals believe that all foreigners are wealthy regardless of the truth. Just by the number of things in a home, or the ability to dine out at will, or to have money on hand without working feeds the myth.

CHAPTER Six

Legends Permeate Culture in Towns and Beaches

Like Fairy Tales of Yore, Witches, Headless Priests and
Wagons without Oxen Fill Legends

"A legend (Latin, legenda, "things to be read") is a narrative of human actions that are perceived both by teller and listeners to take place within human history and to possess certain qualities that give the tale verisimilitude. Legend, for its active and passive participants, includes no happenings that are outside the realm of "possibility", defined by a highly flexible set of parameters, which may include miracles that are perceived as actually having happened, within the specific tradition of indoctrination where the legend arises, and within which it may be transformed over time, in order to keep it fresh and vital, and realistic." Wikipedia

As in any culture, the stories passed from generation to generation lend insight into traditions. While we may feel sophisticated and beyond such beliefs, considering such tales provides diversity and insight into people's mindsets. Escazú, an upscale enclave of architectural sophistication and urban chic including U.S. and British Ambassador residences, North and South American and European immigrants; and trendy bars and restaurants, continues to grow expeditiously despite its fame as the "City of Witches".

Confirming its reputation, the municipal flag and the town seal displayed on the Town Hall each feature a broom-mounted witch, and the local soccer team is named *Las Brujas* (The Witches). In addition, can you believe that cautious locals reputedly still secretly consult modern day hexes before making important decisions in their lives, careers, or relationships?

Apparently, exactly how many people fall victim to frauds and cons by "brujeria" (witchcraft) in Costa Rica is unknown. As a result, the sub-director del Organismo de Investigación Judicial (OIJ) called on legislators to close the loophole in the law that allows the practice of brujeria, including placing misleading ads in the media.

If you scan the pages of the local newspapers in Costa Rica ads offer services from increasing sexual potency, recovering a lost love, to winning the lottery. Often a bruja will ask for a picture of a loved one inferring that magic can bring back that lost love.

In the barrios, a report indicated, tarot card and palm readings cost only a few thousand colones and although no signs advertise the service on the door, everyone one knows where the witch performs the "magic". Some offer services of cleansing one's home, office or business of evil spirits; others use candles, incense and incantations. The darker side where the bruja allegedly places a curse or conjures up spells rarely appears in the ads. Magic in Costa Rica comes under different names that include "sacerdotisas", shaman", and "diosas de la santería haitiana".

Even in the 21ˢᵗ Century, Escazú remains the sleepy, mysterious resting place for pre-Columbian Indian tribes and the legendary meeting place for magical creatures. Plants with certain "powers" and "magical" herbs grow in gardens. Modern day Brujas still use them to make a man love a woman, cast spells, or cure illnesses. In fact, practically all of the town's history links with legend. The native people remain proud of their history, restored edifices, and scenery.

One such Escazú tale includes the story about the unfortunate, but enigmatic *Tulevieja* (literally old veiled hat), probably the area's most celebrated ghostly bruja. Often described as a hideous half-naked hag sometimes with a chicken's body, she reportedly roamed the night-darkened *Calles* and peered through windows in search of the illegitimate baby she starved to death. Allegedly stronger than twenty horses, no one could catch the *Tulevieja*.

However, according to a more recent version, among those still spooking naughty children into more acceptable behavior, a young Escazú daredevil, Liborio Constantino de Jesús Fernández Delgado (nicknamed don Tuto Yoyo), who lived one hundred years (1888-1988), tied her up with a magic vine that grows in the Escazú hills by the enchanted *Piedra Blanca* (White Stone). Allegedly, he tamed the crone and paraded her around Escazú like a pet dog. Does it suggest shades of Taming of the Shrew? Over the years, *Tulevieja*, along with Don Tuto Yoyo, had faded into the dim recesses of people's minds until a group of archeologists excavating near the *Piedra Blanca* unearthed a petrified segment of vine.

Some people feel the discovery has lent credibility to the myth once again and that the mysticism surrounding the town adds a bit of charm to it.

Escazú doesn't stand alone. While the magical rituals vary with the times, witches with large followings practice their craft in other areas of the country. For example, in Desamparados south of San Jose, police discovered photos with pins, hair, ribbons, strings and other objects in a home, apparently the modern answer to sticking pins in dolls. According to the newspaper report, sometimes witches use the power for good; other times for injury. The article alleged that many prominent local citizens sought assistance with situations in their lives.

Catholic priests have long battled superstition of all sorts especially that attributed to witchcraft, because reputedly the sorcerers in addition to causing harm use sacred Christian symbols to invert their power backwards. J.K. Rowling, billionaire author of the Harry Potter series, contradicts parents who find the magic in the books too dark. She said during an interview with Oprah that these kinds of tales survived for hundreds of years, and she predicted that they will continue to appeal to children for hundreds of years more because people enjoy the idea that magic exists in the world.

"I'm not saying I believe magic is real—I don't," she said. "But that's the perennial appeal of magic—the idea that we ourselves have power and we can shape our world."

In Playas del Coco located in the Province of Guanacaste, (named after a national tree), we learned that amazingly both young and old men alike speak in hushed tones about La Mona. Suppressing fear, a man may describe the half monkey, half woman that lives in the forest and appears only on the darkest of nights.

Sometimes the whispering storyteller ends by claiming it happened to him. Rest assured he will warn that if a man walking alone in the dark hears La Mona's laughter, he'd better run for his life. The storyteller truly believes that if La Mona touches him on the head, he will go crazy. What kind of laughter, you might ask? First, it sounds like a child's joyous gurgle the man will answer, but the closer she gets, it sounds terrifyingly hysterical.

Other legends include The Priest without a Head. In it a little church appears at the end of a lonely street where bells peal at midnight. A priest performs mass with his back to the congregation. When he turns to give the final blessing, the congregation realizes he has no head. Supposedly, those that attended the service woke up in the middle of the street terrorized by the thought that a demon had chased them.

Another tale features a painted oxcart without oxen called La Carreta sin Bullocks or Bueyes. Years ago when city streets lacked lamps and appeared dark and eerie (like some areas still do in various rural locations in Costa Rica) and TV only existed in someone's imagination, people went to bed with the chickens. After all, it gets dark about six in the evening year round.

The story traditionally is associated with a parsimonious human. That person apparently heard a cart rumble pass the window without the sound of hooves from an animal and feared something supernatural rode in the cart.

Playa Nosara -- actually several beaches in the Guanacaste province – slopes to the water about six kilometers from the sleepy typical Tico town of Nosara.

Best reached by air it's located on a road that borders the Nosara River that is close to the Refugio Naciónal de Vida Silvestre Ostional where sea turtles nest. During the Colonial period the province belonged to Nicaragua. Annexed and incorporated into Costa Rica in 1825, the boundaries actually changed in 1858.

Sometime in the remote past, a tale developed around how the Chorotegas of Aztec lineage migrated to the Nicoya peninsula that they considered their promised land. The legend included a long tale of love, warfare, buried treasure, and death. It deviated from the traditional Costa Rican legends that like fairy tales deigned to teach a lesson to errant young children.

Depending on the person embellishing the story, the theme states that during full moons, one can hear Chief Curime calling the love of his life, and, most eerily, Princess Nosara's response. Supposedly, she took her own life after an enemy Chira arrow killed him.

In an area near Grecia, the River Poró allegedly once flowed in torrents, and cut off once dominant indigenous tribesmen who cultivated crops of corn, beans, sweet potatoes, squash and more from others nearby. Allegedly, one man sought out a warlock.

Try to picture Satan appearing through thick smoke strong with the smell of sulphur to exact a deal. The cunning and intelligent man offered up his soul in return for a bridge over the Poró. One caveat in the contract stated the devil had to build the bridge in one night finishing before the first rooster crowed the new day.

Sitting in front of a campfire on a hill without nodding off, the man watched as Satan laid stone upon stone. The man realized the devil nearly completed the task even though darkness still covered the area. Reaching into a sack, he pulled out a rooster. Seeing the light of the fire, like roosters in the area of Santiago de Puriscal who can't tell time, it crowed immediately. The angry devil disappeared in a puff of smoke. Today the natural granite wonder still lacks a stone.

Only in recent years has Halloween gained the status of a new tradition in Costa Rica. Some people feel it finds acceptance because of the ghosts, goblins and associated magic as well as coinciding with All Hallows Eve.

To learn more about Costa Rican legends search the archives of the Tico Times, and Google them. Even if you think it all a crock, you may gain some fascinating insights into the history of the Costa Rican culture.

CHAPTER Seven

Will Culture Shock Happen to You?

How will you know?

Having never experienced true culture shock because I embraced the environment of each country where I lived, I have no firsthand experience with the malady. In both England and Germany, I eagerly sought the most exhilarating experience possible although some adjustments remained more difficult than others did. In the end, I blended the cultures and emerged an international person, otherwise known as a cosmopolitan.

Just what is Culture Shock? According to Wikipedia, the free online encyclopedia, *"Culture shock refers to the anxiety and feelings of surprise, disorientation, uncertainty; confusion, etc. felt when people have to operate within a different and unknown cultural or social environment, such as a foreign country. It grows out of the difficulties in assimilating the new culture, causing difficulty in knowing what is appropriate and what is not. Often it combines with a dislike for or even disgust (moral or aesthetical) with certain aspects of the new or different culture. The term was introduced for the first time in 1954 by Kalervo Oberg, a world-renowned anthropologist, who explained the theory of a cross-culture experience to the Women's Club of Rio de Janeiro."*

To explain further, according to Wikipedia three basic outcomes of the adjustment phase result:

"Some people find it impossible to accept the foreign culture and integrate. They isolate themselves from the host country's environment, which they come to perceive as hostile, withdraw into a *ghetto* and see returning to their own culture as the only way out. These (people) . . . have the greatest problems reintegrating . . . after returning home. Approximately 60% of expatriates behave in this (manner).

Some people integrate fully and take on all parts of the host culture while losing their original identity. They normally remain in the host country forever. Approximately 10% of expatriates belong to the group of . . . adaptors.

Some people manage to adapt (to) the aspects of the host culture they see as positive, while keeping some of their own (cultural traits) and creating their unique blend. They have no major problems returning home or relocating elsewhere. Approximately 30% of expatriates qualify as so-called Cosmopolitans."

Having studied Anthropology and Sociology at both the undergraduate and graduate levels, to me the phases one may go through equate to a new love affair. During the honeymoon phase that usually lasts about six months, the differences in cultures appear in a wonderful new romantic light. Just as one ignores faults in a significant other, the initial life experiences in Costa Rica bring enjoyment.

After differences become apparent, anxiety may develop. Cravings for the familiar may envelope the person; dealing with habits and the new way of life may wax untenable. Handling these may result in mood swings and even depression in some cases.

Once a person recognizes that the significant other has more good traits than bad and love prevails, some adjustments facilitate the long haul. In the same way, knowing what to expect in the new environment and the newness having worn off, routines develop so life can return to basic living in the adopted culture.

Recalling my sociology studies, sometimes after adjusting to the new culture a person will suffer reverse cultural shock when returning home. The same phases in adjusting to a new culture may happen to a person returning to his own culture, making re-entry adjustment more difficult. Equate that to becoming disillusioned with a partner and acting more selective in finding a new one.

Canadian world-renowned anthropologist Kalvero Oberg coined the term culture shock in 1954 about the same time as a Frenchman defined Costa Rica as a Third World Country. Actually, the latter described unindustrialized countries. Today Costa Rica has graduated to developing country status. Oberg defined the cultural shock phenomenon as the anxiety and feelings of disorientation experienced when living in a different cultural environment. Tourists may feel things appear familiar, and many assume life will be similar to what they knew before deciding to make Costa Rica their home.

It's the unexpected trials and actual wide differences in cultural understanding that often make adapting much more difficult than expected. In the adjustment phase, some people fail to accept the foreign culture and do not integrate. Personally, I feel people in this category become negative and always find fault with something. Expats who manage to stay for a long time in Costa Rica possess patience and flexibility even if challenged by the different views regarding time, efficiency, and language.

For example, North Americans consider a person late if he/she arrives 10 to 15 minutes after the scheduled time. Latinos give much more leeway. In the U.S., time equates with money. In Costa Rica, time belongs to the individual.

Differences in efficiency strike foreigners especially although if one honestly recalls experiences at home, the dichotomy narrows. The trend in the US leans toward less speed and efficiency in the services sector. When I lived in Santiago de Puriscal, one expat couple told me not to plan to accomplish more than one thing a day. Accustomed to doing many things, I learned how to accomplish more by working within the system. It doesn't mean that I'm not frustrated on occasion and sometimes fail to accomplish as much as planned in one day.

Often problems stem from having to deal with things in Spanish. Misunderstandings often result due to the ways in which people express and understand language content. As a North American born in New York City, I am direct but speak more gently than the stereotyped New Yorker does. Costa Ricans aren't direct because they consider it bad manners, even rude. Expats interpret natives' attitudes as "indirect" or even "dishonest".

Many expats feel they have to decode what their Costa Rican associates meant to say. Are they trying to save face or not to disappoint? If they don't know the answer do they want to give the best guess? A foreigner has to learn to listen carefully and read between the lines.

Despite the numerous challenges and obstacles that expats face in their new homeland, those who adapt are convinced that the wonderful benefits outweigh the drawbacks. The country's strong democratic tradition, innovative environmental programs, museums and cultural activities, and more reasonable living expenses even in the face of rising costs continue to make Costa Rica a popular destination. I emphasize umpteen times the importance of remembering that all foreigners, even with permanent residency status or perhaps even with citizenship, remain guests in Costa Rica. Some people disagree with this point of view. However, going the extra mile helps to make a good life.

Cultural shock also happens when expats fail to realize the importance of preventing certain things from affecting them. One needs to live in Costa Rica long enough to really understand how it operates and to find ways to substitute something that fills the perceived void. When people actually move they may hit a frustration level in six months or maybe it will take longer. It requires effort to stand back and consider the major investment made.

Before you pack your bags and run off again to start life in another country, go back home at least in your mind. Review the reasons you decided to move to Costa Rica. Get in touch with those feelings and thoughts of living in the States (or wherever) and recall and understand the reasons you decided to move to Costa Rica.

Sometimes going on a vacation back home makes one realize how good life is here. At the end of the day, the lack of previous experience with Latino style culture, society, or bureaucracy could affect how comfortable you ultimately feel living in Costa Rica.

Questions to ask and answer honestly:

Are you normally tolerant of other people's habits and cultural differences?

Will you learn the Spanish language if you don't already speak it?

What's your capacity for adapting to new a way of life?

Can you deal with power and water interruptions?

Will your partnership, if you have one, remain strong enough to adapt and withstand the changes?

Can you avoid temptations in order to sustain your commitments?

Most importantly, have you dealt with your life's baggage?

CHAPTER Eight

Laugh at the Lack of Understanding

Fair-Headed Humans Speaking Spanish Surprise

"No hablo ingles," Ileana responded although I had explained in halting Spanish that my cell phone still malfunctioned. She buzzed me in behind the counter in the ICE office and sent me upstairs to Jorge because "el habla ingles".

Having Hispanics think that I only spoke English was not new. With my light hair and fair skin, they assumed that I could only speak English. They didn't make the effort to listen carefully. Jorge and I wound up conversing in Spanglish. This anecdote, however, illustrates difficulties one may encounter in attempting to communicate before learning enough of the local language, especially when not looking like a native.

My host where I was staying who spoke some FK Grade had accompanied me on the first visit to the telephone provider with my malfunctioning low-end cellular. She outlined the problem. Declaring the phone repaired, Ileana had changed the language to Spanish I discovered afterward.

Out came the dictionary to translate the instructions to reset it to English. Subsequently, reminiscent of the ad, I forever asked when I tried to call someone, "Can you hear me now?"

Often the pocket for good transmission, usually outside in the driveway rain or shine, faded before I completed a conversation.

Jorge determined the battery caused the phone's problem.

Therefore, I gathered up the paperwork to prove the warranty and went to the store that sold it. No one seemed to care that the guide who had bought me the phone at my expense so I could communicate at least some of the time appeared as the stated owner. However, the clerk who spoke a little English refused to take it back until after Easter week because the country locks up tight as a sardine can without a key. He feared it might get lost.

Fast-forward the tale to the date to pick up the repaired phone. The clerk shrugged his shoulders and declared, "Come back next week."

A week later, frustrated that I had no cell service for a month, my red headed ire (my original hair color) showed through my now strawberry blond hair. After all, immigrating alone and not able to get a landline to the cottage where I lived, the cell was my lifeline. Wanting to avoid further confrontation, the clerk quickly made arrangements for the delivery of the phone by bus to the store from the repair place in San Jose within two days.

Epilogue: Months later Ileana came to my new abode with the crew to install a second phone line for the Internet. Suddenly she realized that I responded to her questions in imperfect Spanish. I teased her about not listening before and we often laughed about it during future encounters.

In the meantime, I had found a back entrance to Jorge's office and, bypassing taking a fiche with a number to wait to get help, I surprised him with a visit and asked, "Puede usted entender me ahora?" (Can you understand me now?)

CHAPTER Nine

Where Do You come From?

Origins Appear Important

If you have lived abroad or moved from Italy versus the U.S. or Canada to Costa Rica, the transition appears far easier from my point of view. Having a family member move with you may facilitate the adjustment. As a world traveler, you have a feeling for what to expect. On the other hand, if you have lived in one place all your life, you require especial diligence in determining the efficacy of such a move.

One of the reasons I feel my adventure in Costa Rica great stems from my having lived abroad before. While much younger then and accompanied by immediate family, living in England and Germany in the sixties and adapting to customs in each place, prepared me for my move to Costa Rica.

When considering your move to Costa Rica, take into account your origination point and your destination: a city, the country, or something in between. Where will you live happily?

Alajuela, the second largest city in the country although its ranking may change, makes a good measuring stick because it is urban and not as congested as San Jose. Grecia and San Ramon rank more like suburbs. Puriscal to me says country, laid back and more family oriented. Its square constantly has people stirring about, including many students since class schedules vary during the day due to the number of students versus the number of classrooms and teachers. Cartago, Atenas and Puntarenas fall into the same category. The beach towns of Jacó and Playas del Coco as well as Liberia with its recently expanded international airport offer alternative atmospheres.

While the smaller towns feature more mom and pop stores although this is evolving, one finds fancy malls, big box businesses and chains in more metropolitan areas. Walmart purchased a majority of the shares in a company that had markets called Hipermas, Pali, and MasXMenos. After obtaining 51% of the parent company, in 2011 Walmart began changing the stores' names beginning with Hipermas. Whether the prices equal the lows as touted in the U.S. remains debatable.

As anywhere, one has to know the prices of items one buys in order to find the best price, including in the equation the cost of gas to hunt for savings. Price Smart, headquartered in California, is the original US Style Membership Warehouse Club where you can find high quality products. Find out more at www/pricesmart.com. Upscale grocery stores like Auto Mercado and Saretto (recently given a facelift) cater to foreigners willing to pay for the taste of home. Most often, if an item can't be found elsewhere, Saretto, part of Grupo Empresarial de Supermercados (GESSO) (2228-3247) has it. McDonalds, KFC, Wendy's, Subway, and other fast food chains dot the landscape and get blamed for the increasing obesity among natives. TGIF, Tony Roma's, Outback, and Hooters offer familiar fare but at higher prices than in the States.

In the malls like Multiplaza oeste (west), known clothing chains like Liz Claiborne and Tommy Hilfinger with the same high prices cater to the elite. Daum, Baccarat, Kosta Boda and other fine crystal mirrors the cost of such items at Neiman Marcus. Just as in Dallas, the customer that buys these brands here lives in an upscale house. Many people shop as Ropa Americana shops that sell new and used clothing. A chain of Torre de Lobo stores features new clothing for the entire family that they obtain from American stores like JC Penney.

Frankly, I sold my collection of Steuben pieces and the like before moving here because I didn't feel tropical living lent itself to such expensive items. However, I shipped good china and crystal glasses, not a few of which fell to the unforgiving tile floor. My solution: replace old fashion glasses with individual designs. It makes it easier for guests to remember their glass at least in the beginning of the night, and if one breaks, not to worry, a "set" remains intact.

Whether you can live without fine things depends on your preferred lifestyle and mindset before Costa Rica. It also reflects whether you want a simpler lifestyle or seek a million dollar home. My abode (even the one in Puriscal) to some Tico friends appears more luxurious than their homes. A bit of heritage has followed me to Costa Rica.

The apartment that I moved from recently contrasted with the apartment I grew up in New York City but included a few pieces my Grandmother bought in 1920 for her rent-controlled apartment. While I've owned larger homes, I have friends and acquaintances here that live in more luxury than I and have much larger incomes. One encounters any level of lifestyle in Costa Rica. No matter how much income you have, it still should stretch further in Ticoville despite the change in the economy.

During the financial crisis of 2009, I joked that Costa Rica might enjoy good fortune as a result, assuming that more foreigners would migrate here. By early February 2010, Amway announced plans to open new financial operations in Santa Ana near the capital city of San Jose. It joined WNS, Teleperformance, Paysource, McKinsey and Emerson who had announced new operations in the country. International Business Machines (IBM) that first had a presence in 2004, announced in August 2011 that it planned to spend $300 million in development over the next ten years. In addition, it vowed to have created up to1000 additional professional jobs by 2014.

Apparently 95 service companies as of 2009 had set up shop in CR, according to the Costa Rican Investment Promotion Agency (CINDE). They include Canon, Citibank, Hewlett Packard, HSBC, Intel, Panasonic, Pfizer, Scotia Bank, Walmart, and Wrangler. Other companies slated for CR included Boston Scientific, P&G, and Kraft. The expansion in 2009 of the Multiplaza Mall near Escazú offered more evidence of prosperity.

Additionally, Costa Rica's promotional agency, Promotora del Comercio Exterior de Costa Rica (PROCOMER), forecast high expectations for attracting electronic and medical device firms as well as services like call centers, green technology, industrial and agricultural producers, and research and development. Firms like Hewlett Packard that had a substantial presence in 2010 sent foreign employees packing, thereby reducing subsidy and employee costs. Later they recruited employees from the U.S. to teach skills to Costa Ricans. However, from what I've learned, HP currently provides fewer benefits. The second change in policy resulted after Ticos couldn't learn sufficient skills during two-week classes in the States. The company learned It was more cost-efficient to bring an experienced person here instead. HP deserves kudos for giving their North American employees Spanish lessons!

CHAPTER Ten

Social Expectations

What Opportunities for Activities and Friends do You Anticipate Discovering?

What will you leave behind: theater, movies, social clubs, sports clubs, and a religious community? Alternatively, did you live a rural life? Do you need an urban environment with restaurants, bars, and nightclubs, or the quiet life in the country?

Does snow skiing rate high among your pastimes? Then reading a book about living in the tropics will not cut it. Most expats say they came to escape the snow and cold. Living high in the cool mountains means long treks to attend meetings or to gather with friends. One reason for retiring to Costa Rica stands out: to have more free time for doing whatever you enjoy.

In line with pastimes, if you enjoy fishing as a Costa Rican resident or vacationer, contact Lee Swidler who has been a fly angler almost all his life. Although the majority of those years were in the States, his fishing adventures are mostly within the borders of Costa Rica now. On his blog, www.flyfishingincostarica.blogspot.com, he writes about each of his guided adventures. Learn more at FLY FISHING IN COSTA RICA (www.flyfishingincostarica.com). Phone: (506) 2643-1248, Phone : (506) 2643-1248 cellphone : (506) 8889-8113; E-mail: info@flyfishingincostarica.com

Question: Do you have a particular hobby or pastime that requires special equipment? Check out its availability here versus the cost of shipping it. Should you bring everything you anticipate needing to pursue your passion? Other questions: Do you, your spouse or partner and children, if any, make friends easily? How do you intend to find people to socialize with? Unlike lost luggage, how you handle your personal baggage containing life experiences remains most important.

Not unlike believing having a baby will improve a marriage, loving and forgiving yourself will go a long way to making a great new life in a different culture or, in fact, anywhere you live.

Costa Ricans appreciate individuals more. People still give a seat to the elderly or a mother with a baby. Families take care of older people. Same sex relationships are readily accepted. May/December unions of any sort prevail. One note of caution, again if a man "marries" his daughter or links up with a young man, his financial responsibility often extends to the native's entire family. A number of women marry a Tico in order to get a cédula sooner. It doesn't always happen. Often the woman supports the man in return. Immigration looks at such unions more closely now and laws wax stricter in an effort to eliminate marriages of convenience.

Read more about single men and women relocating to Costa Rica in other chapters.

CHAPTER Eleven

Can Xenophobic People Live Abroad?

Can a Person Afflicted with This Syndrome Live Anywhere Comfortably?

If you suffer from xenophobia, you probably are not comfortable wherever you live because the world has grown small and almost anywhere, strangers and foreigners pepper the population. Using precautions in strange places remains prudent. I've never suffered fear or contempt unduly or otherwise of strangers or foreigners especially as reflected in political or cultural views. In fact, I took pleasure in hosting foreign visitors to my Dallas home.

Let's consider some reasons to move to Costa Rica even if you suffer xenophobia:

1. You want to learn Spanish. No excuses. No matter your age, you have the capacity to learn regardless of what you have heard. Remember we all do what we want to do.
2. You can adapt to driving around potholes and on narrow roads without street signs, or live without a car.
3. The lack of specific addresses doesn't put you in a thither. (Actually two banks donated funds for street signs in San Jose and slowly they are being installed.) You don't require street signs or a GPS (although now available and more accurate in Costa Rica than you think).
4. Asking at least three people directions doesn't concern you because you can't remember long instructions. You are not

concerned that the person's eagerness masks the fact he doesn't have a clue and directs you to Nicaragua.

5. You can take the opportunity to speak to strangers to practice Spanish while waiting in lines or traveling on buses and you can read a book, Nook, or Kindle on your feet.

6. You can deal with bugs, snakes, scorpions and spiders, all prevalent in the tropics. Hey, I had to deal with bugs and spiders in Dallas.

7. You retain caution about investing because you didn't leave your intelligence at the border.

8. You can enjoy eating different foods, understanding that a daily intake of rice and beans may add kilos.

9. You take responsibility for your actions, and have no need to sue for every unsatisfactory event. You understand that if you are litigious, it can take years to settle a case.

10. You are aware that McDonalds, KFC, Wendy's and other fast food chains have opened facilities and good hamburgers are sold in more and more restaurants.

11. Many foods you love are available, if for a price, so you won't have as many cravings. Each month more and more familiar products show up on some of the grocery chain shelves. (The down side results when the store stops carrying something you crave, like sweet pickles, for no apparent reason. Patience, a definite virtue in Costa Rica, has paid off. At the end of March, 2013 I found a 16 oz. jar of Mt. Olive sweet gherkins for over $5.)

12. You can find enough ways to make Costa Rica your paradise and fulfill your dream.

Some reasons NOT to move to Costa Rica

1. You believe the move will solve all your problems. Once again, remember personal baggage travels with you.

2. Crime worries you even though drug lords and Nicaraguans are blamed. Actually, it all depends upon what type of crime. Different areas of the country have different rates. Factor in your risk profile and the entity reporting situations. Somewhere I read an article about homicides per 100,000 in Central America in 2009. Costa Rica ranked lowest with 11; El Salvador highest with 76. Even Panama rated higher at 24 than Nicaragua with 13. Guatemala had 48; Honduras almost 67. Just as Dallas police touted since 1970, one has to avoid certain areas, remain alert, remove temptations like leaving a purse on a car seat, look out for neighbors and report suspicions even if they prove false. If you have a problem, you must make a Denuncia at the Organismo de Investigación Judicial (OIJ) to facilitate an investigation and before going to court.

3. You believe you have the answer to others' problems and the need to broadcast those answers.

4. You constantly want to respond, "We didn't do it that way where I come from."

5. People have traditionally conformed to your way of doing things as the best way.

6. Finally, you are unable or unwilling to commit to making a good life for yourself.

CHAPTER Twelve

Can A Single Man Survive the Beautiful Seductress?

Or Even the Not-so-attractive but Cunning Female?

Sex tourism remains alive and well in Costa Rica famous for its allegedly legal prostitution and escorts. Even if a man doesn't come to the country with that in mind, the attention of young women who treat them as they have dreamed flatters and tempts them.

Here's an example. A man I met in a video shop said after a few minutes of casual conversation, "I have to pick up my baby at school."

"Baby?"

He immediately pulled out his wallet to show me a picture of a pretty two year old who he said already had her American passport and citizenship. The Tica mother looked no more than 30.

"I'm 69", he bragged obviously delighted that his plumbing still functioned.

Although I said nothing to him, I often tease older male immigrants that their bucket list included "marrying" their daughter. When a cross-culture relationship ends in marriage the Tico family and friends admire and praise the girl.

Most of the men over 50 falling for younger women haven't taken care of themselves. However, they come with money. Eventually the man awakens to realize that in addition to the pretty young thing living off his pension are her parents, siblings, cousins and maybe even friends. In some cases, these men find themselves having to find a job in order to support the group.

Perhaps one reason for men getting into such entanglements may be blamed on middle-age crisis even if they don't recognize it. It can create depression that leads to toxic relationships. They spend all their money on women or even on forming a new family as if they were young again. If a man wakes up to his situation, he can't go to court. If the woman turns spiteful, he will be sucked into a domestic violence scam or into supporting children for years.

In the book "The New Golden Door to Retirement and Living in Costa Rica", author Christopher Howard has a long section on the topic. He spent 15 years married to a Costa Rican woman, now deceased, and later formed a relationship with an attorney half his age. In his book he provides advice on how to avoid gold diggers and other unscrupulous types. He feels finding fantastic relationships results not as a matter of luck but by approaching things in the correct way. Bottom line, it requires work.

Well-intentioned laws to protect women from abuse can backfire. A sweetheart can accuse a significant other falsely and make his life a living hell. If a woman wants the man out of the house, she will complain and most often, the court sides with the accuser.

As I've said before, the ability to communicate in Spanish helps in understanding the culture and determining the character of a woman . . . or a man.

In addition, looking in the right places -- through work (if any), hobbies, church, and places of interest or having friends introduce prospects -- helps one make the right choices. Meeting women in bars when a man celebrated his 20th birthday rarely ended in a good relationship. Why should neighborhood bars in Costa Rica prove any different?

Men should look for partners that watch out for their financial interests, avoid impulsive marriage, and only pay normal costs of a date. It's a matter again of not leaving one's intelligence at the border.

CHAPTER Thirteen

Can Single Foreign Women Live in a Macho Culture?

Why not?

While the culture in many instances reeks of machismo, more and more independent foreign women retire in Costa Rica. Many Ticas, married or single, have careers. Frankly, when I investigated "retiring" in Costa Rica, macho failed the list as a consideration. Perhaps if finding a man topped my bucket list, I might have considered it. But I knew before I returned to the country a second time that seeking full time male companionship failed to receive goal status. As I have said many times occasionally having a man around the house . . . for heavy lifting, opening doors, and honey "do" lists . . . ranked high. However, my wish list lacks supporting a man just to have a spouse or even a male escort.

Too many tales about male expats seeking women their daughters' ages to live with prevented me from kidding myself that Costa Rica might be a good 'significant other' paradise for finding a man of any nationality. As in other parts of the world, some of best looking men prefer men and feel comfortable about disclosing the fact in Costa Rica. Frankly, I have lived alone too many years to even consider a roommate, male or female.

Uppermost in my mind at the time I researched living in Costa Rica was finding a compatible location, a place where I could meet people from around the world, and in a decent environment that fit my budget. Recalling spoken Spanish loomed as a way to keep my mind even more active. It helped that I had studied the language and could still read and write it. Over time I met single women, some never married, widows, and divorcees, a diversified group. Without naming them, I'll describe a few. A much younger woman made her living from writing assignments and teaching. A British woman writer appeared quite eccentric as only the British can. A Cubana drew sketches and created jewelry. Another lived in the country with some animals, preferring it to city life, and gave shelter to travelling students. One woman joined the single sisterhood when her husband of 50 years died. She joined another mature widow who had moved to Costa Rica after the death of her husband. In fact, a number of widows choose to stay in the country because they live better on their incomes and have friends to support them in their grief.

Another single woman I know houses a variety of pets and looks for creative ways to make extra income. Another works for a hotel part time. She once ran a B&B where most guests recovered from medical procedures done in Costa Rica. Medical tourism grew into a big business because of lower costs than those in the States

Several single women born in Cuba, Panama, or Asia, migrated to the States before eventually settling in Costa Rica. One of them still studies foreign languages. Another has apartments for rent. The third sometimes runs a B&B unlike another single woman who operates a B&B full time. Her trusted employees take over when she visits family in the States. One now deceased widow that approached 100 years old joined the loosely organized single group because she lived alone so many years after her spouse's death. Some married women spend much time alone due to their husbands' careers so they join singles in their endeavors. Living in a macho environment has its pluses because the men often act chivalrously. Costa Ricans respect and honor older people even if they aren't family. The type of woman that needs a man around at all times, has some options including bringing one with her, setting up a relationship with a Tico probably at her expense, or remaining unhappy alone.

Often I'm asked about my husband. Not wanting to lie, I have responded that I live alone. More recently, I have thought it might be wiser to hedge.

The person often responds, "Would you like a novio (boyfriend)?"

To which I say, "Can you afford me?"

One driver asked me if I believed in God and said he would like to be my friend. It's all about flirting. However, a better answer to avoid becoming prey: "I have a novio." Or, "My son or brother lives in Costa Rica."

Single women must avoid bad neighborhoods and seedy places and stay alert to their surroundings. Other precautions include using pirates (unlicensed cabs) only if someone has recommended the driver. I prefer to take a red cab with a meter (nicknamed Maria) even if it costs a bit more because generally the company posts the number of the cab. However, I use a pirate when my butcher calls one for me.

If you have a car, lock the doors and don't leave anything of value that might be seen through the windows. Hide your pocketbook; never leave it on the passenger's seat beside you. Take valuables with you rather than put them in a glove compartment or the trunk, the first places thieves look.

Women, especially over 65 and suffering some disease such as dementia, must be aware they could be targets of caregivers, friends, or relatives who dupe them into letting them handle their finances. One woman's favorite but greedy grandson apparently caused a long-term relationship to falter. Keep in mind that by turning over savings or property does not guarantee care for life.

Take other security measures. Leave expensive jewelry at home when venturing into San Jose by car, bus, or cab. Keep a cell phone or camera out of sight. Deactivate your car alarm when you stand next to the vehicle, key in hand, not from across the street. Avoid repetition of a schedule if possible. For example, don't leave the house at the same time every day and take different routes. Locate police and fire stations, the Red Cross, and other places for potential help so you can drive to them for assistance.

Take someone with you or go to an ATM with a guard. Do not accept help from a stranger. Ask the bank teller to count the money slowly so no one else in line observes the amount, which someone might if you count it.

Keep your credit cards and extra money in a safe place, like a flat cloth holder designed to wear under clothes especially when traveling. Single women especially should utilize the same precautions in Costa Rica as anywhere in the world, even in their hometown.

CHAPTER Fourteen

Personalities Cover the gamut

Like Peyton Place, Small Town Attributes Provide Extremes

Famous writer Maya Angelou once said, "When people show you who they are, believe them the first time."

"Sounds like these women have too much time on their hands," someone whines after some sort of altercation with another person. Looking back to my days in Dallas, I can't recall having to deal with obnoxious, loud, overbearing people, especially women. Why do we have to in Costa Rica?

Let's face it; anyone who decides to live in a foreign country has certain eccentricities. Add these to the type of personalities found anywhere in the world and living closely among them may challenge one's patience. It can resemble Peyton Place that a friend defined at least to her understanding as: people who are doing things not for the stated purpose of the organization, or towards any appropriate or reasonable end, but rather towards satisfaction of their own egocentric, vengeful, jealous or other petty reasons. One friend managed a friendship with a brash, loud, rude woman who butts heads with most people and has few friends, probably her defence mechanism we assume. She told me, "You have to forgive her because she is a New Yorker and Jewish!" Excuse me, another friend and I laughed in response. "Helen was born in New York City," my friend responded, "and although not Jewish, most of her friends were. She speaks softly and avoids rudeness."

Another person talks about people behind their backs and then hobnobs with the very person badmouthed. He never takes responsibility for his actions. It's always the other person's fault.

On the other hand one encounters lovely people who willingly help one another, something as simple as giving a person a ride or as complex as putting a cabinet together. Sometimes one hits it off with someone, whether an expat or a Tico/a. However, I must admit that a very few people might rub me raw if I permitted it but I made the decision to let the barbs roll off my back and to act like the conflagration never happened. I decided they only make fools of themselves and I don't need to feel stress.

It's unfortunate that some people epitomize stereotypes or a living devil but the more mature I am the more I realize that I must regard them as merely flies on the wall that I swat and put in the garbage. I am courteous but I don't have to embrace everyone. I'm lucky to have made several good friends among many nationalities and the number continues to increase. No one better talk to one of us about the other either!

After I moved to Cariari, I began enlarging my circle of acquaintances and friends among both expats and Hispanics from various countries. The diversification pleased me. Some people I encounter only at meetings. Quite quickly, locals accepted me into their friendship circles where I often stood out as the only obvious foreigner hailing from the States, Canada, or Europe.

I feel ecstatic about all the wonderful experiences with my new Costa Rican friends – from dancing at a local restaurant with live music on Saturday nights to attending a Belen municipality boyero sponsored festita complete with food, drink, marimbas, and folklorico dancers not to mention the oxen the size of rhinoceros. I discussed with my Tica friend what made me so accepted. She answered *La Forma,* translated as saying please and thank you and not dictating orders but asking and including the ability to communicate in Spanish, all natural considerations. It also means greeting people you know upon arrival and departure with a kiss on the cheek and a hug, and not turning your back on someone speaking to a group even if the person does not address you directly. Sometimes strangers will shake your hand but if you reach out like a native, the person usually reciprocates.

Another Tica invited me to her home for her birthday party after knowing me only a few weeks. She had encouraged me to attend the Mexican Mother's Day celebration (on May 10th that year, the day after the U.S. holiday). Another Tica, a Nica and a Columbiana went with us. When I go to a dentist in Puriscal, a friend's wife makes lunch for me in her home.

My "adopted Tico son" told me they felt very happy that I visited them when I made the trek (two buses and about three hours each way). Some foreigners have complained that Ticos don't invite them into their homes. Do you think it stems from their attitudes, their lack of La Forma that put off Costa Ricans?

Recently a Tica friend that I go dancing with called and invited me to go to Guanacaste and stay in one brother's house. We stayed from

Friday to Tuesday. It was hot, hot, hot, requiring two cool showers a day but most interesting to visit with a Tico family and learn about their lifestyle. It gave me a chance to learn about places I was writing about and to have lunch at my client's home with my Tica friend. Not only did my client invite us both to stay in her studio, my friend's sister-in-law three times invited me to return to her home. You know people may extend such an invitation once to be polite but with the third one, it feels real.

When you go to a Tico home, one brings supplies like food, liquor (which I do worldwide), bath towels, blankets, and sheets. I discovered I should have brought more shorts; fortunately, I had packed extra tops. Due to the heat, everything should be lightweight. In this home, they washed dishes in the pila in a different "room" rather than in the kitchen sink. Of course, the rice cooker was on the counter. They made coffee in the sock, long a tradition in Costa Rica.

Forgiving people their foibles becomes part of making friends, but the more birthdays one achieves, the less likely one wants to put up with decidedly bad behavior. Frankly, everyone can find people that become good friends even in a small town community. Establishing limits on "putting up with foibles" often results. Some women who have never held a position of authority in their lifetime have it go to their head as the leader of an organization or group. If you volunteer expect to work harder than if a paid employee. It's more difficult to get recognition for your expertise.

If you ever have lived in a small town, you will relate to living in a small community of foreigners. While spread about the country, they amazingly know your business. The only way to prevent stories of your life making the circuit depends on your ability to keep your mouth shut. Sometimes even doing that won't stop a rumor.

When I lived in Puriscal, one rumor suggested I felt lonely. The assumption resulted due to long visits on the telephone with friends reluctant to journey over the mountain to my house. Another rumor touted boredom that I haven't felt since Sunday afternoons when I was 12 years old. In reality, bored and lonely people probably transferred their feelings to me.

In the end the foreign community is large enough (International Living cites 20,000) to afford the ability to form a fine circle of friends. As you have learned in your lifetime, some friends last years, others for shorter periods. If people leave the country, very few stay in touch. However, new people arrive to fill the void. The best advice I can offer dictates having a positive attitude toward the country, its culture, and its people. The reward is many wonderful experiences and an adventure to remember for the rest of your life.

CHAPTER Fifteen

Big City Life Thrives

San Jose Provides "Candy" for the Eyes and Senses

San José, Costa Rica's capital and the seat of its democratic government since 1823, nestles high in the Central Valley (1,253 meters/3,770 feet), between green volcanic mountain ranges. Suburbs clinging to gentle foothills surround the largest city in the country. However, it's not the most beautiful city in the world. One friend quipped, "It's never had a fire or other disaster to eliminate the old places so it could be rebuilt."

The nearby upscale town of Escazú, southwest of the city off an Autopista, boasts the largest population either of North Americans living full-time or part-time in Costa Rica. Escazú and nearby Santa Ana offer many quality options.

Numerous touristic places are located in and around San José. Calle de la Amargura in San Pedro near the University of Costa Rica on the east side has a wide selection of bars, restaurants and discos and caters to University students with food and drinks for relatively low prices.

Margie Davis, also a writer, wrote articles about living in the Central Valley. To summarize she chose it because of the proximity to San Jose and all the cultural amentias in the capital – symphony, museums, and fine restaurants, to name a few.

She eschewed the capital for security, tranquility and green spaces.

As a single woman like me, she wanted to make friends quickly and joined women's groups to facilitate her priority. By having English-speaking people to communicate with and learn from, she could go about learning Spanish at her pace. Later she chose to live farther west from San Jose in Grecia, a town that many foreigners find appealing with its church made of metal imported in pieces.

Come September and October, San José seems to empty out of people I know. The rainiest months makes it a good time to visit 'up North'. Plan these sojourns in advance in order to get the best airfares.

Some people favor living in Atenas, now only 20 minutes from Escazú on the new highway when the road doesn't have problems. While the cost of living in cities seems higher than in smaller Central Valley towns, costs remain much lower in outlying areas than living in or around San Jose. Rentals in Atenas allegedly range from $700 up when you can find one. It's about 20 - 30 minutes to major health care facilities like CIMA but the town has a 24/7 clinic called Linea Vital. On the plus side festivals and parades abound, and reaching the beach by car takes about 30 minutes. The distance to the international airport in Alajuela usually takes less time.

Costa Rica remains not only a land of great variety in its landscapes; it offers a great variety of climates often within short distances from each other.

Geographically the Central Valley encompasses a huge area surrounding San Jose. It's the hub of Costa Rica offering a fine climate, easy access to the US and Canadian Embassies, an international airport in a nearby suburb, extensive products and services, and a wide variety of restaurants.

The extensive bus system enables one to get most anywhere without having a car but requires allowing sufficient time and sometimes taking more than one bus to arrive at a destination.

A circle line designed to facilitate movement by bus around San Jose found opposition from some of the existing bus companies. Never mind considering commuters, the circle line has remained a dream despite signs installed along the proposed route.

If one chooses to live in the more rural areas or near beaches, obtaining many amenities may require driving distances to find needed items. Playas del Coco is an exception and has a busy nightlife as a result of many tourists. You have to decide if you can live in a small community with fewer English-speaking people and exist more like the Ticos. Some areas under construction cater to foreigners. Choosing a small town probably means you will live in a house rather than an apartment or condominium.

While I'm not personally a beach fan, many friends love the sand. Some have second homes at whatever beach they like best; others travel to different ones and rent accommodations. Coldwell Banker has franchisees such as Coast to Coast Properties in Guanacaste that specialize in beach properties: **www.coldwellbankercr.com** It's best to spend time at several to determine which one you like best whether for a vacation home or main residence.

Noise factors into choice of a place to live. Do you love the sounds of the city or prefer barking dogs, roosters who crow at all hours, or awakening to bird calls? Do you rue the chugging of block-long trucks, roaring engines from airplanes, or revving motorcycles? Pick your sound poison.

Living in the Central Valley earthquakes and spewing volcanoes offer less danger but effects feel frightening nonetheless. The quake on September 5, 2012 was the strongest at 7.6 I have ever experienced. (Chronicled elsewhere in the book is dog Leda's experience after a tremor.)

Poas and Irazu, two of four volcanoes I could see from my home in Guachipelin, never appeared menacing. Since earthquakes do occur, concern about the construction of your home remains doubly important.

Take care when deciding which workers you hire to build or make repairs. Needing work and wanting to tell you what you want to hear, sometimes a contractor will take on a job without previous experience. For example, when I bought an on-demand water heater to install under the kitchen sink in the house in Puriscal, the man who had successfully worked on other plumbing tackled the job. Two days later – on a Sunday – I had a flooded kitchen and no knowledge of where to find the cut-off valve to turn off the water. It hid beneath dirt out front at the edge of the property. The man had used cold water pipes! Afterward a friend installed an easily reachable valve in case of another emergency.

Before you start looking, you might make a list of what amenities seem important to have available in your new abode. Keep in mind that you may have to compromise but at least it will enable you to focus your search.

CHAPTER Sixteen

Initial Impressions of Towns Near Puriscal

Country Living in Beautiful Surroundings

Ciudad Colón nestles in the countryside before Santiago de Puriscal, one of four towns west of San Jose in the Central Valley that foreigners find attractive. Escazú (with three sub-towns) wins easily as the most upscale and commercial. Santa Ana with a bit warmer climate features both rural and suburban sections, and Ciudad Colón appears pastoral but not as rural as Puriscal.

Bordered on three sides by mountains and ravines, development and growth in Ciudad Colón remains limited. However, not so long ago, Super Mora (headquartered in Puriscal that will open a store in Santa Ana in 2014; www.supermora.com) opened a modern and spacious (for the country) grocery store by the soccer field. Several developments offer homes and condominiums in a wide price range.

If you drive west along the Autopista Prospero Fernandez (highway) from San Jose toward Escazú, after passing the exits to it and Santa Ana, you will arrive at one marked for Ciudad Colón and Puriscal. Currently furniture stores occupy the buildings to the right before an extra lane leads out the exit.

The four-lane highway curves around to the left but the exit that now has manned toll booths leads to the original two lane road to the more rural towns.

Some commercial and light industrial businesses stand along the road between open spaces of undeveloped land.

On the way, you might notice Essentia on your right, a fine small hotel with a restaurant and bar hidden in a tropical wonderland, then a few other popular restaurants serving *comida típica* or Tico food line the road before traffic must turn right.

At an intersection with a *No Hay Paso* (one way, do not enter) sign, with the Enersol gas station on the right corner, you turn right and then a few blocks later you turn left to enter the center of town (most of the traffic goes this way). To your left before you turn, opposite the gas station, a road leads to residential areas including the Julia and David White Artist's Colony where visiting artists work and occasionally showcase their talents. The one-way "in" street where you make the second turn leads into downtown and continues through town toward the University for Peace and Puriscal.

(The "out" street brings you out of Ciudad Colón and back toward the *Autopista*. Many towns feature one-way streets at their centers.)

Started by the United Nations, The University for Peace put Ciudad Colón on the map. UPaz attracts students from all over the world seeking a Master's Degree in Media, Conflict and Peace Studies. These students gobble up affordable, furnished rental housing, so buying a rental property tempts foreign investors.

Most of downtown Ciudad Colón remains small enough to meet the needs of individuals who run the municipality, including many well-educated Ticos who worked for decades in the United States. On weekends, soccer dominates the main field downtown, starting with peewee in the morning on up in age to adult soccer in the evening. Besides soccer, every Saturday bicycle racers ride along the Autopista into Ciudad Colón from a gathering point in front of the Mega Super supermarket at the Santa Ana exit.

The old market, an open-air structure, stands out as a popular meeting place in town, often for festivals Previously Ciudad Colón's central market featured produce stands, butchers, fishmongers, tortilla and poultry shops, several sodas (hole-in-the wall dining spots) and a taco stand, but they all moved north. An outstanding restaurant, El Establo, open Thursdays through Sundays, features a stable with boarded horses. After turning right at the gas station continue straight and look for signs. It's tucked back in an old neighborhood. If all else fails, ask a native for directions.

Another town near Santiago de Puriscal, La Palma boasts a property called Altos de Antigua that has lots and houses for sale in a gated community. For country living, check out http://www.altigua.com. Obtain references just as you would anywhere.

CHAPTER Seventeen

Early Days Lliving Outside Santiago de Puriscal

Mingling with Ticos

"BAM!"

"It's a transformer," he said in Spanish. "We have no power in the Barrio."

The electrician had just glued the downspout to a short section of a gutter that animals had knocked down.

Fortunately, the outage didn't happen the day before when my neighbor, the eldest son of the woman in whose atypical house I lived, and his wife prepared for the final prayer meeting which lasted all afternoon. Each month for twelve months since his mother's death, he faithfully held an evening prayer meeting on the anniversary of her death. This last time, many more people drove or walked past my door to join the group in singing and prayer. As people departed, they carried food with them.

Not all the family joined the guests. As the world over, squabbles exist in large families especially when circumstances differ. Each of the woman's nine children enjoys a different level of success.

One of the granddaughters stopped by my gate to ask me if I knew anything about Brazil. Even though she said she had researched the Internet, I found a couple of addresses for her where she could get information about it and other countries she needed to make a report for school without doing her homework.

The following written in the first person to a dear friend not long after I arrived in Costa Rica; expressed my feelings at the time.

It's Sunday morning still. I stayed in bed until 7:30 a.m. Most days I'm up by six which is so unlike me. While cool enough to need a cover at night, it gets very hot during the day. Fortunately, a breeze wafts through the house although not in the corner where I'm writing on a borrowed table.

It's amazing how busy my days have been. During the week, two or three men work around the house from six to two for the Ticos, to five for the owner. They break for breakfast at nine. They reminded me of my husband demanding we depart by six a.m. when we took a trip. We stopped for breakfast about the time I felt awake.

Yesterday I tried the pool, a bit cool and slippery with rough paving around it. I'll wear pool shoes in to see if I get a bit more traction because no hand rails exist. It's a long walk down; you're dry and hot by the time you get back up the hill.

The container with my belongings awaits delivery as soon as the funds arrive, a procedure more complicated than anticipated due to requirements.

Verbally orders to sell could be made with the conversation recorded, the instructions for the wire transfer required a signature in writing. Before I left, I received a number that connected me to AT&T; after that, I call a second 800 number, all free. I nearly had a heart attack when I received an email from the mover indicating the cost totaled $1000 more than anticipated. I already had sent orders by Fed-Ex for $200 over what I figured. Fortunately, when I spoke to the representative quoting our agreement in an email, he apologized and called it a typo.

The instructions for the cell phone came in Spanish, which fortunately I could read with the occasional help of a dictionary. However, the inexpensive Motorola phone didn't hold a charge very long and shut itself off when the battery got low. Because of going to ICE (electric and phone company) regarding it, I've made friends with people who work there and one showed me a back entrance. Knowing local people can help get things done.

The owners of the B&B and the house I lived in relaxed a bit when I volunteered to pay any overage due to my use of the Internet. It seemed easier than having to keep track of time, nickeling and diming myself.

I felt it inconvenient and imposing to go to the B&B to access the Internet and to use the phone when mine had no service. The hills apparently blocked the cell radio waves. On Friday, I used an Internet Café that I will do from time to time especially for culling emails.

While in San Jose with an English speaking driver I met with an attorney, got fingerprinted at the Police headquarters for the cédula, purchased a membership in Price Smart (like Costco), and shopped at the Auto Mercado in the uptown mall Multiplaza. It carried lamb (not frozen).

I pick grapefruit, oranges, limes and bananas grown on the finca (farm). I have one tomato plant where I intend to put more, green peppers, and herbs. My seeds made it, so I will hire some men to *dig the dirt and plant them around the casita. Yesterday, the owners picked up a huge head of butter lettuce, a bunch of spinach and a kilo of tomatoes (seven of them) from the green grocer in Barbacoas where they own a large house. They built it before purchasing the farm. The veggies cost about the equivalent of $2.20 and the man gave me a free small mango. He has agreed to deliver to me.*

The acupuncturist/chiropractor hugged me three times when I stopped to say hello. Once again, he gave me his wife's name and home number.

I accidentally left my water can in his office. Not knowing it belonged to me; he took it home but brought it back to me.

The attorney told me I could live like a Queen on my Social Security. I teasingly told him that boded well because I am a Queen. Don't think he understood the humor. Yet when I told another person my name, he said, "Elena de Troy."

Life in the casita lacked conveniences so I moved to Bario Carit outside of Puriscal. Here's another letter written to friends and relatives.

While I camped out at Casita Alturas as work continued on the house, I wrote on a book (second mystery), and dealt with getting my money wired from my investment company so I could pay for my container. I soon realized that the little house lacked space for my things and sat too far in the country with no phone and Internet of my own to live happily. Divine Intervention undoubtedly has guided me throughout the entire endeavor!

When Henrietta, a former first lady of Costa Rica, asked me in my friends' living room in Alabama, "Why are you moving to Costa Rica?," I had only part of the answer. Beyond living well on my Social Security, my purpose grew to include that of helping people especially through their grief and loneliness. (I have seen her several times since when I visited my friends.)

As I contemplated about how to break the news to the couple I rented from that living in their tiny house without basic amenities bothered me, they broached the subject to me. Their assessment enabled us to maintain a friendship and for me to openly search for another place to live.

Shortly after our discussion I learned of a very nicely built 3-bedroom, 1 bath, gated house on an uptown street in Santiago de Puriscal. Only, when the owner presented the contract, it wasn't what we agreed to orally. He tried to gouge me by specifying increases from the initial $350 a month until it reached nearly $500 a month. Listed among the many duped by an American real estate agent, I assumed he wanted to pay back someone.

If a lease specifies dollars, inflation covers increases. A lease written in Colones allows 15% per year increases. Legally written for a term of three years, the tenant may terminate any time with three months' notice, rendering the contract null and void. Fortunately, the owner misspelled my name in the contract written in Spanish so I could to read a copy and consult with the shipper and my attorney. (Subsequently I ran into problems with the attorney and his brother/partner. The shipper left the firm I used. While my experience was fine, some other immigrants had problems.)

About this time, I started riding into Escazú to the International Baptist Church on Sundays with a man I met on tour that I will call John. After a very different service, very unlike any Southern Baptist Church of our youths, we ate lunch Dutch treat at a very nice restaurant, and shopped at Price Smart (like Sam's and Costco's) and the Auto Mercado, a wonderful, large grocery store that has products from home.

I'm lucky that I can afford to shop here because living on a local diet could cause cravings. Even though I ran out of vitamins, I eat more fresh fruit and vegetables, walk, and feel healthy especially because I lost 15 lbs. John said he found them.

Although an Auto Mercado branch in Multiplaza Mall attracts many shoppers, we prefer the one in Santa Ana (pronounced Santana). Many products come packaged in small portions and in squeezable bags. He and his friend of many years helped me by putting holes in my walls with the drill set a Dallas friend gave me. A grandson and his father turned the bulkhead parts into three tables for the pila factory. The aggregate concrete walls in my house make it a challenge to hang things.

By the way, the pastor's wife who has a beautiful voice led half of the church service in song at IBC. The pastor based his talks – they don't sound like sermons to me – on the Bible reading.

I found the people friendly. In fact, one member who has a travel agency came and took me to a women's brunch where I met a number of interesting women. Afterwards, I took the local bus back, which made it a very full day.

The pastor's wife arranged a "Paris Fashion Show," and by the luck of the draw, chose me as one of the models. She and others now refer to me as "the model." Two of us had to put on all sorts of items and our assistants had to prepare and read a commentary.

My items included a mini bikini, fur collar, pointed wizard's hat, toilet paper and Windex. I told John I hoped to get a photo so I could show him what a character I am. He said, "I already know." The bus schedule from Barrio Carit where I lived didn't coincide with the bus to San Jose on Sundays. I needed to take a cab to catch the nine a.m. bus in order to have someone pick me up at Multiplaza and ferry me safely to church for the service at ten a.m., if John didn't drive me.

During the first ride into Church, I told John about my adventure with getting a place to live, and he said he knew of a house for only $200 a month, owned by the heirs from their mother and grandmother. He has known the grandson for over a year.

"My house" was located 2 ½ kilometers east of Santiago de Puriscal, essentially in the country but close enough so I could walk into town. John suggested trying to walk home first because of the downhill route. The bus stopped a short walk up a dirt road to a well-paved road.

My former landlady "forgot" my receipt when we settled up, probably an excuse to see the house, and brought it to me. I had a three-year lease, and the right to renew for a year. The grandson's very nice attorney willingly worked with my attorney to fine-tune the contract to insure it covered legally.

The house had no bars but as one son advised, I put combination locks on the front gate and the side gate at the driveway. So far, I made very good choices about what I shipped. Of course, I seem to own far more things than many Ticos. The house, which has no street address, sits among houses owned by relatives of the deceased woman in whose house I lived.

The grandson's mother, who speaks no English, helped me unpack. After I showed her a photo of Dana at about 21, she said, "Now you have nine children, seven boys and two daughters." They call me the new Abuela (grandmother); I understand they helped me as they had their mother who died after a serious illness at 79 only six months before I moved in. The grandson said that his mother and her sister-in-law talk daily and ask, "Is Helen okay?"

He said they feel happy to have me in the house because they expected that I cared about where I live and that it felt like having his grandmother back. I feel very safe despite knowing some foreign people have had things stolen. Some theft results by not taking precautions like those that we do in the States.

Fortunately, I brought wooden toys, stuffed animals and games as well as the rocking chair from my childhood to fit my new role as "grandmother".

Felipe, one of the seven sons, worked in the garden like a Trojan. He would become my "adopted Tico son." On the first Sunday I lived in the house, he visited me with his wife's cousin who lives in San Jose but comes to the country each Sunday and said he

wanted to do it gratis to restore it to the way his mother liked it.

He likes it because I don't stand over him and instruct him every step of the way. The garden has banana plants (a stalk is almost ready to cut), palm and other trees, poinsettias around the fence which will bloom in December, herbs, roses, other flowers and more. Another grandson, age 15, helped Felipe by "mowing" the garden with a weed eater.

The first Saturday Felipe carried away the debris in a plastic coated cloth cut from a sack. You should have seen his face when I presented him with a new toy, a wheelbarrow that a son-in-law helped me get to the house.

It cost only ¢9000 or about $19. In return, he has given me many flowers, even went down into the farm and picked tropical flowers, including the Canon de Emperador, and lent me a vase in which he arranged them. His wife brought me roses from her garden.

Felipe and his wife have three girls, who address me as Doña Helen, a cat called Kitty who had three babies, a dog and her two puppies. I gave Kitty and the dogs treats. One night, his wife presented me with a good dinner of a type of small chicken (think a Cornish Game Hen), rice, and bananas that I ate for brunch the following day because I had eaten dinner already. The plantains were hard; I like soft plantains but the rest of the meal was tasty.

Okay, so tell me about the house, a friend wrote. Approximately 1300 square feet including inside and outside areas, it had three bedrooms, two baths and a great room for a living room, with a built-in dining table and shelf unit on the wall that separated a square open kitchen with windows on three sides, one looking out on the covered terrace. (Later after I moved, the owner removed the table that made the area more open and the kitchen easier to arrange.)

Large white tiles covered the floors, except in the bathrooms, which had smaller colored tiles installed. Only light bulbs hung from the ceilings just as they did in rental apartments and houses in Europe in the sixties.

The great room was painted a sunny yellow; my office and the two-part bath, shades of blue. The rest of the walls were pale pink. I kept what I wanted of the Abuela's furnishings.

As I settled in, I returned some things. John and the grandson collected my empty boxes. Due to the damp weather, they said not to store boxes. However, that may depend upon where one lives because later I stored boxes successfully.

A small covered entrance patio welcomed one out front where a painted bench and two Adirondack chairs from Sarchi surrounded my metal mesh table.

The rear-covered patio housed a tiled pila, or three–part sink (the family business), a wonderful LG washing machine I bought, and a Whirlpool dryer delivered without wiring and a vent tube. (These weren't sold with dryers then.)

My outside furniture, a shelf unit for garden items, and a small picnic table with two benches that came with the place fill the space. As I don't have a car parked at one end, the space feels very ample.

As an aside, the washer started backing up one day as it drained so I called the grandson because he spoke English but he wasn't home. His mother came down after I explained the problem, picked a branch off a tree, stripped it of leaves and stuck it down the drain. Then she discovered the water backed up through a drain meant for a Tico washer.

She went back to her house and brought two jars of Potasa, an equivalent to Draino, and put it down several drains.

When that didn't work, she removed a tile that covered the hole at the end of the drain in the garden and discovered a toad lodged in it. She pulled him out with my garden tongs and put him in a bag to dispose of so the animals wouldn't attack the dying toad. At night, toads came around the house. In the day, chickens and rooster pecked away in the garden. Of course, neighborhood dogs and cats visited.

My gorgeous bedroom, larger than the one I had in Dallas; holds the Queen-sized bed that fills only about half the room. As I moved the sheers to other windows to make them fuller in the great room, I bought beautiful custom-made off-white sheers for the windows in the bedroom.

The young woman that predicted completing them by Monday called me proudly to announce them ready only two hours later. Ticos have a tendency to tell you what you want to hear, so after the fiasco at Gallo Mas Gallo with getting my cellular repaired, I explained in Spanish that if she couldn't have it ready, to tell me so because I didn't want to make two trips into town. Total cost for the service: ¢8800 or less than $19.

The bath, pink and gray in which my linens looked wonderful, opened to my room and the biblioteca, as the grandson's mother called the combination TV/library/guest room. I kept a dresser and double bed on which I placed pillows to make it look more like a Roman couch. Eventually I contracted for Direct TV.

Both rooms had built in closets with racks and shelves enclosed by curtains. Most of the windows (except the kitchen windows which open wide and I close at night or when I leave) had six inch wide louver windows which I left open. If someone wanted to get in, climbing in a kitchen window seemed more likely but it never happened. As I wrote the original epistle, both the front and rear doors stayed open during the day. From my desk seat I could see the entrance and the back door that had a screen door with a bell hanging from the inside handle. Fearing the ceilings couldn't hold ceiling fans, I bought a large floor fan at Price Smart that John assembled to supplement the two table fans I shipped.

The guest bath opened onto a six-foot wide hall that contained my drop leaf table and their grandmother's china cabinet. Also off the hall are a powder room, in which I hung the mirror framed in shells that a friend made, and a large shower room. Both showers have the heat-on-demand electric water heater heads nicknamed suicide showers. Initially I had to put used toilet tissue in a receptacle provided for it next to the servicios because the small septic tank couldn't handle it. I changed the bags regularly to avoid an offensive odor. (This would be necessary in other houses I lived in. Many public places also require this type of disposal.) I had a fast Internet line into the house and could talk on the phone at the same time but the speed cut in half.

I hired an electrician to ground the plug for the computer (no *grounded plugs in the house), to check the plugs that didn't work, to install 220 for the dryer and to check the shower connections. Even though a plug looks like a proper one does not mean it works or that it has a ground wire connected.*

Once I had my computer center set up and could print again, I expected to get mail, either via the post office or by email. I learned that Customs might intercept packages, except for books, but forwarded mail apparently wasn't opened; at least in my experience. For example, I never got the forwarded vitamins. John told me it took him nine trips to Customs in San Jose and cost him about $400 to get $100 worth of vitamins.

Therefore, my $28 worth of pills rotted in Customs. If anyone sends me anything, I suggested putting it into a card or letter. Two cards, one from the States and one from Europe, arrived without incident to convince me that seemed credible.

Recently some expats reported that items sent by a friend as a gift usually avoid landing in customs. Also, it is wise to use up one's $500 exemption every six months by sending packages of value because customs will use up the entire exemption for one shipment regardless of its worth.

CHAPTER Eighteen

Comparing Life in Costa Rica to the US After the Move

Similarities and Otherwise

So what's life in Costa Rica really like compared to that in the United States? Ask ten people to answer that question, like seeking what happen from witnesses to an accident, and each story differs. I remember a male friend who refuted my life in Germany. His memory of his sojourn varied because he lived there after World War II as part of occupying forces but my experiences in the late 1960s remained valid although widely different from his. Please note that my adventure in Costa Rica probably varies from what you or any other person moving here may experience.

To begin with, several opinions exist about what to bring when moving to Costa Rica. The guide who showed me towns in the Central part of Costa Rica in August 2004 preached, "Sell everything and buy down here." At that time, airlines allowed more bags weighing more on flights and for a couple, such a choice was more feasible if they wanted to buy everything new.

Another retiree I met brought everything, filling a 40' container and part of a 20' container, which he shared with another person. I had 153 items ranging from a large desk to an outdoor table and mostly boxes of all sizes that didn't quite fill a 20'container.

(See Appendix C.)

If you have room, possibly in a garage, you could measure an area 20x20 feet and 8 feet high to help you determine what will fit in a half container. It's possible to pack a container tightly if it's not full so everything survives the journey. By using a mover in Costa Rica – I had great service using ABC Mudanzas, S.A. – the price would have remained constant even if I had filled the container to the brim. Other people I know weren't so lucky with the company. Check out current experiences from expatriates before selecting the firm you trust and request everything in writing as a guarantee of terms.

From researching as much as I could during my exploratory visit, I determined that high quality furnishings here could cost as much or more as shipping treasured pieces. Many of the fabrics and designs were different, especially in the rural areas, and some inexpensive pieces of furniture felt extremely uncomfortable. Despite my old things locals saw them in good shape, and as I've noted before thought I'm rich. What impression might result if I had brought the 80% I sold or gave away?

Of course, the amount you bring limits where you can live. After you have investigated areas and know where you want to settle and about how big your abode will be, ship your goods.

Check with your potential neighbors to determine their experiences rather than taking the word of someone who lives in a different climate. For example, a couple that own a B&B outside of Puriscal said that the rubber seals in jars deteriorate. Having seen these items for sale at Cemaco, a store that sells household goods, I shipped mine to protect foods from bugs. The seals still function after eight years.

Knowing how great Costa Rican coffee tastes and preferring freshly ground beans, I included an old coffee grinder that after 30 years fell apart. So I bought a name brand version at Cemaco that lasted about ten months and wound up with a ¢25000 credit.

Returning things to stores has changed in just the years I have lived here making it far easier. The common policy five years ago essentially stated that if you bought it, you owned it. However, in reality what was/is the legal guarantee? Does it mean that the seller will replace a defective item or accept an unwanted item for exchange, refund or credit?

For all I know, the law may have stated all along that no matter what the retailer tells you verbally or in print, every retail purchase in Costa Rica, even those bought at a discount, comes with a 30 business day guarantee (or about 40 days if the retailer isn't open seven days a week) from the date of purchase. The key: have the receipt and the original box in pristine shape. Although legislation forces retailers to provide a guarantee with every sale, confirmed by Kattia Chaves, head of the Comisión de Apoyo al Consumidor (Consumer Advocacy Commission), it often remains unclear what the guarantee means. In many cases, a retailer will do their best to make a customer happy, refunding or exchanging a defective or unwanted item. Nevertheless, not all stores accept returns; some impose time limits not quite in tune with the law.

For example, EPA has a 30-day return policy, but not 40 since it is open daily. Cemaco bases it on the warranty, if any.

When I needed to replace the grinder, I went to the repair center where the person told me to go when I called.

A clerk informed me that I had to go to the Cemaco branch where I bought it. About four weeks later, I received the credit. If you think you might need to make a return, ask about the store's policy before you buy something.

Rust sometimes creates a problem. Bring rust remover just in case. Keep in mind that solid wood furniture made in Sarchi looks lovely but some soft wood tabletops scratch easily. I covered mine with a glass top and deal with keeping it streak free. Prices for handmade pieces may cost less than in the States. However, you might choke on some of the prices for electronics, linens, pots and pans and items found in discount stores back home. You might not find the quality you seek either. While you can buy candles here, you might ship them as a starter because they come in handy when the power goes out at night. I wrapped my large collection in wax paper in case they melted but they didn't. I moved in March.

If you are adamant about making what amounts to a radical move and your spouse sinks his or her heels in like a donkey refusing to budge, putting stuff in storage and renting in country for at least six months might solve the disagreement. It's far cheaper than shipping round trip. You also will learn firsthand about what things to bring when you make the decision to retire in Costa Rica.

If you don't have a spouse, don't despair. Many single people have retired in Costa Rica. Some couples aren't jealous of one another and befriend singles.

Some people solve their different needs by spending six months in Costa Rica and the rest of the year in their original country. One man I know plans his year so he gets the best from both locations.

Make sure the medicines you take are available at the CAJA when you sign up for the benefit as some meds are available only in local pharmacies, if they are available at all. You may find out you can order them from Canada addressed to a U.S. mail service that will forward them to Costa Rica. Compare costs and benefits prior to ordering. Also, check the latest laws because some items can't be shipped but must be carried in.

As I had heard wood and the tropics don't mix, I sold most of my antiques. The drop leaf table my grandmother bought in 1920 at the Lord and Taylor store in New York City remains in great condition. In Puriscal, a mildew film coated it but spray furniture polish cleaned it up. In Guachipelin and Cariari, I found *no hay problema.* I had also heard that skirts on couches reduce airflow but I decided to leave the one on the loveseat I shipped. In over eight years, it never mildewed. One friend found his leather couch needed frequent cleaning due to mold. I bought two lovely bar stools more than three years ago and the leather seats on them remain as good as new. Lots of leather living room sets grace homes here.

Let me point out that one of the benefits of moving to Costa Rica is the opportunity to cull out things you don't need, especially those items not used in a year. I can't tell you how many large black bags of trash I filled. I had to carry them to different dumpsters on the property to spread them out.

So what's the answer to what to ship? Whatever you feel most necessary. When in doubt, let your children inherit now --- provided they want the stuff --- or sell, sell, sell. If you can't decide what to part with you could always follow in one man's footsteps and construct a large barn to store stuff in. Alternatively, sell those items you discover you don't need to expats and locals in Costa Rica.

Areas with damp climates affect old, veneered wooden pieces but not if you live in a warmer area or where you have AC. Some of my furniture arrived scratched because when customs unpacks the original container, they don't rewrap the furniture when transferring it to a local container. One friend said he found his movers' quilts worth $500 neatly folded in a corner of the second vehicle.

I wrapped the drop leaf table with shrink-wrap available on rolls as I did two of three small bookcases. The one that wasn't wrapped got scratched. The clear wrap enabled customs to view the items inside (area rugs) and no one removed it.

Every piece of furniture or box needs a number. If a table has two parts, it gets two numbers. If you miss a box, Customs may confiscate one of their choosing. The son of the mover told me that one man lost three large flat-screen TVs due to faulty numbering. Apparently, I missed one box but my mover added it to the list. At least I still haven't missed anything significant to suggest customs confiscated one. I had numbered the three pieces of bulkhead that didn't fit upright that a friend built to keep things from shifting.

The U.S. mover securely installed them across the bottom near the door but didn't have them on his list because the man I dealt with said it wasn't necessary. The son said differently. When in doubt, number and list all items.

Use the Kiss Method when describing box contents. For example, "TV" – even if you have other items in the box, only note the TV.

Identify office supplies as "Paperwork" so it won't look like you are moving a business especially if you plan to apply for residency as a pensionado/a. Books are duty free.

The inspectors who opened some boxes resealed them with Customs' tape so it was clear which ones the officers had inspected.

Am I glad I sent my old sewing machine (made of metal and recently serviced so it worked like new) and related sewing stuff (fabric, ribbons, thread, etc.)? As brand name sewing machines made of plastic cost a lot here, you bet. One friend brought back three different machines on one of her trips back to Canada. I haven't sewn so much in years! The other alternative: hire a seamstress.

Before moving, I had my love seat reupholstered, the perfect size for a small Tico house, with a washable fabric I bought at a closeout sale. With the large remnant, from which I already had made pillows, I covered the seats of three dining chairs belonging to the owners that I had refinished for about $50, and made shams and bolsters to coordinate in the guest/library/TV room. Before moving from Puriscal, I took the fabric off the chairs for future use, replacing it with a simple inexpensive fabric.

Having sent many pillows, which served as packing materials, I turned the matrimonial (double) bed that came with the house into a kind of couch where occasionally I fell asleep while watching TV.

Even worn out linens (more packing material) came in handy; the dogs loved their beds made of plastic crates obtained from the local grocery store and lined with old towels.

The two plastic outdoor furniture and grill covers that I bought in Dallas to cover the two white on white upholstered chairs to keep them clean, although a little damaged from the duty, served to cover the dryer and grill on the covered terrace/carport.

While it took time to use all the pots and pans at least once, I rejoice I sent them. I use the small appliances regularly. I sold my large cookie sheets because I assumed ovens were small and had to buy another to cut the time on baking cookies. Ovens come in 20" and 30" widths. Some models of the larger one have grills and broilers. When I made the first batch of chocolate chip cookies that I had not made in years, I wished I had the larger sheets. When in doubt include the things you might use if you have the room. You can sell or donate what you don't need.

Located at least 3000' above sea level, I had to experiment with time and temperature. (Cooking with different cuts of meat, etc., at the higher level, and with available herbs resulted in a learning experience.) I also regret not sending the burner size flat utensil with holes that one uses on a stove to spread the heat under a pot.

Later I bought two heat spreaders among the many things on my list during a vacation trip to Dallas.

My friend and I managed to get a hose for the grill I bought here and sent it without customs interference by including it with other forwarded mail.

While some people ship cars, think twice and investigate the pros and cons. Someone told me the duty could equal its value because Customs determines a value. I chose not to ship one.

To be able to drive everywhere in Costa Rica, buy a 4-wheel drive vehicle. Cars cost about half again as much as they do in the States due to all the taxes. Gas and diesel prices overall keep climbing.

However, one can afford to buy a used vehicle and have it repaired because labor allegedly remains relatively cheap. I question this viewpoint based on friends' tales. It may depend on the brand and the availability of parts.

A friend told me that he imported his 20-year old rice cooker. When it stopped working, his gardener took it apart and found a kernel of rice inside the mechanism. It took him about 20 minutes to make the repair. I paid about $23 for a large Daewoo rice cooker figuring if I entertained here, rice would be a part of the menu. Entertaining on the terrace became necessary because locals bring their kids regardless of what the invitation says, and I never have childproofed my home.

I rarely use all the china I brought but I couldn't buy the same quality here for what I paid for it. Having to wash dishes by hand, one tends to use the same ones repeatedly.

Ceramic and plastic dishes fill shelves in local grocery stores and a discount store called Pequeño Mundo sells dishes, glasses and more. Having books, photos, artwork, and albums with me makes my house a home.

Put cleaning tools on your list. When a mop broke, I used the Tico type. Fold two cheap hand towels bought at the grocery store into the device where string mops (available in stores) are usually installed on a pole. You can easily remove them for cleaning in a washing machine after each use. First, I bought a super, programmable LG mid-size Fuzzy Logic washing machine and then a Whirlpool dryer. However, the dryer didn't come with an electrical cord or the exhaust tube.

It was necessary to go to Cemaco – at the time the store-combined hardware and household goods including china and crystal departments – located in a suburb of San Jose to buy the vent kit, part of which I didn't need. The electrician connected the electrical cord when he installed a 220-volt line for the dryer. Cemaco eliminated the hardware department subsequently.

If I hadn't sent the three old TVs, I could have justified buying a new TV sooner even though they cost more in Costa Rica. Without a satellite or cable connection, only a few local stations with poor reception broadcast.

Even at Price Smart, sort of like Sam's or Costco, prices for TVs and other things often seem high, sometimes higher than local stores. In some cases, prices are better. Share the membership for two that costs $30 a year with a spouse or friend.

In Puriscal, I had Direct TV (satellite dish on the roof) on only one of the TVs due to the cost. Later in Guachipelin, I hired Amnet and paid 75 cents a month for an additional TV. Shortly after moving to Puriscal, I gave one TV to a friend. When I moved to Guachipelin, I bought a larger screen TV for downstairs.

My house in Carit was larger than the standard Tico home but certainly smaller than many owned by rich locals and foreigners.

White tile that covered the floors throughout the house made it brighter and helped it to appear larger, the colored tiles in the bathrooms showed less dirt. Tile is easy to sweep, vacuum and mop. The dogs and cats left footprints outside, making it a challenge to keep those areas clean even with help.

Mildew appeared here and there and needed constant monitoring. Some houses, like the first one I lived in at the B&B, had painted concrete floors.

It's interesting that on the farm dust accumulated rapidly on concrete floors and required sweeping, vacuuming and mopping at least once a day. Periodically I applied colored wax. Dust in Carit outside Puriscal seemed less than in the apartment in Dallas. Having area rugs helped to soften the look. Tumbling them on the air cycle in the dryer helped to remove dust. The tile, slippery especially when wet, didn't require wax.

Garbage service in Carit cost less than $3 a month for a once a week pick-up. Mostly I put one bag of garbage mid-week outside on a shelf that animals couldn't reach until I had a canasta (metal basket) made to hold trash. Then I added a second bag at the end of the week so I didn't have a foul odor in the kitchen.

With a small septic tank, one dropped toilet paper into a covered trash can. I transferred the plastic bag lining it to the garbage in the kitchen every other day. One does not need to do this everywhere but in public places receptacles sit by the toilet for this purpose. When a friend remodeled his house, he put in a large septic tank to eliminate the need.

Incidentally, gray water such as that coming from the kitchen sinks runs to ground or river through pipes. My neighbor said that in the Carit house the water diverted to a creek rather than to the far corner of my lovely garden filled with everything from tropical flowers to roses. Poinsettias, which bloomed in December, grew to ten feet tall along two sides of the fence. When the roses and gladiolas started to bloom, one cut them for the house to prevent rain from destroying them.

After the rainy season starts, like Indian Summer, *el* veranilol *de San Juan* (San Juan's little summer) breaks the rain pattern for a couple of weeks. To learn more about tropical gardening check out Tico Times Columnist Ed Berhardt articles. Contact him at **http://www.thenewdawncenter.info/products.html** For herbs check out the Ark Herb Farm **www.arkherbfarm.com** 2269-4847.

One neighbor often sent me a bouquet of tropical flowers. One Saturday another friend cut me seven Birds of Paradise from a wooded area on part of the original farm that at least six houses currently occupied. He's not afraid of the snakes there but fears toads. Another neighbor sent me several gingers, and other flowers, expensive bouquets at a florist in the States. Later I discovered such tropical flowers for sale in Costa Rica cities.

While some places have central hot water as we have in the States, my house only had heat-on-demand showerheads. Some locals don't even take hot showers.

When I added a water on-demand apparatus for the kitchen in order to have hot water I had to install a 220v line for it. The one plug that looked like a switch for an electrocution and appeared to be 220V was only 110v for the small electric stove that came with the house. I bought light fixtures with two receptacles as only single bulbs hung from the ceiling. Many natives don't seem to require good lighting.

Actually, the cold water feels more tepid that cold. It doesn't get freezing the longer you run it, at least not where I've lived. In addition, dishwashing soaps are available to clean with cold water.

Brasso made in Mexico (not the brass cleaner) makes a product that removes grease. I used it to clean up the plate on the little coffee pot stained with coffee and restored it to near original condition.

Another neighbor owned a high-end clothing store in Puriscal. He protected his very large, well taken care of property with a security gate and four large mean dogs that he caged or tethered except at night. The family owned other dogs, a cat, geese, and had a pond with Tilapia. The living/kitchen area of the house seemed small – I wasn't shown the bedrooms – but the lovely Rancho, a house essentially without walls and a wood fired stove in the "kitchen" for entertaining probably equaled the size of the house.

La Nación delivered my paper to their store because our barrio lacked home delivery. He brought it to me. It cost about $10 a month depending on the exchange rate compared to $15 a month for the Dallas Morning News. In 2012 it cost around $12 -$13.

The third son who had a good job in a pharmaceutical company in San Jose lived in a typical Tico house. Three of his dogs and a cat adopted me because I fed and petted them. I took the two puppies, part Chihuahua, to the vet.

The adopted son in the Costa Rican family who just built a home next door before I moved in (he inherited the land from his mother) and his wife both worked in grocery stores, two different chains, in Puriscal. I don't know if he availed himself of it, but the government provides funds for couples to build a house if they have land or if not, to buy land. The house must be built to government specifications, hence the typical floor plan, and the owners can't sell or rent it for 15 years. Later owners may add rooms.

Another son had a lovely looking home with a well-tended lot and a security gate, presumably to protect the car. Their son and I visited one day. He and his parents work for Super Mora, a grocery store, which an uncle owns. Dad works as an executive; his mother, who speaks some English, works in the office

Just up the hill, a daughter and family owned an older sprawling property that included two houses and a large covered area with a commercial bar. The family owned a lumber and pila (local sink made of concrete, sometimes tiled) company. I had a lovely three-part tiled version on the terrace, a bit large for the space.

One daughter, the most successful of the clan, lived in Alajuela and owned a farm up north. At a party I went to, one aunt (not sure on which side of the family), an attorney, drove a $100,000 vehicle, a Lexus I believe. Another son lived in Florida.

As I mentioned earlier I went to a brunch for women of the church I sometimes attended. Held in a new high-rise condominium, I felt transported to the US. The owner said she had all the furniture made in Costa Rica. The kitchen sported large appliances such as a two-door stainless steel refrigerator with outside ice/water access and a dishwasher. I estimated the price of the condo at $350,000 that illustrates that rents and costs of buying run the gamut.

Barrio Carit, in which I lived, owned its own pure water system. It cost ₡1500 (about $3) a month paid annually before the company installed meters. In Puriscal central others paid about ₡2000 a month for water. Rates may vary by neighborhood or an association's bill that will include maintenance and security with a fee for water.

Originally, high-speed Internet service served an area within five kilometers of central Puriscal. (It changed after a few years.) The owner of a B&B had a private phone line that a former owner installed. As a result, they could not switch the phone to their name or have the high speed Internet because they lived about eight kilometers from the source.

The deceased grandmother's name remained on my phone line in Carit. Once I had a cédula (ID card that even the locals have) I could have a phone in my name. No one questioned my paying the bills in other folks' names. I went to the Red Cross to pay them or to ICE, the provider of many services. One could pay at a bank, at a drugstore, and online, but interacting with locals and practicing Spanish prevailed.

Companies don't always send bills. It's up to you to learn the due dates and pay them accordingly. Not having a physical bill does not excuse your lack of payment and no sympathy results if the supplier turns off your electricity or water.

The popular dentist I visited required making an appointment a month in advance. The local native had the latest equipment made in Germany, and charged more than other dentists. He personally cleaned his clients' teeth.

Not long after I moved into the house in Carit I met Rosa who came to my house to give me manicures and pedicures. She painted designs on the nails, something new for me. As I moved from place to place, she followed me. I arranged for others to get their nails done since she had to drive from Puriscal to wherever. Sometimes she or her daughter cleaned my house. Over the years we became friends and exchange Christmas gifts.

Under the impression that I needed to have a will here I contacted my attorney. He explained that when I acquired some property, car or land, and formed a corporation, he would write a will under the corporation. In the meantime, my US version remained valid there but not here. If I write one here, it will negate the US Will according to him. He told me that I should use the money instead to enjoy myself.

When he learned he called on what would have been my son's 40th birthday, he apologized. Knowing I have no relatives, he invited me to come to his house on Christmas Eve – he'd even fetch me – and said I could stay at his Mother's house.

The invitation was incredible! On top of that, attorneys don't charge for emails, phone calls or faxes. Unfortunately, the attorney made excuses so I never went to his home. Later, thanks to actions by his brother, also an attorney, I demanded removal from their client list even though I didn't blame the man I worked with.

Sometimes I saw a multi-colored Hummingbird feeding on flowers outside my office window. A beautiful black and red bird, called a Cacique (ca-seak-ee) and a yellow-breasted bird (Pechoamarillo) often flew into the garden. They often filled the country air with their songs joining the sounds of roosters who couldn't tell time, dogs barking, cows mooing, parrots squawking and cats meowing.

More and more butterflies flew into the garden. People often rode horses down the dirt road outside my house about 50 meters from the paved road that led directly to Puriscal up a hill.

Most of the children seemed very well behaved and they enjoyed my company. Apparently, all these relatives seemed happy to have me living in the house.

What might I have left behind in the U.S.? Maybe the new three-shelf Elfa unit had I known the thin walls made of aggregate concrete defied its installation. Later in the next house, I gladly had it installed because the walls could support the weight. Beyond that, I can think of nothing else. I wish I had brought more of the curly light bulbs. While available here, they cost more and usually came in the cold white variety so I hauled them back in my suitcases when I visited the United States until the soft light bulbs became available in stores here. Sometimes they don't last in Costa Rica as long as the packaging claims.

Allergic to insect bites all my life, I constantly had itchy, red blotches in various state of healing until I bought Off Botanicals made by Johnson and Johnson. I feel I got bitten a lot because I lived outdoors more and petted animals that lived outside. Fewer insects flew inside the house, considering that only the doors and large windows had screens, than on the farm where I lived briefly. I couldn't figure out how to screen the jalousie windows because they jutted out.

However, the sheers on the windows acted somewhat like screens. When it got dark, I closed the drapes. In my bedroom, I had a plug-in device made by either Raid or Baygon that attracted mosquitoes. However, mostly flies, ants and spiders bit me. At the farm the flies turned counters black, especially in the B&B. Eventually some bugs bit me so badly on a day trip to Puriscal that I developed immunity and suffered less although some bugs still found my blood sweet.

Feeling very safe in my area and not wanting to heat up the house that had no HVAC, I left the narrow (about 6" wide) jalousie windows open all the time.

I placed nothing small enough near the windows that someone could reach in and take. I had combination locks on the gates at the front and side, merely to act as a barrier especially to people trying to sell things. I had lightweight chain link fencing installed along the barbed wire fence to keep out strange dogs and chickens. The two table fans I brought with me and the new floor fan I bought here sufficiently cooled the place on warm days. Sometimes I had to turn one off because I felt chilly, usually when it rained.

One thing I've learned since living in Costa Rica: be wary of foreigners who have to earn a living and skimp by. Understandably, some Ticos feel jealous of what foreigners have. I've often explained how one accumulates things over the years from working, from inheriting and from receiving gifts. I also told them how we could buy things at a discount in the States.

Sales in Costa Rica happened only a few times a year at first but more pop up now: a few so-called discount places exist. In Puriscal and other rural areas, normally purchases rated about a 10% discount for paying cash.

American Standard bath fixtures in the house were a far better grade than those installed in the farm. The refrigerator operated but I had to defrost the freezer. Newer frost-free models existed but at least I didn't have to buy a refrigerator until I moved to Guachipelin. The new one had an icemaker, a feature you might not miss.

Some stores carry better quality linens, like Yamuni in San Jose near Universal (has office supplies and more) on Sabana Sur, but it takes a while to locate them.

Alyss has clothing, linens, dishes, and bath and kitchen supplies. Americana Ropa stores feature new and used clothes that fit foreigners. Stores like a chain called Torre de Lobo that buys leftovers from chains in the States and upscale stores in malls carry some items made of cotton and silk but more synthetics line the racks. Most people shop "back home" to supplement their wardrobes and for things like bras that are made differently in most cases in Costa Rica.

You soon learn what you can find in Costa Rica and adjust. Find malls and shopping centers in Costa Rica here: **http://www.infocostarica.com/travel/shopping_malls-op.html**

CHAPTER Nineteen

Communicating

Learning Spanish Affects Adventure

"Español es en mi computadora de mi mente pero no puedo enviar las palabras a mi boca!"

This is what I tell Costa Ricans when I can't remember a word or phrase in Spanish. It was especially true when I first settled in Puriscal because Spanish words hid in the recesses of my brain.

Years ago, Americans living in Europe lamented that the natives did not speak English! Even then, I felt that as guests in the country we should make the effort to speak their language. Therefore, I first learned British words. Friends told me they sometimes had to look up words to understand what I wrote in my letters home. Later I attended three semesters of classes to learn German, receiving a certificate. We learned and promptly forgot parts of German that only graduate students used.

Even though I had studied Spanish in high school and college, and later had taken group and private conversation lessons, I entered Costa Rica without the ability to say much. Fortunately, I could read and write it that made recalling the spoken language from the computer in my mind much easier. Luckily, I lived in Puriscal where few natives spoke any English. Little by little, I could make myself understood even if for a time I suffered from present tense-"itis". After a while I could even communicate over the phone and started thinking in Spanish. Nearly every day I learned or recalled a word heading toward conversational fluency if not perfection.

For example, one day I asked a cab driver what the word in Spanish was for the wide street with tall trees in the middle of the parkway that led to my house.   He said, "bulevar" but I imaged it as boulevard.   Obviously, I knew the word from English and French. Just one more example of knowing a word in Spanish but not knowing I know.

Costa Ricans have used the phrase "Pura Vida" since the mid-fifties when they adopted it as they often do with words they take a fancy to.   As noted before, the phrase denotes a greeting, farewell, or an expression of a philosophy that includes enjoying life and having good spirits.   Ticos delight when foreigners use the expression and such responses as "con mucho gusto" that replaces "de nada" used in other Spanish speaking countries.

Many people who have lived in Costa Rica for years never learned to speak Spanish; some think they do, which causes people to laugh.   I wish I could do a study to determine whether a person's inability to communicate correlates to their tales of bad experiences. When I needed to transact business in English, I began in Spanish and then asked for assistance in English.

When I have to transact business in Spanish where the words aren't in my Spanish vocabulary, especially over the phone, it sometimes requires extra patience by the person on the other end of the line. People the world over become more helpful, I have found, if you first make the effort in their native language.

Some people feel that Spanish presents a learning challenge but compared to German, it's a piece of cake thanks to my experience learning both languages. Spanish has nowhere near the two million words that English purportedly contains. Actually many Spanish words are similar to English. You already know quite a few which gives you a head start to having a vocabulary of about 600 words when you can certainly begin to communicate at least according to the experts. One man I knew learned essential vocabulary words and infinitives and managed to convey basic information.

Words you know include those that end in "tion" in English because they end in "cion" in Spanish. Accents show the emphasis rests on another syllable other than what would be the normal pronunciation. Check p 557 in *501 Spanish Verbs* for clues about pronunciation. Change nation to nación, action to acción, and repetition, repetición. How many words can you list ending in "tion"? While not every English word appears the same in Spanish, you'll delight at how many exist.

Words ending in "ly" in English end in "mente" in Spanish. Words ending in ssion like passion translate to pasión. To me it's interesting that Spanish will drop one of the double letters from an English word, but will make a double letter in some cases, for example Hellen. The meaning of some words like *difícil, gasolina*, and *garaje* seem obvious, even if pronounced differently. Words that end in "al" like special usually end in "al" in Spanish. In this case *especial*. *Espinaca* that means spinach essentially contains the English word. Sometimes adding an "a" or an "o" to an English word nets the correct Spanish word but then most often not.

A couple of examples: form translates to "la forma" and document, "el documento". Another hint: each syllable generally ends in a vowel or ga-so-li-na. Just remember the "i" sounds like an "e" so natives pronounce it as ga-so-lean-a.

Another hint, the vowels are the same as those in English. Spanish does not have the letters 'K' and 'W". However recently I saw the word Komplete on a cereal product advertised in the newspaper. Spanish used to have words starting with a CH that separated them from those beginning with C but they are fading from the language. In any case, in order to learn even basic Spanish the secret remains practicar, practicar, practicar. It doesn't matter if you don't say it correctly, just that you communicate. Ticos differ from the French who allegedly don't care what you say as long as you pronounce it correctly.

My accent sounds American no matter what language I speak although my dialect comes across as more International than from any particular area of the States. Investing in a Spanish/English Dictionary and the 501 Spanish Verbs volume that includes some grammar makes an excellent beginning to clear communication. A source for vocabulary is: **http://www.costaricaspanish.net/**

With these tools, you can make a list of words you know that end in cion, mente, and words you suspect are correct in Spanish and verify them in the dictionary. While you may speak in the present tense to begin with, you can learn the simple past or preterit in the Verbs book. One way to start speaking in the future tense is to use "yo voy a" before an infinitive. You may even drop "yo". For example, I am going to go. "Voy a ir."

Think about this! Whether the sample appears large enough or the findings accurate, AM Costa Rica in November 2010 reported a study of about 200 patients by a Canadian science team, the Rotman Research Institute at Baycrest, a University of Toronto affiliate. The results, reported in the research journal "Neurology", suggested that learning a second language or more could help stave off Alzheimer's for up to five years.

Kate Galante, on November 4-10, 2011 in The Tico Times wrote a column about various virtual programs available for studying Spanish. Some of her suggestions included www.1to1languages.com, www.bbc.co.uk/languages/spanish, For more, look up her article at www.ticotimes.net

While I haven't used online programs, you might want to check these out, keeping in mind that the resources could change: http://www.visuallinkspanish.com/index.html , http://www.spanicity.com/beginner-spanish.htm, http://www.emagister.com/ejecicios-espanol-cursos-1057164.htm , http://www.mansionspanish.com/, and http://spanishfree.org/Audio/Activos/Audio.php.

CHAPTER Twenty

Communication Choices

Latest Communication Devices for Worldwide Contact

Amnet, (now Tigo) CableTica and Direct TV offer cable and Internet services. (Millicom International based in Luxembourg that provides mobile services in 13 countries owns Tigo.)

In my experience, the companies generally provided okay service with limited connection losses or problems and offered a variety of connection packages. Consider that cable frees up landline phones, often at a premium in many areas. Some people have satellite dish connections. In Puriscal, I had Direct TV, the only company serving my area at the time. It delighted me to get Amnet in Guachipelin. The company had a good basic package and offered three different speeds for Internet service. Unfortunately, one had to pay RACSA for a telephone line, the only choice then for Amnet users. Now Tigo subscribers can choose either one or the other.

It may seem a minor point, but parts of the country still lack access to cable television. If you like to watch TV but end up living outside a cable TV area, ask yourself if you will understand Spanish well enough to view only the local channels. You could consider installing a satellite provided it functions in your location.

Foreigners' favorite gripes targeted RACSA, the subsidiary, and ICE, the parent company regarding phone service.

Whether your business depends on it, or you are a computer nerd who gets nervous without broadband connectivity, how these monopolies will deal with competition opened up conjecture. In 2011 thanks to CAFTA Latin America's wireless carrier American Movil's subsidiary Claro and Spain's Telefonica Movistar began to compete with Costa Rican Electricity Institute's (ICE) service called Kolbi, ending the cellular monopoly.

The jury is out because Kolbi has been pushing service and the others' run full page and double truck (2-page) ads trying to attract customers. In some areas like Playas del Coco, according to reports, Claro has not been able to open due to lack of cell towers. Now they have a presence.

My service with ICE or Kolbi is basic, 60 minutes a month that I rarely surpass because I use a landline and Internet services, for about $7.00 a month. Many friends have jumped on the bandwagon with the latest phones that do everything but brew morning coffee and the service costs more.

Cellular phone coverage varies nationwide. If you choose to live in an area that doesn't have landline connections either, then you could feel pretty isolated without good cell service. As detailed before when I lived in Barrio San Juan outside Puriscal for a few months, I only had a cell that had terrible reception. A landline wasn't available.

A phone line existed in the house in Carit in the deceased mother's name. I had a second line installed for the computer because the new owner didn't want me to use the existing line for Internet service. I never understood why.

A few years ago, phone numbers increased to eight digits from seven. Landline phones added a 2 in front of the existing number and cells, the number 8. Increasing the length enabled the country to keep one area code: 506. Even if the message sounds garbled, leave your message after the tone. Of course, it wreaks havoc when online forms won't accept the extra digit. My solution was a Magic Jack number in the U.S.

When I moved into the Cariari apartment, I had no phone line so I used my cell. For the first time my bill cost much more than the minimum usually charged. If you check your landline phone bill, notice that the amount you of the bill is based on usage. It's one rate for calls to other landlines and more when you call a cell. Occasionally I have used prepaid local and international calling cards. At one time using a card cost less per minute than to call overseas from home. Now with Magic Jack and Skype, I don't use the cards or the home phone. Everywhere people walk, ride in buses, or drive cars with a mobile device growing from their ear. Some don't have landlines.

Email and public pay telephones, a dying breed, still rank among the ways of contacting people. Internet cafes dot the landscape especially in tourist areas, with prices varying by location. Some of these offer long distance calls over the Internet.

Although unlocked cells and prepaid SIM cards make public phones and calling cards dinosaurs, some still exist. That is why I define them here. Pay phones include Chip, Colibri and Multipago types. The information appeared correct at the time I collected it.

Chip phones allow you to insert a chip-type calling card into them and make your calls. Avoid buying chip cards sold in small denominations that are insufficient for international calls because they malfunction, and you can use them only at the few-and-far-between chip phones.

Colibri phones have a small swipe bar for a scratch off type calling card referred to as a Colibri calling card available from 500 colones up. The swipes often don't work; you nearly always have to enter the calling card access code on the keypad. Regardless the Colibri calling card remains the recommended one to buy as you can use it in any of the payphone types.

Multipago (multi-pay) phones accept coins, chip cards and Colibri cards. Most public phones around the country were switched to this type of phone. They also allow you to send SMS messages and emails as well.

The phones list instructions in a mix between both languages and have some icons to help the non-Spanish speaking caller. First, you lift the receiver and listen for the dial tone. Next, you deposit 5, 10, 25 or 50-colon coins, insert a chip card, or use a 197 or 199 calling card. Dial the number and then talk. Four buttons provide the option to go to another call (siguiente), to change the "volume", to indicate the language (idioma), and to change to another phone card when the first one runs out of minutes.

Tarjetas para llamadas nacionales (domestic calling cards) come in denominations of 500 colones and 1,000 colones. Phone-card rates are standard throughout the country, about 2¢ per minute; a 500-colón card provides about 50 minutes of landline calls.

The minutes decrease sharply if calling a cell phone. *Tarjetas para llamadas internacionales* (international calling cards) come in denominations of $10, $20, 3,000-colón, and 10,000-colón amounts (amounts inexplicably split between dollars and Colones). It's harder to find the 10,000-colón cards; look for them at a Fischel pharmacy or an ICE office.

Phone cards are sold in an array of shops, including Cruz Roja stations, MasXMenos and other supermarkets, post offices, offices of the Costa Rican Electricity Institute (ICE), pharmacies, Internet cafes, souvenir shops and at any business displaying the gold-and-blue "tarjetas telefónicas" sign. Look for International cards in downtown San José and in other areas popular with tourists. Purchase them from the government phone monopoly ICE. Certainly it seems a much better choice than using a credit card or a US calling card.

Domestic calls are quite cheap; with only one area code a call costs the same wherever you live within the country. . Calls to cellular phones cost significantly more.

International calls are expensive from home lines. Calling over the Internet using a service such as Skype or Magic Jack keeps costs in line. Some people use Vonage phones.

Mobile phone service in Costa Rica provided by Groupo I.C.E. uses GSM technology. Roaming with a GSM handset costs more. Note that the GSM phone systems in the United States and Canada allegedly use different frequencies and travelers from those countries will need a "world" handset. You should check with your provider beforehand.

All reports indicate that most of the country has very good GSM coverage (including most of the capital). Non-residents may rent cell phone service (for example a friend bought a SIM card good for 60 days), and of course anyone can buy a cell phone, but traditionally only a documented resident of the country can own a cell phone *number*, and even then you will only get one if numbers are available. Prior to establishing residency, a corporation can receive a number. Determine in advance, if the fee for establishing a corporation warrants getting a cell number.

The Costa Rican phone system works well as judged by the standards of other developing countries. The dial tone sounds similar to that in the United States. For people without Skype, Magic Jack, or an international phone service, the cheapest way to call internationally is from a pay phone using an international phone card. You can also call using your own long-distance calling card; or call from a telephone office. The cost for dialing directly from a hotel room or recruiting an international operator to connect you might jolt your senses.

To call overseas directly, dial 001, then the country code, the area code, and the number.

You can make international calls from almost any phone with an international calling card purchased in Costa Rica. First dial 199, (or 197 depending on the card) then the PIN on the back of your card (revealed after scratching off a protective coating), and finally dial the phone number.

When requesting a calling card from your phone provider, ask specifically about calls from Costa Rica.

Most 800-number cards don't work in Costa Rica. Check out **www.callingcards.com** , a great resource for prepaid international calling cards. At I wrote it listed at least one calling-card company with rates of 1¢ per minute for calls to the U.S.

You may find the local access number blocked in many hotel rooms because the facility adds surcharges for having a hotel operator make the connection. It's sort of like putting your money in the garbage. First, ask the hotel operator to connect you. If the hotel operator balks, ask for an international operator, or dial the international operator yourself. To reach an English-speaking operator, you'll have more luck dialing the international operator (1175 or 1116). You may improve your odds of connecting to your long-distance carrier by signing up with more than one company: a hotel may block Sprint, for example, but not MCI. If all else fails, call from a pay phone. AT&T, MCI, and Sprint access codes make calling long-distance relatively convenient but ultimately very expensive.

Most car-rental agencies have good deals on cell phones, often better than the companies that specialize in cell-phone rental. If you're not renting a car, a number of these companies will rent phones.

In 2011, rates ranged from $7-$10 per day, plus varying rates for local or international coverage and minimum usage charges. You'll need your ID (passport or cédula), a credit card, and a deposit, which varies per phone and service; some rent only to those over 21. The deposit then drops significantly with companies that can hook you up with a rented local chip for your own phone. Check at an ICE office.

Rated brusque but professional by users on web groups, Cell Phones Costa Rica will get you hooked up, whether you fly into San José or Liberia. Cellular Telephone Rentals Costa Rica has higher daily rates but free local calls. Reach Cell Phones Costa Rica by phone at 877/268-2918 in U.S. and Canada; 506/293-5892 in Costa Rica, and on the web at http://www.cellphonescr.com/; and for Cellular Telephone Rentals Costa Rica: call 800/769-7137 in the U.S.; 506/845-4427 in Costa Rica or visit www.cellulartelephonerentals.com, where you'll find the most up-to-date info . . . probably. The quality of your cell phone, and where you are located will determine how well it receives a signal. At my home high on a hill, I usually got a clear call. Yet my neighbor with an inexpensive phone complained about her reception.

You can make international phone calls, as well as send faxes, from the ICE office, Avenida 2 between Calles 1 and 3, in San José (tel. 2255-0444). The office opens daily from 7am to 10pm. Radiográfica (tel. 2287-0087), at Calle 1 and Avenida 5 in San José, also has fax service. Note: Numbers beginning with 800 within Costa Rica are toll-free, but calling a 1-800 number in the States from Costa Rica costs the same as an overseas call.

Using Skype in an Internet Café offers a solution. Avoid adding attachments or photos to avoid bugs. The cost for accessing the Internet remains extremely affordable in cafes and they abound. Check to see if your hotel offers free Internet services even including WIFI. Buying a cup of coffee entitles you to several hours of Internet usage at restaurants like Bagelmen's.

Traditionally one needed to buy a cell phone in country and carry the receipt to ICE. This has changed. However, unless the person has a cédula, the government prohibits owning a GSM cell phone number.. The same rings true for landlines and they can take time to acquire depending upon the location and availability. I recall having a similar problem in Germany in the mid-1960s.

Keep in mind that competition in CR means the entire communications system will evolve. Already ICE offers 3-G phones and 4G found in the States. Apparently, people utilized the technology even though not certified until approval in July 2010 by the Superintendencia General de Telecommunications (SUTEL). If you use 3G or soon 4G technology, some users recommend not using Edge but choose HSDPA or WCDMA. As I repeatedly write, Google, ask, and ask again to avoid costly mistakes. As I have not used this service, I cannot recommend one over the other.

By the way, the last time I was in the US I bought a Sim Card with time on it and added to it when it got low. I had ICE put my CR Sim card in the phone, a more recent model, and it works well. With an unlocked phone, you should be able to buy a limited use Sim Card here. Some residents use these.

CHAPTER Twenty-One

Will You Need to Supplement Your Income?

Oops! What are your Chances of Success?

You've probably heard that the cost of living in Costa Rica compares favorably with that of living in the States or Canada. Lately some expats are convinced this has changed. Like the world over the cost of living increased combined with a devalued dollar. The Tico Times reported that the Exchange Rate in 2001 equaled ¢317 to a dollar. In 2006, it rose to ¢495 and early in 2011 to ¢506. However, the dollar slowly dipped later in the year, then fluctuated between ¢495 and ¢510. When figuring what something costs it's best to use 500 as a dollar.

From 2001 to 2011 in Costa Rica inflation accumulated during those years totaled 101.72%   Panama had a total of 27%. In some States a low cost of living may exist or not. Therefore, with a limited income, check out your options before choosing where to settle and the residency to select if you opt to live in Costa Rica.

An example of how some things cost a lot more in Costa Rica allegedly due to import taxes is the Magic Jack phone system. I paid about $40 with tax in Dallas, TX in October 2009. In August 2010 Radio Shack in CR offered it for about $60. If you have a mailing service, ship it that way, factoring in mailing costs and the possible hassle with Customs. Alternatively, maybe a friend will bring it in for you. If you have a limited budget, knowing the cost of something will help you decide whether you can live without it.

If you will need to supplement income in Costa Rica, follow the safest road as an entrepreneur. Laws are very specific about foreigners obtaining employment. One of the posts on Costa Rica Central Valley (Digest Number 1943) on July 22, 2011 from *Costa Rica Builder* detailed the subject. Another article to check: **http://www.costaricalaw.com/can-i-legally-work-in-costa-rica.html** Begin by reading the posts to determining what is available to you if you need to work. If you will work for a U.S. firm in Costa Rica, the company may assist you in handling procedures.

Even if you don't have a cédula, get a business cédula number by going to the Tributación office in San Jose located behind the funeral home JARDINES DEL RECUERDO. Fill out a form and provide a copy of both sides of the cédula if you have one or of all of the information pages in your passport. When I applied, I had Pensionada status and paid no fee. Afterward I went across the street to a printer to have invoices made. I ordered the minimum 200 that for a nominal fee arrived at my door two days later. Such services are especially valued when you are sans a vehicle.

Start your own business in a field (even a hobby like making chocolate as a Minnesota couple have) that you have experience in after investigating how businesses are operated in Costa Rica. Using techniques learned in the U.S. or Canada probably will lead to failure. However, if you market online to clients up north, you have a better chance of success using those skills. Remember fewer consumers exist here because about 25% of the population lacks the discretionary funds to spend.

According to La Nación in February 2013, 4,301,712 people live in

Costa Rica based on the 2011 census. Of these 2,106,063 are male that means females have a slight edge. However, since I participated in the census along with other expats and not all Ticos did, the total probably requires adjustment.

One woman I knew invested with close Tico friends in building a number of houses in a development. With expected delays in finding property and obtaining permits, the project never happened. If you go into development, have sufficient funds to allow for unforeseen problems. In fact, the government denied this woman her application for residency and she had to return to the States.

Another friend found a job in an accounting position. Fluent in both languages and an experienced bookkeeper made her invaluable to the investors in a multi-unit housing complex with a combination of owner and rental units. The owners agreed not to treat her as an employee and aided her in getting a business cédula.

Personally, I'm an editor and writer and work as an independent contractor. While I don't expect to invent a Harry Potter character, the prospect of selling books that will help future immigrants pleases me immensely.

If you start your own business, be sure you have some experience in the field. Turn a hobby into a company. Buy a franchise. If you want to live part-time in Costa Rica, think about renting your property when you're not in the country.

Regardless of how you find that extra income, file a Costa Rican tax return for income received. Even if you have minimal sales that don't require paying taxes, you don't want to cross the IRS in Costa

Rica. In 2011, it became necessary to download a program to your computer so you can pull up the correct form. After filling in the blanks print three copies and go to Banco Costa Rica to turn in your return. You can get help from the Ministerio Hacienda but most people find it easier to hire an accountant. Make sure the people who have used the services recommend him or her. Whether you have to file an income tax return in the States on what you earn requires investigation with the U.S. IRS.

Questions to ask: Will my retirement income provide enough to live on at my preferred level of comfort, keeping in mind that living abroad may not afford certain amenities I'm used to without a higher cost?

Am I willing to live at a level that doesn't require extra income?

Do I want to go into business for myself or find an employer, U.S. or Costa Rican, if I have the correct residential status?

Will prices going up require adjusting my standard of living level downward?

Will I have enough discretionary income to return to my country as often as desired or needed?

If I find I don't have enough income and my job choices are limited after I've moved, will I have enough funds to move back home?

CHAPTER Twenty-Two

Transport Choices

Public and Private Means of Living sans a Car

With yo-yoing gas prices, potholes, drivers who break the laws, fearless motorcycle riders called pending organ donors, lack of street signs, one-way streets, foreigners who break laws inadvertently or on purpose, does driving around in Costa Rica by car frighten you whether you drive or not?

Perhaps you will join the bus corps, an informal group of Gringos and Ticos who make their way around by bus supplemented by taxi rides. Some of the members use the extensive bus system out of need. Those over 65 years old simply present their cédula and ride free except on long distance trips (over 25km). The cost is discounted for longer rides. Seniors may become exempt from paying train fares with a decision in 2010 by the Sala Constitucional (Constitutional Court) that ordered the Instituto Costarricense de Ferrocarriles (Incofer) and the Ministerio de Obras Públicas y Transportes (MOPT) to adjust their fare schedules.

The Autoridad Reguladora de los Servicios Públicos provides *for* seniors 65 and over to get preferential treatment on buses. The Defensoría de los Habitantes has received complaints from seniors that drivers have kept the cédula or otherwise treated them badly. Anyone who files a complaint should include names and if possible contact information from witnesses (difficult to obtain). The free informational number that I have called is 8000-273737.

An English-speaking employee helped me after I asked in Spanish if someone spoke English. This is often the case as sometimes the person knows some English but is reluctant to speak it.

Most of the time bus drivers are helpful. They take the card and write down the number or simply say "pasé" without taking it. If they have a scanner, they run the card through it. Buses in San Jose tend to have these. In Puriscal, a reader hung on the wall. If the driver takes it at a major stop, he walks back through the bus to return them. If he keeps it en route, you have to remember to pick it up when you disembark. I almost forgot one time but the driver reminded me. Carrying a cane to help me get off the bus usually emphasizes my age that luckily I don't look. I call it my costume.

One time the bus driver gave me back my card, railing something in Spanish that I didn't understand. A passenger explained that he said he had to pay for my fare whether or not he wrote it down. As I believed that the government benefit for mature people by law (later verified) required acceptance on every bus line – and I had never had a problem on the Guachipelin route before – I didn't offer to pay. Another time the driver said that I had to be a registered voter it is not the case.

Later I inquired about it with a fellow bus corps member. She said that not every Costa Rican likes foreigners and perhaps the driver numbered among them.

She encountered a driver who said the cédula number took too long to write down. Later she tried to pay but he waved her away. Most of the time drivers wait for seniors to sit but one time the driver shot off. Some passengers kept her from falling.

When I first arrived, pensioners traveled to San Jose to fetch tickets to ride buses without a fee, the day on which one accomplished this determined by the initial of one's last name. Representatives only distributed five sheets of twelve tickets to a supplicant. One had to decide the length of trip needed and select the appropriate tickets. Technically the tickets lasted a month but actually remained valid as long as one had them except for the year when the government issued a new series. When a native ancient went to court, the tribunal decided that elderly people needed only to present a cédula. The law regarding senior citizens instructed the bus companies to change their fare requirements. Switching to accepting a Cédula as proof has undoubtedly saved the government money.

One day I took a bus to Alajuela to go to a store to shop – got off at the correct stop with the help of a passenger – and then met with a friend for lunch. As I boarded the bus for home, I told the driver where I wanted to disembark. He said to sit behind him so I assumed he planned to let me off at that stop. When I realized he drove too fast to stop, I tried to press the buzzer unsuccessfully. I had him take me several stops into San Jose where I knew the pedestrian crossing (four flights of stairs up, four down) and took a bus back. Despite ringing well in advance, the driver by-passed my stop and I got off at the mall. As no cabs stood along the drive, I walked across the pedestrian overpass and started walking toward home. Fortunately, a cab came by. He didn't use the meter but charged me ¢1000 (about $2) which was fair.

The time I reported the incident occurred when I took a bus from San Jose to Cariari. Somehow, the scanner failed to read my card.

The driver shut the door at my stop and waited until I paid the fare to let me off the bus. His company received a letter from the authorities.

Some expats travel by bus like many Costa Ricans because they fear driving or don't want the anxiety of dealing with Tico drivers. The kind native people change their personalities when they sit behind a wheel. As mentioned before, bicycle and motorcycle drivers as well as potholes add to the motoring challenge.

Some rent cars for a special outing. Having only rented a car with a driver, I can't vouch for any company. However, in one of the chat groups a couple wrote, "My husband and I are almost at the end of a two-month SUV rental from Dean Krieg/4x4CR. Prior to this trip we had always used one of the big name rental agencies. Since we were staying for two months this time around, we needed to find a better deal."

While the old car they rented had a leaky door, she noted the mechanical condition was good and the tires new. Add prompt delivery to their hotel made them feel they blended into the landscape.

They explained that the muffler blew out near the end of their stay. Hugo at the rental place delivered a replacement car to them within two hours but the second car wasn't up to their requirements, so they called again. The next morning the first car appeared at their doorstep repaired and washed, sans the leaky door. I found Dean's website that contains other clients' recommendations: **http://www.renta4x4incostarica.com/.** Search online "rental cars in Costa Rica" and "4x4 rentals in Costa Rica" to encounter choices.

One of the buses on the Guachipelin Road to San Jose took me through Escazú where I could get off at favorite haunts like Don Fernando's meat market that sells beef prepared more like U.S. cuts. He owns his own cattle ranch. With prices higher than local meat markets, his products sustain a high quality. Another meat market of the same ilk is Don Melchor 2260-6028; **www.carnesdonmelchor.com**. The only complicated destinations were getting by bus to San Antonio de Belen and Cariari beyond unless I took a cab at least at some point. The problem reversed itself when I moved to Cariari.

In Santa Ana Carnicería Olando, on the old road headed toward Escazú, has good meats and will cut to order. I've been told they have their own farm. It's across the street from the Hermanos Montos service station. Call 2282-9557

To get to Puriscal for a visit now entails taking the bus to San Jose and then the express back west, or going to Multiplaza to catch a local, a two to three hour jaunt depending on how long one waits for buses and the amount of traffic.

However, the long trip let me read a book or practice Spanish with fellow passengers. In the past, I garnered valuable information about a topic. For example, when my computer continually presented the so-called blue screen of death, I learned the cause. My experience riding the bus has included drivers from surly to extremely friendly and helpful. When I used to ride a bus to the PC Club (**pcclub.net)** meeting at the Pan American School, one driver always flirted with me. He showed me a photo of his novia that he called Cleopatra. In San Jose, a bus (not the one I was on) blocked traffic by stopping at an angle so I could safely cross the road. On a Station Wagon bus company route from Alajuela toward San Jose, I witnessed drivers waiting for passengers, some obviously regulars getting off work. In one case, a driver saw me coming and waited for me. On the negative side, a few drivers didn't stop at obvious bus stops. Perhaps they were express buses. Some drivers are patient about answering questions and giving directions; others not. In the latter cases, I ask a passenger in Spanish what I need to know.

In Costa Rica people offer seats more often than not to the infirm, aged, or women with babies. I've had many a hand extended to help me off a bus even without a cane. I have never felt threatened when people offered assistance.

However, like everywhere in the world when one uses public transportation, one must keep an eye on belongings. Don't wear jewelry except for inexpensive earrings if you have pierced ears and a cheap watch. From time to time one hears about robberies on buses even though most people assume that bus riders don't carry much cash or wear expensive jewelry.

In some areas bus stops are not obvious, just places in front of a store or at the side of the freeway. In some cases, a covered stop with seats stands on one side of the road but not the other.

After I fell and injured a knee, I started using a decorative wooden cane for particularly uneven streets or when riding a bus. I've always felt that watching for holes to avoid falling makes one more vulnerable because it's difficult to watch the people around you at the same time Using a cane provides extra security. The grade of the lower step on most buses is usually very high to allow for sidewalks, mostly non-existent. Many buses have few handles to hold onto so the cane helps one negotiate that last step down. Carrying a cane adds to deference shown mature and handicapped folk too. Many places still lack handicap accommodations although progress looms hopeful.

Online "AM Costa Rica" columnist Jo Stuart ranks among the bus corps. In one column she pointed out that she usually arrives on time as opposed to those who drive themselves to an appointment. In fact, I'm often more than prompt too because like Jo I take an early enough bus to allow for traffic jams and late buses.

The situation reminds me of when I had a job that required me to arrive on time. I chose to drive the long distance rather than move to a small town and always clocked in on time unlike those employees who lived just blocks away. Jo has figured out how long it will take to walk four blocks to the bus stop (and which bus stop to walk to) and how much time different buses will take to deliver her where she wants to go. Occasionally when her small and lightweight bus book eludes her, she might miss a bus.

Used to having my own vehicle over the years, not having a car in Costa Rica harkened back to my childhood.

Some people here value the freedom of doing chores, exploring the country, or scheduling appointments without waiting for buses. As one guide asked, "What do retirees have but time?"

Some friends do not own a vehicle and happily and safely move around the city and country on public transport as I do. We bus riders also hire drivers, use taxis and gladly accept rides from those with cars. As one friend explained, "No one without a car will turn down a ride." (That's not true if the person drives poorly.) The well-established efficient network of city and country wide public transport provides low cost transportation regardless. Airline flights within the country have increased.

Red taxis have meters. Expect to pay tolls if any when hiring a taxi. A driver doesn't expect a tip but if he (have never had a woman chauffeur although I understand a few exist) does something extra like haul suitcases or grocery bags; he appreciates a few hundred extra colones.

If you use private taxis called piratas or porteadores, negotiate the fare beforehand. Use those recommended by friends. Cultivating a friendly 'pirata' driver in the neighborhood to cover regular outings or early morning trips makes life easier. Have two or three to call because one driver is not always available. Excuses run the gamut from taking time off to attend a wedding or funeral or some other event because family comes first.

Some drivers are more reliable, something you learn by trial and error. Sometimes, unbelievably, a taxi service company may not have an available taxi. Keep in mind, a public transit lifestyle still works out cheaper than owning a car.

Your transportation requirements will depend on whether you live in the city, in the country, or at the beach. You also have a choice whether to buy a new or second hand car or even whether to bring your car in from abroad. In addition, what's the deal with motorcycles?

They frighten me because moto drivers weave in, out and around cars and cause many accidents. They often don't follow traffic rules. Yet friends who own them, even those who received injuries while driving one, have to have one.

Russell Martin and his wife Kattia own WheelsCR.com, the English pages related to the Fijatevos.com auto database for Costa Rica. It offers used vehicles for sale from direct import dealers. It's a resource for deciding whether to import a car, the pros and cons of doing so, the costs, the popular brands, the laws, and more. Again, remember your friend Google and research, research, research.

Buying a car from a dealership with a posted price or from an advertisement means a foreigner probably will get a fair price, a short warranty, and perhaps the assurance that the car wasn't shaken over the many potholes decorating the roads in Costa Rica. Dealers offer financing, accept trade-ins, and assist with registration.

Warning: Watch out for higher prices for Gringos versus Ticos when purchasing from a private owner. It's a good idea to have a native handle the initial inquiry. Remember to exercise caution even when buying from someone you know. Despite what the owner might say, have the vehicle checked out by a reputable mechanic, one recommended by several people.

At one time, I thought about buying a car since I lived up a hill that took me 15 minutes to walk down, steep and slippery after rain, to get to a bus. A couple I knew through a club offered for sale a car whose model year dated ten years before. Unhappy that I insisted on having it checked out by a dealership, they nevertheless accommodated me. The $100 cost to learn of many repairs saved me several thousand dollars. It's not a matter of mistrusting someone you know, it translates to protecting yourself.

Lawyers advise if one owns something, including a car, to put it in a corporation to protect the owner from personal liability. Check the pros and cons especially now with the new tax on corporations.

When considering buying a car I had about decided to put it in my name because I own nothing else but personal belongings in Costa Rica. Several friends told me they own their cars in their names and have not had a problem.

In the spring of 2011 train service from San Antonio de Belen to San Jose began for a cost of less than $1.00 each way. Several secure public parking lots are within blocks of the train station located in the center of Belen near the Catholic Church.

For more information about rail service in the country, including the schedule from Belen station, check this link: **http://horariodetren.com/cr/index.php?lang=en**. Here is a link of one person's experience riding the train to Heredia from San Jose: **http://www.eldoradocostarica.com/English/News/art.php?nNew sCod=2247** Websites to check out about the bus system: **Costa Rica By Bus** (also has a book) and **Costa Rica Bus Tickets**

Recently some bus companies have introduced the Tarjeta Tapachula, a card read by a small card reader at the entrance of the bus. It saves time boarding. You have to have a cédula and apply for one. I went to the Municipality in Escazú, presented my

138

cédula and had my photo taken one day. The following day I went back for the free card. The day you sign up happens every two months because they have different days in different locations according to one of the clerks running the signup. The number I called to inquire in Spanish was 2289-8007, x131.

Questions to ask if you decide to buy a vehicle:

What does establishing a corporation cost?

What corporate paperwork is needed to handle the annual requirements when owning a car?

Must you file a tax return?

What annual stamp does the corporation need to purchase?

What liability does a corporation have in the event of an accident?

What hassles might I have in proving I'm the corporation owner?

Will requirement of naming board members create a problem?

What happens if the lawyer proves unscrupulous or careless?

Name the advantages of having a company own the car.

What type of vehicle will you need depending on where you live?

What brands are best to buy?

How does one pay the Marchamo (Google for current requirements) and inspections if a corporation owns the car? Beware that passing the Riteve (Google too) does not guarantee the condition of a car.

CHAPTER Twenty-three

To Ship or Drive a Car to Costa Rica?

Pros and Cons – Your Adventurous Quota

Look around as you travel the streets of Costa Rica. What brands do you see most often? Why Toyota, Nissan, and Hyundai?

These vehicles tend to hold their resale value and parts although often more expensive than in the U.S. are readily available. Mechanics have the equipment to service them. Do your research if you are interested in another brand. Remember if you buy a used car, Costa Rica has no law against rolling back the odometer. However, buying a previously owned vehicle costs less. Regardless mechanics traditionally have charged reasonable prices for repairs.

Shipping a car has pros and cons. Customs imposes import duties (allegedly at least half the value of the car or more). Add to this cost the price of insurance and shipping and the hassle of clearing the car through customs. It had impounded a used car I considered buying for a year when the owners shipped it ten years previously to Costa Rica. They wanted to reduce the age of the car because it wasn't driven in its model year. However, whether driven or not, the age included that year. When I had a dealer check out the car, the long list of repairs, some serious, equaled the price the coupled asked for the car.

"This dealership is noted for high prices for repairs," the female expat owner said firmly.

"Even if I could have them done with a reputable independent mechanic for half the price," I responded, "it puts the price beyond my budget." Although I run into her, the woman remains cool because she "wasted" a day.

Keep in mind when shipping a car, damage could occur in transit and parts could be stolen that insurance probably won't cover. In addition, new car warranties are not valid in Costa Rica if you import one. If you buy a new car here, it will have some coverage. In addition, since insurance company competition is relatively new no official Blue Book, the bible of car worth, exists in Costa Rica. Caveat Emptor is especially pertinent when it comes to cars.

The dilemma of whether to register the car in one's name or that of a corporation to protect assets looms a consideration. Check out the choices carefully. While putting it in a corporation excludes your personal assets from liability, you have to pay an attorney to form the corporation. Choose board members carefully. Remember you will need papers showing you have the authority to have inspections at Riteve, and pay the annual road tax (Marchamo). The corporation has to file a tax return (the fiscal year ends September 30) and to buy a stamp in March whether or not it generates any economic activity. On the other hand, a corporation permits the declaration of expenses, and protects the individual. Employ the services of a trusted lawyer or accountant.

A post on Costa Rica Living in September 2010 noted that Oscar Diaz (506/8844-6151, OscarDiaz@gmail.com) can help with buying or selling a car, getting parts, having a vehicle checked out, and with all the logistics as well as translate!

If you elect to use his services, ask for current references, get his rates in writing, and find out how long it takes – anything to make your experience good. I have not done business with him.

Giovanna Barrantes posted on Costa Rica Living in August 2010 a list of car models/years with the estimated amount charged by Customs in Colones. Remember these estimates are not current and the exchange rate varies daily. However, these estimates might help you in deciding whether to ship a car or buy one in Costa Rica.

Mitsubishi Montero Sport 2000 2.116.000

Toyota Rav 4 2000 - 1.615000

Toyota Rav 4 1999 - 1.545000

Honda cr v ex 1998 - 1.695000

Mitsubishi Montero sport ls 1998 - 1.710000

Chevrolet Tracker 2000 - 1.410000

Suzuki grad Vitara jlx 1999 - 1.820000

Toyota Yaris 2008 - 2.405000

Toyota Paseo 1996 - 1.015000

Toyota Echo 2000 - 1.050000

Chevrolet Tracker 2003 2.- 385000

One has to learn to ask directions from at least three people if you don't have a GPS because even if a person doesn't know how to tell you the route to your destination, he or she feels obligated to give you an answer. One friend who has trouble remembering more than three turns makes it a practice to go so far and ask again. She avoids going far out of the way by this practice.

When I acquired a accurate map of Alajuela I asked patients waiting in the eye doctor's office for the street name but no one in the waiting room knew. The doctor verified it from landmarks nearby. Several people feel the map of San Jose and Costa Rica from ARCR rates among the best available because the country generally lacks good maps. The GPS system here may be changing that.

Quite accurate GPS maps have arrived in Costa Rica at least according to friends who successfully used them. Check out: http://www.navsatcr.com and GPSTravelMaps. One person on a chat group felt the latter useless; another felt it his favorite. One post warned not to use the auto-routing feature because you may get dizzy as the GPS reroutes you around construction, one-way streets, and other barriers.

Apparently at one time you bought the GPS hardware in the States (last information: $100 on Amazon or Craig's list) and then acquired the map in CR with provision for updates for about $150 which included downloading it into your machine after you provide the serial number to the supplier.

The computer woman, the voice that I dubbed Athena for the fact one successfully finds the way, tells you where to turn giving names of streets you have never heard of because few posted street signs exist, at least not yet. Sometimes you feel you drive the long way around following "her" instructions but if you requested the fastest route, you encounter less traffic. In Costa Rica, people measure distances in time due to much traffic congestion. The pink line on the map on the GPS keeps you on course. Check: http://www.costaricamap.com/ing/infomanejar.html

CHAPTER Twenty-four

Need a Driver's License?

Serves as Identification at the Very Least

"Read the eye chart," the man ordered after asking a series of quasi medical questions in the mobile home where a "doctor" performed the "exam". It cost ¢5000 then. I walked back to the offices. The same procedure existed a couple years later when I went to renew. Only now it's streamlined and the requirement was added for some evidence of your blood type obtained locally. I asked for mine at the CAJA; private labs can also provide yours. New applicants also need a photocopy of a foreign license, a passport with a valid visa, or appropriate immigration documents.

The agency, Departamento de Acreditaciön de Conductores, is located in La Uruca. Be aware that requirements keep changing. Let me point out that I got a driver's license because it serves as an ID, prepared me in case I had to drive in an emergency, or decided at some time to get a car.

Keep in mind that I had a much quicker experience the second time when I renewed. Other expats tell stories of spending hours to complete what they consider a chore. Do their experiences correlate to their ability to speak Spanish or having a Spanish-speaking person with them, and the time of day or day in the week they go to the office?

During school vacations, or mid-week, appears the best time to seek a license but no guarantees.

Many years have passed since I had to apply in person in Dallas so I can't equate it to the time spent there. I recall that I had problems passing the eye test with the machines in use at one time. Here doctors bend over backwards to help you with the eye exam.

The license place hides way back in a building called Consevi in Pavas, a part of the CSV or Consejo de Seguidad Vial offering little parking in front. Banco Nacional where you pay your fee is just a couple of doors past the entrance. If you are driving you have to go past the turn to the right (Sign indicates COSEVI) so I would recommend paying at another branch.

The street to turn right on is near the Subaru dealership. Go down the street until you come to a guarded gate on the left that is the new entrance to place. You drive past a car graveyard on either side but many more parking spaces up ahead are closer to the building you want to go into. If you are over 65 or disabled go to the head of the line.

You sit in one place and play musical chairs to turn in your information: old license if you have one; foreign license if it is your first time, ID, copy of official exam, official blood type report, and bank receipt for fee payment. Then you go to another group of chairs to have your photo taken. After usually a short wait, you get your new license. It behooves bringing a book to pass the time just in case you have a longer wait.

You can have your medical exam in advance although places near the front entrance offer the service. The pharmacy I asked about an exam referred me to a doctor with offices behind them when I thought my license needed renewing.

I read the date as January 11 when actually it is in November because the day appears first on documents here. When I had the exam redone in September, it cost another ¢15000, the exact rate the government allows now. In June 2013 I cost ¢18,000. It may change so be sure to check out the fee.

You may pay the license fee at any branch of Banco Nacional and save your receipt. The fee is ¢10,000 for five years; first time licenses are for two, possibly three years (someone said theirs was recently three years) and cost ¢4000 now. Blood type reports must have an official stamp. If you don't have one, it will cost ¢5000.

Avoid the help of lingering Ticos at the entrance seeking to earn some colones. You do not need their assistance.

Normally one receives a B-1 license for passenger cars and light trucks. If your license from your home country has a motorcycle endorsement on it, you'll receive it here.

Replacing a stolen license for a fee requires first reporting the theft to the Judicial Investigation Organization (OIJ).

Apply for a license within 90 days of arriving in Costa Rica (double check the timeframe). You need to present your existing driver's license from your country (only valid as a license in Costa Rica up to 90 days). You keep your foreign license. An unlicensed foreigner will have to take weeks of classes, a written exam, hands on training, and a practical test. I didn't do it within the allotted time initially but waited until I left the country again for a trip so I had a new entry date in my passport. They weren't computerized then.

Currently locals can make license renewals three months in advance at Banco Costa Rica (BCR). Medical exams are valid for up to six months. Foreigners have to go to Consevi in La Uruca. Start the process before it expires in case a hitch develops. (Foreigners can renew cédulas at BCR.)

Recently (2013) it was determined that unless you have a cédula you can't get a Costa Rica driver's license. This means that in order for your original country's license to be valid, you have to have a new visa stamped in your passport every 90 days. Overstay, have an accident or get stopped for a ticket, and you could be in deep you know what.

For all the current regulations, check out **http://www.twitterbuttons.biz/es/www/csv.go.cr**. You can translate it at **https://quest-app.appspot.com/** or with Google translate, not perfect but good enough to provide the information you require.

CHAPTER Twenty-five

Choices for Attending Worship

Beyond Catholicism

As evidenced by the fact that Christmas and Easter are major holidays, literally shutting down the country, the Catholic Church remains alive and well in Costa Rica. While some men attend services, females constitute the majority of the church's congregation. It tickled me that the mother of a friend attends services everyday but will yell, scream, and curse worse than a sailor. Sometimes constituents don't practice their beliefs, like anywhere in the world.

Preparing for Semana Santa or Easter week, a major undertaking, gives locals a break from work and time to spend at the beach, in the mountains, or working on their homes. San Jose resembles a ghost town. In Costa Rica, the legal holidays include Maundy Thursday and Good Friday but not Easter Sunday itself. At this time, the law prevents selling liquor in restaurants or bars and grocery stores. An effort is underway to change this rule. In 2013, authorities waved the rule but it may not be permanent. Police visit bars to seal their doors and proprietors block or empty liquor displays.

Banks usually close early on Wednesday, may open on Saturday, or not until the Monday after Easter. ATMs work until money runs out. Incidentally, banks charge fees ranging from $1 to $30 for using ATMs unless it happens to be your bank's machine. Check yours.

Many large retail stores and supermarkets have limited hours on Thursday and Friday or close on Friday. Smaller establishments shut down for the entire week. Although on the menu year round, ceviche ranks as a favorite dish during Holy Week.

A post on Costa Rica Living noted, "a Catholic Mass (is) celebrated in English every SATURDAY at 4:00 pm at the Cathedral Metropolitano in the large chapel to the left of the main altar. The Cathedral is in the very center of San Jose across from Parque Central at Calle Central and Avenida Segunda about one block from Gran Hotel Costa Rica.

Other sects exist including ones that have at least some services in English like the Episcopal Church in San Jose. English mass at the Anglican Good Shepherd begins at 8:30 a.m. on Sundays. Iglesia Buen Pastor where the services are performed is located on Ave. 4 between calles 3 and 5, one block south of Teatro Naciónal across from the Colegio de Senoritas (high school). The phone number of the church is 2222-1560. Its number in Zapote is 2253-0790.

Across the Autopista from Multiplaza in Escazú, the International Baptist Church holds services and Bible study in English in the morning. To get more information about the church call 2215-2217 or Pastor Paul's cell: 8365-1005. This church unlike any Baptist church I knew in Dallas in my opinion provides a place to make friends and worship in your own way.

IBC shares the building with another English-speaking congregation, The Escazú Christian Fellowship that meets at 5 p.m. Contact Stacy Steck for further information: 506-8395-9653 or website: **http://www.ecfcr.net/index/Contact.html**

The Unity Piedades Church in Santa Ana holds Sunday services at 11 a.m. Contact: jet@UnityCostaRica.org Click on the flag at the upper right for English. (506) 2203-4411 or (506) 8381-5147-cell.

Calvary Christian of Jacó (2643-0125 or http://ccjaco.org/) holds services in both English and Spanish.

The Atenas English Speaking Church worships in a non-traditional building, a rancho at Finca Huetares in Los Angeles de Atenas. For those who base their faith on the Bible, worship takes place Sunday mornings at 8:30 a.m.

Bible study takes place on Thursdays at 7:30 p.m. at Kay's Gringo's Pastries. http://gonzosincostarica.blogspot.com/2010/02/atenas-english-speaking-church.html

A church in Orosi began services in English on July 4, 2010. The pastor Robert Melton and his wife Lorita worked as missionaries with Missionary Ventures International. Find the non-denominational church in the heart of Orosi, 200 meters east of Coto's Restaurant on the road toward the swinging bridge. Service begins at 9 a.m. following fellowship and Bible study an hour earlier at 8 a.m. Call 8859-0574 for more information.

Jehovah's Witnesses worship in Spanish and English at different times. https://watch002.securesites.net/e/contact/submit.htm

Guadalupe Missionary Baptist Church Costa Rica, located at Calle 6, Avenida 2, (100 meters south of the Municipal Palace of Guadalupe on the corner) holds services in English every Sunday at 3 p.m. Telephone numbers: 2222-4757 / 8848-3987. Contact Pastor: Kent Ward at: www.guadalupembt.com.

Iglesia Sol de Justicia, a Wesleyan church in Grecia, has an active congregation that meets at 8:15 a.m. every Sunday morning for a service in English. A Spanish service begins at 9:30 a.m. For more information, call Pastor Luis who is bilingual at 8827-2035. He also holds Spanish classes on Tuesdays and Thursdays.

In 2012 Robert Williams, who wrote me about this church, sponsored a Thanksgiving Day Feast cooked by Gringas and held at the church. Over 100 foreigners attended and many donated to the church. Check Costa Rica Living for details for Thanksgiving 2013.

Don't forget the very special Jewish Synagogue under tight security located next to AYA on the same road as the U.S. Embassy. Not only does it offer members a place to gather and worship, it features a wonderful museum depicting the history of Jews in Costa Rica. Contact: Bet Midrash Morashá in Rohrmoser: 506-2912940, Fax: 506-291.2937. For more synagogues check out this website: http://www.mavensearch.com/synagogues/C3371Y41525RX

Here's a blog that may provide more information about churches: http://www.costaricachurch.blogspot.com. Check out Religion at http://www.ticotimes.com/costa-rica-society-culture/religion. Here you can link to a Directory of Protestant Denominations in Costa Rica.

CHAPTER Twenty-six

Moving Within Costa Rica

Chore or Possibility

You may arrive in the country believing you want to live in a city or at the beach where you might require air conditioning at times, but wind up in the end high in the mountains with a chill factor that sends you hunting for heaters. Alternatively, like me, you might settle in a more rural area, only after a year or two, have life direct you closer to the action. Based on my experience and that of friends, I'm convinced everyone should initially rent until finally settling in a given area, whether renting again or buying. Find the best location where you will reach your paradise goal.

As I have written, I initially chose to live near Santiago de Puriscal. A good choice at the time, I'm grateful for all the friends I made in the area, especially my Tico neighbors. As I joined organizations, got involved with subgroups, and made more friends from various countries who lived closer to San Jose, I rose early and spent hours waiting on buses. My body ached at times due to the often-uncomfortable seats and the high steps to manipulate getting on and off buses, especially when I carried many bags. I sometimes jokingly referred to myself as "the bag lady". Sometimes I took cabs.

Friends urged me to move closer to San Jose. Exiting the simple but comfortable house in Barrio Carit outside the "city" of Puriscal – thanks in part to a very long list of improvements I made at my expense with rent only $200 a month -- needed much consideration. Neighbors took care of me. One said in Spanish each time I went on a trip, "The house was sad without you."

I'm sure he thought the house lonely as it sat empty for many months after I moved out and later when tenants came and went. Another brother, my "adopted son" that helped me in his mother's former garden, wondered at how the garden grew so well and how many banana stalks grew on the plants (not trees). He said I had green hands. He commented one day as we had drinks on the patio, "I was waiting for you to come."

The thought of moving finally took shape at the end of 2006. Living near Escazú, despite rumors about high rental costs and infrastructure lagging behind development, appeared at first the most logical location because moving to Cuidad Colon or Santa Ana wouldn't cut my bus commute time significantly. I had yet to make friends in Santa Ana.

Escazú has three villages: San Rafael at the lowest level, San Miguel or Centro and San Antonio up the mountain. Many foreigners choose to live in one of these towns.

San Raphael, filled with a variety of commercial establishments, camouflages neighborhoods tucked behind them. In Centro one steps back into time before Escazú spread out and diversified. It resembles many small towns dotting the county.

If you move into San Antonio with its magnificent views, having a car becomes an essential necessity in most locales although buses run regularly. It has a center like a small town in Costa Rica.

A woman I met through one of the women's clubs hooked me up with an agent that her Tico friend and she used in some of their real estate dealings. It wasn't until mid-January 2007 that the agent finally set up an appointment to look for a place per my wish list. The big hurdle of finding a place that allowed my three dogs loomed in their minds. Later I sent the larger dog back to a home in the country where he had more freedom.

The first place we went to had no appeal. The agent discovered the owner had rented it only when her key failed to open the door. Next, we went to a new place that cost an amount well over my budget and didn't accept animals.

"Let's look so I can tell you what I like and don't like," I suggested.

I knew that showing her rather than telling her made life easier because she spoke very little English and my Spanish, although better than she spoke her English, wasn't always sufficient to describe my wishes. Finally, she mentioned an apartment in an area called Guachipelin that took me a while to learn to pronounce and spell. The landlady accepted dogs and cats but it cost too much also. I reasoned in my mind that it might be possible to negotiate. Having worked in commercial real estate in Texas for about 25 years I knew more than the average person and knew how to negotiate well.

The two story attached end unit, one of four attached and one free-standing, had three bedrooms, two baths and a bonus of a tremendous view for miles of city lights and four volcanoes. Even with negotiating a lower rent, it still surpassed my budget.

Back in Carit, I figured that with some adjustments, I could squeeze the rent out of my income even though the third bedroom lacked phone connections and temperatures rose in the afternoons when the sun sank into the West. We returned a second time when I measured, tested for grounded plugs (none existed), and more in an effort to determine if the townhouse suited me.

Just as we walked out of the townhouse after I had said to draw up the contract, the neighbor next door, also a single woman, popped her head out the door accompanied by her super puppy. After explaining her friend decided not to rent it when she moved out the end of January, she showed me her place. The moment I walked in the door I found my next home. The agent called the owner and the rent, although higher than the current tenant's rate, fell within my budget. The landlady suffered anger at first because she thought she had both units leased. Soon after we came to an agreement, a Tico, 50, and his sons, 28 and 26, rented the larger place (vacant six months) making us a completely adult community.

The former tenant told us stories that painted the Landlady as an ogre. I later discovered a tough young woman, one with several experiences in common with me. Down the road, she lived up to her reputation because she lacked communication skills even though she spoke English, and delayed making repairs. Later I was told she had become a born again Christian!

Since my acquaintance didn't speak Spanish, I dealt directly with the young agent in the business for three years. She sent me a copy of a lease (not written for my unit) as a photo scan.

At the signing, she showed up with a properly typed version of the lease that I had requested. As I had taken the time to copy the skewed version into WORD, make some changes, show it to my attorney, and to read the rental law it referred to, I said, "I have the lease."

The agent appeared to have trouble dealing with strong clients. Further complicating the deal my attorney at first thought I had taken over his job by writing the lease myself. I had merely revised it.

"You shouldn't be the Landlady's lawyer," he admonished.

He started to revise it by e-mail but then said he wanted the owner and me to come to his office but I knew she wouldn't. She had her own contract. Allegedly, she was recuperating from an operation. Frankly, I didn't want to run up a fee. In the end, the owner and I came to an agreement with a few handwritten clauses to my version of the lease, and signed with no pet deposit required.

Her contract referred to la Ley de Arrendamientos Urbanos y Suburbanos de Costa Rica Ley # 7527 del 17 de agosto de 1995. The agent said she didn't have a copy but that I could get it off the Internet. Another drawback was the agent didn't have e-mail at home. I read all 73 pages in Spanish and discovered similar laws to those in Texas even though Costa Rica boasts a Napoleonic form of government. If I had to live by that law, I decided, so did the owner.

More than one attorney told me that by law, the term of a lease is three years (even if some people believe that one year leases are okay now) but tenants may break the lease legally with three months' notice.

Contracts for payment in US Dollars lock in the rent for the term of the lease. If stated in colons rents may increase (traditionally 15%) each year. When the value of the dollar fell owners lost too. Before you sign a lease, please double check the law that may have changed.

Not wanting to carry cash around that I couldn't afford to lose, I wanted to get the equivalent of certified checks, one for the owner and one for Century 21. However, the two women helping me felt I would offend the owner. If I gave her one check, they feared for their commission because she spends much of her time in Guanacaste, the northwest province of the country. So I paid cash (my friend accompanied me to the bank) and received a receipt for the rent, and one for the deposit. The owner paid the agent her commission, who paid the other woman for the referral. Everyone wrote handwritten receipts.

Of course, in Costa Rica rules and contracts bend like a tree branch in a storm. For example, the law states a tenant must give three months' notice to terminate a contract. In Puriscal I gave essentially six weeks but left about three weeks later, leaving the deposit as the last month's rent even though this wasn't copacetic. The owner acted very cordially knowing all I did for her property and how slowly court cases precede.

In the subsequent contract, I wrote in a two-month notice. I left sooner and didn't take my deposit, also leaving it for rent. Owners don't have to come up with a deposit amount which they have probably spent long before.

Frankly, at one point when things dragged on regarding the

Guachipelin lease, I thought about chucking it. After some consideration, I decided to see what transpired . . . as it turned out, I felt ecstatic that I held on even with future problems.

The owners' elderly and frail father slept in the guardhouse until his death nearly two years later. He enlisted the aid of fellow guards at neighboring properties to help with repairs. You should have seen us hanging my portrait high on a wall above the staircase where a hook existed. He brought my newspaper to the front door each day. I called him "mi amor" to his delight. If you use the phrase, you need to learn how to say it so it sounds sincere.

While my descriptions paint pictures of affordable places to live, let me assure you that all the amenities in the high end homes found in North America are for sale here -- for a price. Some people feel prices stated for foreigners have remained constant and are usually stated at a cost higher than that quoted to Ticos, even with the state of the economy. Ferret out unadvertised lower priced homes through native friends or by driving neighborhoods.

One woman I knew had her large townhouse on the market for about $250,000. We guestimated that other friends sold their newly constructed home for well over $300,000 due to asking prices for homes in the development.

They had plunged into building immediately upon arrival and then discovered they rued moving to Costa Rica. Both their homes, depending on the neighborhood in Dallas where I worked in commercial real estate, could fetch two to three times as much. On the other hand million dollar homes may be purchased or rented for several thousand dollars a month here.

Keep in mind that when I described the Guachipelin house, many of the amenities included ones we take for granted in the States, like central hot water.

In Puriscal, both showers earned the nickname "suicide" because the water through these showerhead devices only heated up upon demand and the force was weak. If you tried to increase the intensity, only cold water came out. They ran on electricity and initially lacked grounding.

The terrific Transporte Mudanzas Villalobos handled the move. The five men, all Spanish-speaking although sometimes one of the crew spoke English like the owner, showed up ten minutes early, worked diligently, and even waited for me to arrive at the new house. The price they quoted didn't change despite extra chores; nothing disappeared or broke. The person in charge showed me an empty truck. I provided drinks, lunch, and gave them a tip. Total cost about $300.

Please note that this local company received kudos from another friend who also had experienced smooth moves with it. However, I make no promise that the business will exist years later or that another's experience will equate ours.

One person's pleasant adventure might be another's nightmare. So ask for current references and check them out as you do in your home town. One thing that impressed me: the company keeps records of your moves with them. They seem to value repeat customers.

One of the advantages of living in the development in Guachipelin was the streets had names and the houses had numbers. A mail carrier on a moto delivered mail and publications, often a rare service. Citizens have endeavored to install a street system, at least in San Jose, for some years but reported that locals stole the street signs. Signs are beginning to appear on buildings.

Establishing five number zip codes facilitates the beginning of giving everyone a "real" address. Don't hold your breath! (In fact my Santa Ana zip code is the same number as one for a small town in upstate New York.)

Memory of junk mail dimmed. Sometimes a letter didn't find its destination. However, when it arrived, recipients welcome it because the lack of junk eliminated a time-consuming chore to sort mail.

My townhouse stood about half a kilometer up the hill affording a view that extended for miles. At night, the various towns' lights looked like twinkling jewels except when it rained and fog masked the valley. All day the changing weather provided a show.

At the street level, on the road that leads to the Autopista (highway) and Multiplaza Mall about seven minutes away, two entrances to the residential development featured manned guards 24/7. They sporadically monitored who passed through the gate including my neighbor's Tico husband who got questioned about where he was headed. Cab drivers might have to report their destination. One of the guards toured the neighborhood on his Moto (motorcycle) several times a day. The gate to the five-unit townhouse complex, operated by remote control, led to two parking places per unit.

One bi-lingual neighbor who has lived in her unit since the 1990s reported before I moved in, "We've had no problem with crime."

The level of crime demands top priority in choosing where to live. Other than a few insignificant items disappearing when service people entered either house, I feel fortunate not to encounter any significant problems.

However, some friends have had house invasions at gunpoint (a business that the perks scoped out), being followed into the house when getting a glass of water for a perk, or car windows broken and a purse on the passenger's seat grabbed. Like any place one lives, one has to take precautions, remain aware and protect valuables.

To give you an idea of properties rented for a lower cost, I'll describe my Guachipelin home in detail. The development contained five units, four attached and one freestanding. All had about the same size public rooms with similar configurations. The great room as I called it had an ample kitchen for one, a bit snug for two, separated from the rest of the room by a long counter. The remaining area provided sufficient space for a combination living and dining room.

One wall of windows enabled an unobstructed view. Features lacking included the absence of cabinets under the length of the counter and a pantry. My neighbor had more cabinets installed over the overhead cabinets, and had a couple of other cabinets squeezed into small places. A freestanding cabinet and a bookcase for cookbooks placed under the ledge of the counter provided solutions for me. I made a pantry area in a section of the bodega (storeroom) that I accessed from a covered patio. (It would have made a great half bath because one had to go half way to the second floor to a bathroom.)

When I moved friends made a point of assisting me. One took me to an appliance reseller and I found a Hotpoint refrigerator with ice maker that looked new except for a few dents. Later another one took me to Price Smart to get shelving for storage in the bodega.

At Monje in the Multiplaza West mall, I found a great combination GE gas and electric stove; have not seen the model in the States or online. I achieved my dream of an electric and gas kitchen. However, like Carit, dishes needed washing manually. My friend from Puriscal not only dug up plants from the old place for my small walled garden, he came and planted them, and installed a number of things for me. Periodically he visited and I cooked for him like his mother did.

The kitchen window over a two part stainless sink with one water control and vegetable spray, provided a view of the covered patio (which housed a pila – a two part sink -- my washer and dryer) and of the walled garden beyond.

During the rainy season, people called it a jungle, as many plants grew wild. I rigged what I called a "sprinkling system" contrived with hoses and soakers to keep it green during the dry season.

The bodega provided a "house" for the dogs. The place felt cool enough at night to sleep under a comforter; sometimes when it rained sweats felt wonderful because the jalousie windows let the wind whistle through the cracks. No AC or heat required.

The staircase curved and more than half way up a small full bath with a large shower that provided easy access gave guests privacy.

I installed hand railings along the steps because with tile steps, I wanted something easy to hold onto and some friends who had difficulty climbing stairs needed them. At the lower level and up a few steps ledges enabled displays. The upper one provided an extension of the Rogue's Gallery, or collection of family photos and my portrait. Over time I hung many of my framed photos of places and things I photographed, fulfilling another dream.

On the second level, two bedrooms faced an ample hall. The irregular shaped room contained a closet with louvered doors equipped with the more modern Elfa type fixtures inside. It served as an office and guest room. Both rooms opened to a small balcony; both had large windows that framed the wonderful view. The rectangular bedroom with a walk-through closet large enough to accommodate my sewing center previously had been papered with a "daubed" blue pattern.

Because someone removed a section of wallpaper, I painted and daubed paint on the white cement wall to make it less apparent, and glued the places where the wallpaper had lifted.

The larger bathroom off the master closet had an enormous tub with a sloping back. One of the things I had missed in Carit (and again in my last two homes) includes the ability to have a soak. The shower initially sprayed powerfully, like fingers stroking one's back. As the side of the tub stood taller than normal, I installed safety railings to hold onto getting in and out. Because the unfurnished place had more space, I had fun hunting for a number of items.

In Carit all kinds of bugs prevailed, especially spiders; one becomes accustomed to dealing with them in the tropics. In Guachipelin, fewer darted or flew about. Someone on the chat group Costa Rica Living questioned the high instance of roaches that year. Before I moved in I sprayed with the lethal Baygon, and did so every time I traveled. As a result, I saw afterward mostly dead beasts. Garbage men picked up trash twice a week that one stashed safely in the pickup space any time; they only fetched it once a week in Carit.

While in some areas of the country scorpions, killer bees, poison dart frogs, and various species of caterpillars exist that may cause serious and painful injuries, in the central valley toads abound. They have a serious poison that seeps through their skins that may be fatal to other animals. I had them in Puriscal but nowhere else.

Anticipating another move, I kept looking at ads in La Nación and Tico Times. Frankly, it is better to drive your desired neighborhoods and get recommendation from friends.

Lo and behold, an ad for a house just above Escazú Centro appeared and I jumped on the chance to see it. While it didn't meet all my requirements – not quite in walking distance to amenities but near a bus stop with two lines, had no tub but most Tico older houses don't, had a tiny kitchen that couldn't accommodate all my kitchen stuff – it had many pros.

However, the trouble began when the owners didn't always answer the phone. Never mind the frustrating details because finally the the owner emailed the contract to me. We had agreed to a price in dollars that can't be increased. He wrote it in colones with increases. The document stated that the house was in perfect condition. Like my Spanish it wasn't. In fact, I couldn't test that everything worked because the electricity was off. I questioned more clauses and felt under pressure because the property owner said more than once that he had another person interested in renting it.

Both my friend and I thought this a ruse and I didn't bite. The day I finally got the contract, an ad for the house appeared in the paper again. That said that he was not serious about negotiating. During this episode, I kept in mind what I told my clients when I worked in commercial real estate in Dallas and didn't marry the property.

I called his bluff when I wrote in Spanish that if he didn't want to work with me, "Qué sera!"

This experience and a few others in looking at properties assured me a place that met a good portion of my wish list was out there. This time around, I've learned even more about CR real estate practices. Patience is the key in Costa Rica.

Another agent that I learned about through a dentist that friends went to when they lived in Costa Rica took me to a place in San Antonio de Escazú.

After going through a difficult divorce, the owner had split her house into two apartments. I looked at the front one where the living area was great with light from windows and skylights; the kitchen was okay but the one bathroom and two tiny bedrooms weren't good. She ordered closets that would make the two rooms smaller.

Other deterrents were no on-demand water tanks, no bathroom shelves or cabinets, and she would not allow a doggie door because she had spent a fortune on the front door. She said she had no money for improvements and while I might have shared some expenses, I wasn't going to make do or pay for all the improvements.

My client that I write for suggested I contact her agent that worked the Escazú and adjacent areas. He had a furnished place for rent with all-inclusive bills save phone and cell. The owners removed most of the furnishings but I kept a few pieces including the LG refrigerator and Maytag washer-dryer pair to use and sold mine.

Once again, I used the same moving company. This time eight men moved me for the same $300. It would have been less but the distance to my house from the street increased the price.

The rooms in this house are large, and the kitchen eat-in. The two baths are small; one is off the living room due to the expansion of the home from a small Tico typical house to a larger one. Two on demand water tanks provide hot water.

It has lots of natural light, few steps (the Landlord put a handle in one place to facilitate the stairs into the master bedroom), wooden ceilings in some rooms, lots of ceiling fans, and more.

An exhaust fan is in the master bedroom. It's cool enough at night to sleep under a comforter. The owner put up a fence in the corner of the garden (shared expense) so my two little dogs could go in and out the kitchen door where he installed the doggie door I provided. He hung all my art, shelves, etc. which was part of the lease. Some of the walls are wallboard but many are concrete and I didn't want to damage them. He has several techniques for facilitating installations.

All the windows face a large garden with flowers and fruit trees. It's my hope that this is my last move because I can walk to amenities and friends give me rides. The proprietor drives me places for gas money. In fact, for Easter, people who live in the compound had a barbecue. The compound includes the owners' house, a hostel with 9 rooms (now two apartments but one serves as a hostel), and my abode plus bodegas that contain the owner's workshops. My lease is for three years, renewable with 90 days' notice, and if the place sells, the lease goes with the property.

When the property owner in Cariari totally closed in the wall dividing our patios he sealed my interest in moving. The owner on the other side had increased the wall height by three cinder blocks several months before. It lessened the light and air and the odor from the river intensified. I called it a cell without a door. As every window had bars, the only escape route was the front door. The Landlord shrugged and said that was true in apartments.

A real estate broker said I had a legal right to vacate because the place wasn't this way when I moved in. In defense, the Landlord said the roof on the patio wasn't there but I gave him a picture showing it was installed when I moved in.

For the last year, many things went wrong in the apartment. (A list two pages long details problems I had over two and one-half years.) While I was finishing packing the drain under the sink kept overflowing. During the previous 12 months, I had watered the property owners' plants at least four months, while he had watered mine less than a month, an arrangement we had agreed on. His wife usually took care of my pets but I had to find someone else to take care of the dogs during my trip because she was in the States.

During the last year, the couple seemed to become less friendly. We fought over notice. I told him in January that I was leaving; he kept pushing for a specific date that I couldn't provide until I had a new place. Actually, I left before March 1, a date he preferred. He had a For Rent sign up the entire time. He brought back a secretarial chair I had given their daughter rather than disposing of the now damaged chair.

When they inspected the place the day I vacated they could find no damage because I had repaired and painted over the repairs where I removed art, photos, and shelves. The only damage was the mess he made on the patio floor when installing the wall. I left a few items I had paid for that I didn't remove. The wife asked where the bottom rod was from the front door window. It was a cheap suspension curtain rod where a curtain had to hung for it to stay in place. I had placed the rod in the cabinet.

The Landlord had agreed to return the deposit but in the end we agreed he would to keep it instead of my paying more. I also paid the association fee for the month although I wasn't there the entire month. It disappointed me that our relationship changed.

Since the phone with Internet was in my name (it took nearly three months to get the phone), I had to arrange for its disconnection. When I moved in, I shared Internet with the Landlord for an extra fee. It took much effort to get it to work on my computer but he had problems so he changed providers and I had to get my own Internet at an increased cost.

168

The first ICE office I went to couldn't terminate my phone service because it offered minimal services. I had to go to another office.

Even though normally it would be three days before they could collect the modem in order to close the account, technicians showed up on Thursday because I wouldn't be there on Friday, the third day.

Amazingly, eight days later technicians showed up at the new house and installed the new line as promised.

Later I would receive a call asking me to correct my address so that I could receive an invoice at the house.

Part of the package at the new house included WIFI. It took less than five minutes to hook up and I could access it throughout the house. Only the connection from my Router was not secure. The Landlord bought me (at my expense) an adapter and no hay problema anymore.

Other good experiences include the owner introducing me to a pharmacy where the price for the medicine I have to buy resulted in being less and the service better. He showed me a great meat market; my bank has a new location. I easily got a PO Box. The CAJA clinic has medical personnel that also have private practices. You can read about the CAJA system at **http://retireforlessincostarica.com/2012/03/the-ebais-where-healthcare-starts/** All these are in walking distance. The bus stop is about three blocks away.

As I have two medicines not carried by many of the CAJA clinics, I had to arrange for delivery of them from one in San Jose. It takes 15 days for the meds to arrive. At first, we thought it would come to my main clinic but then I was told it had to go to the Cooperative Clinic in central Santa Ana. Another 15 days later, despite being told on the phone that I had only one med, my order was found. The pharmacist ordered next the month's and told me to come around the 15th to pick it up. They keep orders 30 days.

Amnet (now Tigo) in Guachipelin provided a variety of channels including CNN News, Headlines and Español; Fox News, CBS, NBC, ABC, and Deutche Welle. Three other channels broadcast in French, Italian, and Chinese. Most movie channels repeated films, same as in the United States.

What cable/internet company one uses depends on the location of one's abode. In Cariari, the provider was Cable Tica and it came with the apartment. During my sojourn, it changed the programming and I lost a favorite channel. Even though his wife liked it too, the Landlord wouldn't opt to increase the service. In Santa Ana, once again I have Amnet or Tigo.

Of course, one factors in Daylight Savings Time in finding program schedules listed online for ABC, NBC and CBS. As cell competition, heats up I anticipate new TV providers.

CHAPTER Twenty-seven

Shipping stuff

From Local Post Office to Mailing Service

"This weighs more than two kilos," the clerk at the post office said in Spanish. "You'll have to open the package."

Flabbergasted I rambled on about not having a car, having paid a high cab fare due to construction on the Autopista and detoured traffic, and suffering from el gripe, but he remained adamant. I knew that even if I could repack it, the less secure package would not weigh sufficiently less.

"Do you have tape," I asked in Spanish. He handed me a nearly used roll of opaque tape and a scissors. Looking at the insufficient tape, I whined in Spanish, "I don't know where to buy more tape." An older couple filling in a form on the counter near me asked the clerk the cost of a roll of tape and her husband (I assume) gave her ¢1000.

She left to buy the tape, saying in English, "I can get it up the street." I offered him a replacement note but he refused.

I carefully cut the paper covering the box and opened it as peanuts bounced around on the counter and onto his computer keyboard. I showed the clerk, who speaks a little English, where the "cow parade" appeared inside the box. I explained in Spanish that my friend teaches dyslexic kids and wants it for a teaching tool. He accepted my explanation without asking me to remove the inside box squeezed in tightly to protect the fragile cargo, and I began to recover the outside box. The woman came back and handed me the tape; she and the man left. When I looked at the tag I saw that it cost just under ¢1000, not the ¢500 the clerk had estimated.

Once I resealed the packaged -- the tape kept sticking and we both worked on getting it to unwind -- he announced a fee of ¢14,060 or just over $25.00 at the then rate of exchange. In addition, I had to fill out two forms, one where I had to give an alternate address. I didn't want it returned to Costa Rica and have to pay for the return as he indicated, so I wrote down an address in California realizing that my friend there could forward it if push came to shove. I put the recipient's address in the box, on it, and on both forms, one of which he gave me, scribbling a word that I believe meant inspected.

The package made it safely to its destination about three weeks later. Subsequently my friend's daughter repacked it after checking for damage and shipped it to Columbia where it has an honored place in my friend's living room. Never before had I needed to open a package. From then on I carry my tape gun and other supplies with me and seal packages at the post office.

Of course, the padded envelope containing a stack of vintage postcards didn't weigh more than four pounds but I showed the clerk the contents anyway before sealing it. It arrived in Canada within eight days. I had expected it to take about two weeks.

You may discern that the postal system in Costa Rica operates far differently than the one in the U.S. When shipping an item to the U.S. or Canada, warn your recipient that it could take up to six weeks to arrive. With changes happening in the U.S. system, it may take even longer.

Postmen don't pick up letters from your house in Costa Rica even if you're lucky to have a "real" address and not an address that describes your location as so many meters east of the fig tree chopped down ten years ago. Mail boxes aren't placed on corners and post office branches are not in every town.

Exceptions exist. After I moved to Los Arcos, I asked a dear Tica friend to inquire about picking up mail from me because I don't have a car. "No hay posible." Fast forward a few weeks when I encountered the postman and in my usual friendly manner, spoke to him in Spanish. I asked him about pickup and he disclosed he doesn't work out of an area post office. Rather he picks up mail for his route from a central location. A few days later when he delivered a magazine to me directly because the mailbox on the fence wasn't large enough to keep it dry, he announced that his next stop was at the local post office. "Do you need to mail something?"

Unfortunately, I wasn't prepared with letters but he gave me his name and cell number so we could coordinate in the future. He said, I'll take the mail, money, and bring back a receipt because we are friends." I expected to tip him.

When I lived in Barrio Carit near Santiago de Puriscal, I had to go into town to the post office where I had a mailbox because a postman rarely delivered on our dirt road. In Guachipelin, a short bus ride took me to town and the closest branch. Initially, the bus that went into Escazú central didn't stop in front of the shopping center down the hill. One walked 300 meters (three long blocks) to the next stop where the route began or took two buses. Published bus schedules essentially remain non-existent and subject to frequent changes even if one had an inkling of the timing.

When the Ministerio de Obras Publicas y Transportes (MOPT) widened the tunnel under the highway the bus "depot" moved and the two routes now stopped at the closest bus stop down the hill from my home. Even though a supervisor created a timetable for me during the weekdays, it wasn't always accurate BUT it helped.

Options at the post office slowly improved. A service called "certificado" provides a means to track lost mail. However, some letters and packages from the States never made it to my Guachipelin home even though a postman delivered mail. I never received notice that customs may have intercepted a package for ransom. Why a letter went astray, I haven't a clue. In Puriscal, everything seemed to arrive. Both addresses contained San Jose, which some explained, facilitated receiving mail. Costa Rica also has a mail service called EMS that delivers throughout the country, much more cost efficient method of shipping packages.

If you need to ship stuff to Costa Rica because it won't go into your luggage, consider using the services of DeliverToCostaRica.com located in Port Manatee, Florida if it is feasible. A five cubic foot carton of *used* items in 2010 cost $90 for delivery to the warehouse in Alajuela, Costa Rica located about a mile west of the International Airport. It took between four to six weeks. Get current information at: http://www.delivertocostarica.com/

What other options exist? DHL, UPS, and FedEx, all money gobblers, offer various services and delivery times. The cost might be justified for important or urgent mail and for sending or receiving something in a timely manner. Weight plays a factor. Check prices online to help you make your decision. **www.fedex.com/cr_english/** or call 800-Go FedEx, **www.ups.com/latin/cr/engindex.html** or **www.dhl.co.cr/publish/cr/en.high.html**. DHL's main number in CR is 2291-2472. Please note again that telephone numbers have eight numbers in addition to the nationwide area code 506. When I ordered a proof of this book, Create Space sent it by DHL rather than to my PO Box. Even though books are supposed to be duty free, I was charged 1% of the value but the total DHL bill was ¢11,624.80 or nearly $24 for handling the shipment!

One can also rent a PO Box in Florida from such companies as Aerocasillas (**www.aeropost.com/sjo** or 2208-4848) that will forward mail and packages to Costa Rica. It requires picking up the mail from one of its local offices. The organization ARCR also provides mail service through Aerocasillas. It's a free service except you pay per letter or package depending on its weight. Mail Boxes Etc. is also in Costa Rica. **http://www.mailboxesetc.co.cr/**

For shipping small quantities of stuff, send packages to family owned Cargo Tica in Doral FL. They are a freight company with facilities in SJO near the airport. About 350 pounds cost around $100 plus some fuel charges according to the latest information in 2010. Contact them in San Jose: 2443-7058 or in Doral FL: 305-477-5508.

Other services include:

Correos de Costa Rica; **http://www.correos.go.cr** (No phone numbers were available.)

Jet Box: 2253-5400; http://www.jetbox.com

Mailboxes at local Post Offices or Correos rent annually, with the fee due in January. If you forget to pay it, you lose the box in March. Some of the Post offices will have mailboxes available only sporadically so maintain it once obtained. The first payment includes a deposit for the key, reimbursed when you return it.

Location of some of the branches: *(While accurate at the time of research, please note change is constant.)*

The Alajuela Post Office is located on a corner about 100 meters south of Parque Palmares and 200 meters north of the cathedral. 2243-3265 or Fax: 2441-0122.

Escazú Post Office Fax: 2289-9564: located 100 meters al norte de la Municipalidad de Escazú. Boxes also are available in Escazú Centro in Plaza Roble y Plaza Colonial, 100 meters north from the Municipality of Escazú.

Santa Ana Post Office 2282-7403 Costado Norte Plaza de Deportes (sport arena). Boxes are located in the Downtown Santa Ana Office and at the Forum Correo.

Rohrmoser & Pavas Post Office 2232-0333 costado escuela de Pavas. P.O. Boxes are for rent in Plaza Mayor next to the Pavas School and in Pavas Center.

The post office in Ciudad Colon 2249-1966 stands on the north side of casa cural.

San Antonio de Belen: 2239-2254. From the Church 300 meters west and 25 north.

The lack of junk mail is one great benefit of a less than efficient postal system. In fact, the PO in Santa Ana has a trash basket for recycling junk mail and discarded parts of mail like envelopes. With the advent of all sorts of services online, hard copies also died. You learn how to work within the system and friends and family back home adjust. Visitors carry stuff in their luggage. Friends bring back coveted items for one another when they travel depending on size and weight and ever-growing airline restrictions.

CHAPTER Twenty-eight

Education Considerations

Choices Exist

Moving here without family and not needing to select a school, I'm out of the first-hand loop regarding education. When I lived in Europe, my son only attended a pre-school on base because of my husband's indirect affiliation with the military. We lacked the need to choose a place to live based on availability of good schools until we moved to Dallas.

If possible, investigate schools of interest before moving. An important factor in choosing an initial place to live underscores the need to rent first. If you rent in a place without easy access to the school of your choice, or the school close to your home disappoints, you can move much easier if you rent. Or you may elect to home school as several people I know have.

Understand that your child may need to learn Spanish in order to do well. Consider that as one of the benefits of dwelling in Costa Rica rather than bemoaning the fact.

For a Directory of Schools, Universities, and Language Institutes, check out the Tico Times Weekend, page W8 on June 4, 2010. The newspaper excerpted the article from the Tico Times Exploring Costa Rica guide. Buy the guide online at **www.ticotimes.net** or call in country 2258-1558. (You might need to find a used copy because the newspaper terminated its print format on 9/28/12.) Order a daily e-mail from the paper on the website.

To begin your search, Google schools in Costa Rica. Also check **http://www.therealcostarica.com/health_education_costa_rica/private_schools_costa_rica.html**

Questions: What do you know about the availability of bilingual schools?

Did you know that the main vacation in Costa Rican schools starts in December and runs through January, with a shorter summer break in July?

Should the school calendar coincide with that in your country of origin?

Can the school offer the curriculum options that your child had back home?

CHAPTER Twenty-nine

Facing Boredom

Demon Boredom Follows Some People

What defines boredom and how can one experience it in Costa Rica? As I mentioned in another chapter, the last time I recall boredom dates back to my teenage years on Sunday afternoons. We'd return home from church, have dinner, and the hours to bedtime stretched endlessly. Mostly I read books. My father didn't buy a TV because he felt a need to avoid distracting me from homework or maybe it wasn't in his budget. Only when friends invited me over did I watch the boob tube.

Do you recall how many idiotic TV series aired in the early years, many reminiscent of the stunt shows or soaps shown on Costa Rican local channels currently? Nevertheless, we watched them, fascinated by the newfangled box and having nothing better with which to fill the time.

Even in "retirement" I keep "to do" lists because I have so many interests, meetings, and projects. Perhaps the accuser in Puriscal that claimed I suffered boredom projected his feelings to me. While living there I spent many hours editing another's book, co-authoring a children's book, working on a second mystery as well as reading books, handling household chores, gardening, and traveling into town for meetings. I made time to chat with friends even if it interrupted progress on a project because I didn't want to appear rude by hanging up the phone abruptly.

When I moved closer to San Jose, I joined more organizations and learned to play Bridge that replaced editing someone else's book. Unlike some Bridge players I didn't become addicted and stopped playing when other interests took precedence. Writing for websites increased as well as entertaining because a mountain no longer divided me from friends.

Yet foreigners here have confessed boredom to me.

Let me try to analyse why.

As I have said many times, curriculums lack How to Retire 101. One day a person works and maintains a routine; the next he's in another country without an agenda or purpose and unable to speak the language. Even when I lived in England (yes, British English almost rates as a foreign tongue) and Germany, boredom belonged to others. While other dependents sent abroad bemoaned the loss of a disposal and a dishwasher (I had a portable), I celebrated the opportunity to live in a different culture and travel as much as possible. Rather than acquire many things, my family spent money-seeing Europe.

Among the foreign population in Costa Rica are people assigned here for a couple of years or less. Unless they find interests -- joining groups to meet people, traveling, have hobbies or possibly a career handled on the Internet (not available during the 1960s when I lived in Europe) -- left to their own resources boredom may rear its dull head.

Foreigners seeking foreign companions at the local soda where Gringos congregated ranked among the bored in Puriscal. They frequented the local bars, coffee shops and restaurants, or sat in the square. Did they fill time by corresponding online in groups with repetitive topics that at times appeared downright silly? I surmise boredom followed them from wherever they came from and that they didn't realize the malady doesn't change with location.

Some Gringos fill their time by joining service, interest (like Bridge and computer), church groups, and veterans' organizations as well as committees that organize events. Women seem to have more options because two women's clubs feature sub-interest groups. One club now has a men's division. Some people teach English (and probably learn Spanish at the same time). Smart foreigners use part of their time while settling in to the new routine to learn some Spanish.

Probably the secret of ending boredom requires following the same path in any place: living a meaningful life. Retirement offers a time to enjoy the freedom from a structured existence no matter where you live by giving yourself permission to deviate from a routine, swing in a hammock while sipping a cool drink, and studying Spanish along with your omphalos.

CHAPTER Thirty

Cultural and Other Activities

Going from Bored to Too Busy

While the tour books contain much information about what activities exist in Costa Rica, from those for the athletic to restaurant sampling, let me reiterate that CR offers things from art to topes to keep you busy, maybe too busy. Other sources for information include newspapers: in Spanish La Nación and the English weekly Tico Times (now online only). You may find current contact information in these periodicals in case any phone numbers or websites cited here have changed since publication.

Costa Rica has one of the best symphonies in the world. I can say that having attended performances in England, Austria, Germany, and Russia. The symphony dismissed a recent director after a few concerts in 2011. He hired more musicians to increase the size but maintained a diverse age group of both male and female performers. Twelve performances begin as early as February and end in November. Season ticket holders receive a discount for up to 12 concerts. Outstanding guests perform. In between, the National Theater (Teatro Naciónal) in San Jose features other events. Tourists and residents enjoy touring the facility.

Art galleries, tours, and events abound. One interesting event was a textile exhibit. Held in 2010 at the National Museum in the former dungeon, it featured a variety of creative textiles and mixed media linked together by kilometers long fabric rope chains.

Those signified ties between artists, artists with people, and people with other people. Some pieces were quilted; others feature 3-D portions, while some appeared woven. Others had handwritten messages on them, the narrow panel flowing down the wall and onto the floor. Another display resembled large overstuffed whimsical pincushions.

Beyond the displays and the architecture, the exhibitors seamed the event together with music composed for the show that drifted in the background. It's amazing to contemplate that prisoners lived in the tiny windowless cells where some of the creations were displayed. After viewing the special exhibit other permanent displays in the facility beckoned.

The Little Theatre Group (LTG), was founded in 1949 by Englishman Bert Williams -- hence the spelling of "theatre" the British way. Despite earthquakes, financial disasters, loss of costumes, sets, and performing spaces, it is the oldest continuously running English-language theatre in Central and South America.

Currently, the group puts on a minimum of four productions a year, offering the English-speaking community a choice of modern, classical, comedy, serious, and farcical plays, plus special events that include hilarious skits as seen in *Midsummer Madness*. The expanding repertoire has included such productions as The Birdcage, Twelve Angry Men and Same Time Next Year. For a "Hallowe'en Costume Party" members and friends donned costumes and spooked each other.

At the annual Christmas concert, musicians from the *National Symphony* donate their time and talent to raise funds or gifts in kind for the *Hogar Tom & Norman*, a home for abandoned old folks in Guapiles. The group regularly sponsors school drama festivals, trains new directors, and takes productions on the road to other areas of the country.

Auditions (open to all) for LTG productions appaear in the membership newsletter and the *Tico Times*, and new members are always welcome on both sides of the footlights.

In the early days, LTG presented plays at the *National Theater* and later at the *Eugene O'Neill Theater* in the *Centro Cultural Costarricense Norte Americano*. Unfortunately, in preparation for the visit of the then United States First Lady Rosalyn Carter in 1977, LTG's sets and properties were mistaken for rubbish and discarded by workers cleaning the center.

For many years thereafter, the LTG was homeless and like roaming troubadours produced in many different theaters or whatever space they could find. Rising rents heralded financial doom and the final curtain call appeared imminent in 1998 until the then President Blanche Brown, who passed away on September 20, 2011, came to the rescue. She proposed the group covert the back of her house into a theater. Members contributed to LTG's new home by purchasing a seat for $100 in *The Blanche Brown Theatre*. Once again in 2012 LTG began the hunt for a new performance hall. Check out the website for the latest information: **http://www.littletheatregroup.org**.

Other performances and art exhibits happen at the Centro Cultural Costaricense-Norteamericano in Barrio Dent in San Pedro de Montes de Aca.

185

The center, which celebrated its 65th anniversary in 2010, includes among its services exhibits by artists in the Galería Sophia Wanamaker and performances in the Teatro Eugene O'Neill. Several people tout the Metropolitan Opera performances shown in high definition in the theater as far better than seeing them live in New York City. The ticket includes a discussion of the Opera. The center also contains a library with English books.

From time to time major groups like Bon Jovi. Julio Iglesias and the International Guitar Festival that celebrates strings make appearances. Various recitals include those by the National Youth Symphony.

Bridge lovers can play at the Bridge Club on Sabana oeste close to Pops across from a branch of the La Bruja liquor store. Computer buffs meet once a month at the PC Club held for some time at the Pan American School near Panasonic in Belen. Once a month, members and guests gather at a restaurant for the Wine Club luncheon. The Women's Club has a men's subgroup, a website at **wccr.org**, and a presence on Facebook **http://www.facebook.com/WomensClubCostaRica**. The Newcomers Club (some members have attended for 35 years) offers regular programs **www.newcomerscr.org**

These two groups have interest groups from book clubs in English and Spanish, gourmet cooking, gardening to golf. In various areas organizations like the Cariari Coffee group meet so women can get to know one another and exchange information. The Professional Women's Network (PWN), a subgroup of WCCR, focuses on business women. Website: **http://www.wccr.org/text/sigs/pwn.shtml**

Men also may join a weekly luncheon, Shriners, Lions Club and the American Legion as well an investment group, Bridge (Club and private games), Rotary, Chess, and the Canadian Club (members are not all from Canada). One may also work with various volunteer groups like those that work for animal rights. The fact remains that you can probably find a group that focuses on your interests with just a little effort.

Of course, if you live outside the central valley, you'll find other interest groups locally because of the difficulty in attending meetings in town, an important issue to consider when deciding where to settle.

CHAPTER Thirty-one

Internet use and choices improve

Keeping in Touch Worldwide

Unable to get a phone line to the casita I moved into shortly after arriving in Costa Rica meant no Internet access. For someone who stays in touch with people all over the world, this predicament frustrated me extremely. If I didn't have my writing, books and the ability to get online at the main house or at an Internet Café, I might have gone stir crazy. Not! Nevertheless, having to coordinate use of the telephone line in the main house with the slowest Internet connection ever was debilitating. Add tying up the only phone line to the B&B business caused stress, not so much for the owners as for me. They were more concerned about the increase in cost. I asked them for the regular amount of the bill and paid overages.

Moving into a larger house at half the rental with a phone already installed seemed the answer. However, for some unknown reason the owner didn't want me to subscribe to Internet on that line. Through perseverance, the Internet provider agreed to install a second line. Only the modem for dial up conflicted with something in my laptop computer. The blue screen of death appeared regularly, a dilemma I learned happened because the computer and type of modem weren't compatible. Once again, I dogged the supplier for ASDL as soon as available in Carit and had no more problem modem. No more blue screens but with all the procedures performed on the laptop, including wiping the hard drive twice, the computer lacked greatness ever after.

Tired of commuting to towns close to San Jose to attend meetings and friends rarely visiting due to the drive over the mountain, I moved to a townhouse with a great view. AMNET could provide cable and Internet. However, when I decided to try WIFI, it functioned sporadically. I returned happily to cable that provided the Internet at a more consistent speed and stayed connected.

Part of the agreement when I later moved to a one-story apartment included sharing the WIFI connection to the Internet provided by Cable Tica. My new computer (same brand but not same model laptop that had problems in the country) had a built-in program that took hours to overcome to make it possible. Saying, "I'm bigger than you!" I doggedly worked at it until I made the connection.

Only it took about three months to get a landline . . . the same provider for phones in the country served the new place. The provider had no lines even with a doctor's letter that stated I needed it for medical reasons. In the end, I received a phone connection without the letter. You should have seen my cell bill even faced with sporadic access!

My excitement at finally having a phone dimmed because the person who had the number before me had a recording set up to refer callers to his new line. Sometimes calls went to the recording.

Part of the time when I attempted to call out I'd get a recording and no dial tone. It took repeated phone calls from me and a friend more fluent in Spanish to have the recordings removed. During one of the calls we learned about caller ID, and call waiting services and ordered them at no charge.

Later the Internet setup changed because the cable provider had poor service. When the owner changed to ICE, I had to seek my own ADSL service from the same company.

Look for Information you need to help you make your decision about Internet service and Costa Rica on various websites or from information sites. Keep in mind the postings of importance to you may be up-to-date but take readers' information with five grains of salt. While their experiences appeared accurate at the time they wrote, double and triple check information from several sources.

Some people adamantly claim that they "know" something, but really, their knowledge terminated at the time their experience ended years ago. Daniel who edits escazunews.com does a good job of keeping up with changes in his database where he lists sources in the Escazú area in both English and Spanish. Just like getting a second opinion for major surgery, it pays to question before acting.

CHAPTER Thirty-two

Medical Services Matter

The Older we Get, the More Important

Hairs stood up on the back of my neck because I knew I could figure out how to apply on my own for Caja Costarricense de Seguros Social (CAJA) benefits (the socialized medical system). At that time after getting a Pensionada cédula, I could opt for it if I wished; now it is mandatory for residency.

Soon after I received my first cédula as a pensionada, I applied for the insurance. With limited Spanish, I called someone who had gotten the benefit in Puriscal to see where I should go first because I misunderstood the man in the location where I stood. Rather than tell me, he advised abruptly, "Get someone who speaks Spanish to go with you."

Tell me I can't do something I want to do and I want to shout, "Stand back and watch me." A long past example of my trait, call it stubbornness if you want, dates back to high school when adult friends predicted that I would smoke. When I went away to university smoke free, many said, "She's too sophisticated. She'll learn to smoke in college." Not.

Taking a deep breath and again asking the clerk in poor Spanish what to do, I finally understood that I had to make the application at the clinic on the other side of town, no more than ten blocks away as I recalled.

The clerk that befriended me in the other location helped me to make the application. Later I walked back to the larger location for my carnet that enabled me to use the system.

In Costa Rica, we have good public and private medical care and can choose which to use. Under the new law, anyone with a cédula has to pay for CAJA benefits even if he or she elects not to use the benefit. To me, it's a good place to go for preventative medical care and emergencies. Once you've paid your monthly fee, based on income, visits to doctors and specialists and available medicines are included. Some medicines are not available; some prescribed on a very controlled basis. Hazards include doctors going on strike that cause delays for appointments and surgeries.

As you will read, in some cases I chose private medical care even though I don't have health insurance beyond the CAJA. In some areas of the country, quality medical care looms hours away, a consideration when selecting where you want to live depending on whether you have children or many medical problems.

During June 2103, a post on CRL indicated that Traveler's Insurance is offering coverage from five days to one year. Apparently, the company serves clients worldwide in more than 170 countries, including vacationers, business executives, missionary groups, entertainers, fortune 500 companies, schools and universities, professional marine crew, expatriates and local and third country nationals. For immediate quotes and details, go to http://travelerfriendlyinsurance.com/ (I have not investigated this insurance opportunity.)

INS (the Instituto Naciónal de Seguros) had the monopoly on

insuring vehicles, health, personal effects, house and boat requiring no shopping around for coverage. With competition entering Costa Rica, check if your US insurance, like Blue Cross, will cover you abroad. Retired military may have other options like Tricare. In addition, some international insurance plans are available for a fee based on age.

Costa Rica compares very positively in the region with up-to-date clinics, well-trained doctors (often schooled in the U.S. or European medical schools), and widely available resources.

Private care costs are all much lower than in the North. If you have special health considerations, consider how close you must live to a doctor or a clinic with specialists.

Are your special medications available in Costa Rica? How does your health insurance and available plans work for the main hospitals and doctors? Do you use alternative medicines? Do you need a chiropractor or homeopath?

Sinai Medical posted a response on CRL on November 2, 2010.

"We thank you for your interest in Sinai Medical and hope that we can find a solution that suits your needs. Please allow me to elaborate on our product and services and allow you to ask any questions concerning your needs. Sinai Medical intends to offer a high-end medical service at accessible prices.

"Our initial plan, Sinai Essential, consists of a membership to our growing network of proprietary medical clinics that utilize the highest standards of care. Our doctors are English speaking and our medical director has implemented US (American Medical

Association and World Health Organization) medical protocols to ensure the highest possible levels of care and standards in the country.

"With your monthly membership, you will receive unlimited access to our clinics to enjoy strong primary care services, preventative medicine and disease management. Sinai maintains a culture of service and deploys a US delivery model with an affordable cost for patients. Among the benefits that you will receive, aside from unlimited visits to our facilities, (include):

"Annual blood work to include metabolic panel, lipids and glucose, Mammography, Pap smear, PSA, Medicina Mixta (if you have CAJA benefits, you may obtain prescriptions for free). Deep discounts are provided by a network of pharmacies, top specialists, hospital and all ancillary services. All care meets AMA and WHO standards."

"The monthly charges for the plans as of November 2010 were as follows:

Monthly Fee Individual $36.67
Individual y wife/partner $73.33
Children from 0 to 12 years old $20.00
Children from 12 to 21 years old $25.00
Family of Four $99.00"

For up to date information contact Adrian Acevedo G. at 2248 1280, 2505-5656 or at acevedo@sinai.cr

For services in Costa Rica published by the Susan G. Komen for the Cure Foundation, link to: globalkomen.org/news-press/news-archive

Another   website   you   might   like   to   consult   is:
http://www.guiaverde.info/localizacion/costa-rica/cl%C3%ADnicas-
costa-rica

While I can go on about people's experiences with health care, both good and bad, I feel that recounting some personal experiences with the CAJA and private doctors, and facilities might convince you that health care in Costa Rica rates overall good to great and remains far less expensive than in the United States.

In the next chapters, I relate stories about my TIAs (Transient Ischemic Attack), cataract surgeries, and more.

CHAPTER Thirty-three

Personal Medical Experiences

What You Could Encounter

"Am I dreaming?" I heard a strange voice say.

"What is happening?" I spoke again, testing the voice. It sounded vaguely familiar but the words seemed a bit slurred.

Slowly coming awake, I silently wondered if I had slept on my left arm because my fingers on my left hand tingled although I felt nothing else. No pain! Sleeping on my arm had never happened before I recalled. I lifted my left arm with my right one and let go. It dropped to the mattress like a Raggedy Ann doll's arm.

Finally, I willed myself to scoot up even though my left leg felt like a dead weight. Thankfully, the two stacked pillows hadn't shifted apart while I slept. I reached with my right arm and clicked on the light that hung over the bed. I tested my left arm again. It really wasn't functioning. I couldn't reach the phone although I didn't know who to call at midnight. If I called 911, respondents needed to break in, first through the gate to the parking lot and then in my townhouse because the lock bolted the door. I'd probably injure myself if I tried to get down the stairs.

Jill Bolte Taylor came to mind, a woman that I had learned about from a friend who lives in Columbia. Was it a coincidence that on March 23, the day of my second mini-stoke, that Oprah's online magazine that I read after returning from the hospital ran a story about Jill?

Jill had studied the human brain since childhood, and worked as a Harvard-trained neuroanatomist when she had a massive stroke at age 37. A blood vessel exploded in the left hemisphere of her brain. She managed over seven years, with her mother's help, to recover. Somehow she remembered what she felt during her life-changing event and eventually wrote *My Stoke of Insight: A Brain Scientist's Personal Journey.* Alternatively, you can listen to her story on YouTube. Search *Jill Bolte Taylor my stroke of insight.*

Thinking about Jill made me force my brain to remember what I was experiencing. I began massaging my left arm until the hand stopped tingling and the arm functioned again. I foolishly fell back to sleep. Underline foolishly.

The next morning I felt fine as I began to dress. In the middle of it, I struggled to put on my left shoe. When I tried to walk around upstairs to open blinds, my left leg dragged, and my fingers tingled again. Finally, after several calls I reached a friend, formerly an operating room technician, who told me later that my speech sounded slurred. She ordered, "Go to the Emergency room now.

Just then, I heard my neighbor revving up his car in preparation for leaving for work. I carefully went down the steps, holding on to the hand railings I fortunately had installed. I explained to him my problem and asked him to drive me to CIMA, a nearby hospital that had a fine reputation, allegedly associated with Baylor in Dallas. He dropped me off, making sure he had my cell number so he could call me.

Having had a mammogram in the hospital because the gynaecologist I frequented had offices in the building, I went to that desk to ask where to find Emergency. She told me in Spanish and I endeavored to make sure I understood when a man standing at the counter said in Spanish, "I'll show you."

Thankfully, he did because fog filled my brain. In retrospect, the person behind the desk should have ordered a wheel chair for me.

Somehow, I managed to explain in Spanish what had happened to a clerk in the reception area of Emergency. He told me to sit in a chair in front of an unoccupied counter. After what seemed like ages, a man finally came to sit in the empty seat across from me. He took my information and asked for a credit card for a deposit. Later a clerk credited it and charged the actual amount of less than $600. I could have had another episode while I waited. Certainly, he could hear my slurred speech.

A friend later explained that since I waited alone I had to take care of business. It's my belief that a nurse should have put me in a wheel chair or bed and a clerk sent to me. Later hearing stories of overcharges, wrong codes used for bills that meant difficulties in obtaining insurance benefits, reports of infections and more, I decided that CIMA lost face in my eyes.

The first blood pressure reading practically broke the machine; subsequent ones tested down and up. The young doctor, who probably graduated recently from medical school, scheduled blood tests. She did not include one for the liver. Then an EKG, a CT, and an Ultrasound of the arteries followed. On and off my left hand tingled. No one gave me water although I asked several times.

Fortunately, I had had some while I waited to check in. Later I sucked on a Tic Tac I had in my purse to assuage my thirst.

The doctor wanted me to see a neurologist and admit myself but since my friend with medical experience and her own heart attack scenario had recommended Dr. Juan Carlos Elizondo Urrutia, I called him (2522-1000, x 2075-2076, or 8392-6246). What did we do without cell phones? Gratefully mine had sufficient power left to make many calls. I hadn't charged it that recently. I didn't have a jacket with me (it was very cold) or a toothbrush.

After signing a release, I left CIMA and took a cab to the emergency room at Clinica Biblica in San Jose. I experienced no problems but CIMA prudently should have had me hire an ambulance. (As an aside, subsequently I signed up for a service called Emergencias Medicas that provides ambulances with medical personnel and medicine on board.) As instructed I told the admissions clerk at Clinica Biblica to give the tests results (one gets the originals here) to the emergency doctor. After he reviewed them, he was asked to call Dr. Elizondo. No one asked for credit card information.

A few minutes later, a nurse appeared and showed me into the emergency room built years ago, old but clean. Dr. Rafael Guerra León attended me. When I asked for a blanket because I felt cold in the room as I did in the Emergency at CIMA, he ordered one and came back stuffing a pillow in a case for me. After he consulted with Dr. Elizondo, a clerk came to me to fill out my information and collect credit card data prior to admission. The amount charged equaled half of what would have been required at CIMA for admission. In the end, the bill at Clinica Biblica totaled less than anticipated, so it covered three doctors' fees and I received a small refund.

My very large room in the new section of the hospital in addition to the hospital bed had a futon that made into a bed if someone wanted to stay with me. A chair and a lounge chair as well as cabinets, safe, and a flat screen TV furnished the suite. The bathroom with walk in shower accommodated a wheelchair.

Later Dr. Guerra, the emergency doctor at Clinica Biblica, brought Dr. Franz Chaves Sell, a neurologist, to see me. Dr. Chaves said that Dr. Guerra had taught himself English. Discussing the problems in English facilitated matters. All the staff was helpful. If one couldn't understand my Spanish, s/he found someone who spoke English. Meals featured low sodium but mostly tasty food except for some very thin white porridge like substance served at breakfast that I couldn't eat.

Another blood test determined a baseline regarding my liver (in excellent shape). An echocardiogram showed a strong, normal sized heart. By the time I left the hospital, my blood pressure returned to normal even though I hadn't taken any medicine for it because I hadn't brought any not anticipating staying in the hospital overnight. Incidentally, before the doctors discharged me I had to walk around the room in my "designer" hospital gown. To prove I maintained my balance, to the surprise of my doctors, I kicked my right leg waist high, something I could do since I took dancing lessons as a kid.

Dr. Chavez told me that one should get to the hospital immediately after a first occurrence because available medicines may prevent a massive stroke if taken within the first three hours. Perhaps that's what was in the IVs they gave me. Luckily, the second stroke proved milder than the first. I tell everyone to seek medical attention immediately, even if waking up someone at the crack of dark.

My phone and cell now sit at the edge of the nightstand next to my bed so I can easily reach them. For nearly three years, a list of names and numbers in large type hung on the end of it.

If I suffered another stroke, 20-30 % possibility in the first year afterward, I planned to go immediately to Clinica Biblica and then transfer, if necessary, into the Social Securidad system. Through the CAJA, I have received regular check-ups, medicines that they carry, and tests. The first EKG I ever had was administered in one of the branches in Escazú. I simply removed my bra and blouse, and the male doctor hooked me up. In the hospital, the orderly applied connectors without my removing clothes. One simply lifts one's blouse or shirt.

Initially I had my annual female check-ups with a private gynaecologist who offices in CIMA. Like in the US, one changed into a hospital gown and the procedure was similar even to a disposable plastic spreader. No more freezing metal. He also did an ultra sound. In the CAJA, the attendant applied no cream resulting in a little bleeding. The doctor there told me if I had a problem, I would hear from a doctor; otherwise, the report arrived in three months. I decided to go back to my private doctor the following time because through the CAJA system, one can only have the test every two years and I liked the private doctor's services better.

The CAJA offers free services after the monthly charge but one has to follow the rules. For example, one brings samples from home (like urine) and must arrive early enough to get a number. Seniors with a Ciudadano de Oro (gold card) or with a Cédula that shows one age have a special line that speeds up the process. One needs to fast but fasting was not necessary for every blood test in the hospital.

At the Ebais clinic, I went to in Guachipelin 1 turned in prescriptions one day and picked them up the next. The system permitted turning them in up to three days in advance or after the date on the form and one had three days to retrieve the drugs. If I went on vacation, I could show proof and get up to 3 months medications filled; although normally doled out monthly. In some clinics like the one I frequented in San Joaquin, one can wait for the medicines. In Santa Ana at a cooperative clinic where the medical personal work for the CAJA and have private practices, I order medicines in the morning and pick them up that afternoon. Since I have special medicine needs, I pick those up at another clinic in Santa Ana (the clinic in San Joaquin had them) and I am allowed to order the next month's meds then. It has been my experience that Costa Rican doctors provide cell phone numbers and email addresses whether private practitioners or those part of the CAJA.

After I moved to Santa Ana in 2012, I went for my blood test and follow-up appointment in San Joaquin where I went when living in Cariari. My lab work was perfect with Cholesterol down and all tests in the mid-range, a sign I made a good choice moving. The doctor gave me a referral letter to the new clinic. A few days later, I went to there. The receptionist that was filling in that day was most helpful. He signed me up and gave me an appointment for a few hours later to see a doctor; asked what days wouldn't be convenient for another lab test which is "required" when you are new. He stretched it to June 4 at 8:30 a.m. It's in walking distance in central Santa Ana.

This new clinic only carried two of my meds; the other two meds have to come from Clinica Morena Canas in San Jose. One day the owner of my new home drove me there and the doctor at the Pharmacy gave me both meds and said I could order them from my clinic. 15 days after turning in the order, after getting another doctor to rewrite the prescriptions (we didn't know why the first doctor didn't do it) the forms were returned and I was told I had to go to the Cooperativa Famarcia in town near the Casa Blanca store and Banco Nacional.. The clerk said it would be another 15 days. I called before going (yes a phone number) and learned that they only had one med. I walked down there and it took at least 15 minutes for the staff to find my full order. Each time I ordered I had to include a copy of the transfer order that came back with the meds I collected.

When I went to get the results of the lab test (8 days later at 7 a.m. for adultos mayores without an appointment), a doctor wrote the prescriptions for the two meds for three months, in addition to those for the meds at my clinic. She made an appointment for three months rather than the six months as before.

Affordability, accessibility and quality comprise basic reasons for medical tourism. Tourists seek nip and tucks, dental care and operations such as hip and knee replacements. If one needs home care, options include hiring a nurse or even a live in. Costa Rica fortunately remains free of many endemic diseases that afflict other tropical countries.

A friend visiting Costa Rica slipped on a hanging bridge during a tour on a Saturday and cut her left eye. The tour guide took her to a clinic in a tiny village and she said the cute doctor stitched her up beautifully. She didn't have to pay for it. The doctor said, "The hanging bridge will pay for it."

La Nación reported in 2009 that 937 compatriots lived for at least 100 years, up from 231 in 2000. The article noted that some locations produced more long-lived citizens than others. Therefore, my goal to live to 107 in order to finish all my projects is a possibility although I wasn't born in Costa Rica. Genes might count because relatives on my mother's side actually lived long lives; my great grandfather died just short of 95 when I turned 12 years old.

When I first arrived in Costa Rica in 2005, I heard rumors of the demise of the Ciudadano de Oro (gold card). Rubbish. I didn't apply for about two years and missed a lot of preferential treatment (discounts, going to the head of lines, free bus rides). Once again, you need a cédula and proof of living at least 65 years. So if you hear rumors of the elimination of the card, check it out for yourself. Don't cost yourself benefits because you want to hide your age. Go to the Social Securidad building across the street and down the block from Teatro Nacional to the office downstairs. Bring your cédula, passport, evidence of your address, the usual stuff, even if you don't need it. The clerk inputs the data into his computer and if all goes well you return in two weeks for the card.

"One place I have not wanted to go recently is the Hospital San Juan de Dios," (an ancient edifice in the CAJA) wrote Jo Stuart in a Living in Costa Rica column for AM Costa Rica. The newspapers worldwide including those in industrial countries had reported bacterial infections in medical facilities. Her column went on to describe the daylong tests she endured.

It didn't make her feel any better when she read an article by Cici Connolly about efforts to improve medical care in the U.S. Regarding older patients, Jo quoted: "'Much of the evidence suggests that the more doctors, more drugs, more tests and more therapies given to patients, the worse they fare – and the unhappier they become,' said Donald Berwick, president of the independent research group Institute of Quality Improvement." It led Jo to vow to allow tests only accomplished with a stethoscope.

CHAPTER Thirty-four

What Happens if Medical Complications Occur?

Depends

"The cataract in your left eye has grown substantially and you will soon need an operation," my eye doctor since 1972 informed me when I saw him in Dallas, Texas in October 2009. For a person without insurance, the tab for the operation amounted to $3,000; with insurance, $5000. Due to follow-up after surgery, add the cost of staying three weeks, probably making the cost about $5,000 with airfare and accommodations. Read the details of my experience with complications here; I wish I had known the details of what might have occurred in advance. Costa Rica has good private doctors that charge less than in the States.

Less than two months after I returned to Costa Rica in 2009, the cataract grew like a weed, literally blinding me in one eye except for shadows, making surgery most urgent. Doctors in Costa Rica agreed the impaired vision contributed to two falls. About the time a large bruise on my right thigh faded from a fall up some steps in the Cariari Mall, on the way to the bus stop near Los Arcos I careened face down onto the sidewalk after my foot stubbed a raised portion on the concrete sidewalk. It resulted in multiple bruises and aches. Due to the injury to my left knee, I limped along wearing a brace on it that a friend lent me. It slowed my pace but after eschewing the brace I carefully walked an open air art show with my friend two weeks later with a golf umbrella as a cane.

Despite some discomfort on the day I fell, I kept going like the battery bunny. Another friend and I went to Immigration anyway and turned in letters requesting Permanent Residency. We received preferential treatment due to my condition. We checked that I wouldn't need to have another accident for it when we have to return to get appointments for the new cédula. Presenting Tarjeta de Oro cards put us first in line!

Despite admonitions by friends, I didn't have an x-ray but I called a pharmacist I know and he prescribed medicines that put the knee on the road to recovery. I knew by the feel I hadn't broken a bone. Later when I had a massage, the knee clicked into place. With the knee nearly well I went to a chiropractor who uses pressure and deep breathing to adjust the body. I bought a cane that helps me fend the high steps off a bus and provides me with preferential treatment. It also helps in negotiating broken sidewalks. I call it my costume because sometimes I use a golf umbrella because I don't need a cane to walk.

Since the fall, as noted before, I signed up for an ambulance service with medics and medicines on board an ambulance called Emergencias Medicas. When I fell if I had the service, I could have called for immediate attention. The ambulances used by the socialized medical service known as CAJA provide transportation only. Unfortunately, drivers here don't give way readily to ambulances like they do in the States. My new service will determine what problem exists, treat it if possible, and if serious enough, will transport me to a hospital. Fortunately, I haven't had the need to test it.

After much research through friends and online, I found Asembis, a clinic that specializes in a number of exams and operations. A friend from Puriscal had used the clinic about four years before. He remained pleased with the results of two cataract operations. Locals also praised the facility. My neighbors took me to one of the locations close to where we live.

The doctor couldn't see if the retina appeared healthy enough to warrant the operation. For the second appointment, we went to the main facility where doctors perform operations. I saw the doctor regarded as the best eye surgeon in the clinic. He performed an ultrasound on the eye; "Like they do for pregnant women," he said. The blood test proved me fit for the operation. During the weeks before the procedure, I cleaned and washed, doing the things not permitted immediately afterward.

"Don't worry," a friend whose husband practiced as an eye doctor said before my exams, "Cataract surgery has fewer deaths than tonsillitis."

From my experience, I responded, no simple surgery exists no matter where it happens. "If my eye can be repaired, the doctor will schedule an operation. Otherwise I will be blind in one eye."

During the day of appointments for a blood test and consultation with the doctor my Spanish speaking neighbor/friend who drove me and I attended a lecture in Spanish about what to expect and I received a flyer in Spanish that fortunately I could read. Doctors prefer someone accompanies the patient. All tests declared my health fine and my blood test excellent so the clerk scheduled surgery so I could stop taking Plavix for eight days.

Please note that with Spanish the language of choice, my neighbor helped to translate what I couldn't understand.

Before the surgery she and I signed the consent form listing the things that could go wrong but I don't recall what happened to me listed as one of them. Later I requested copies of my records, which they freely provide in Costa Rica. A letter from the surgeon, which could not be mailed or e-mailed, I picked up in the Alajuela office that I could go to by bus. The form wasn't attached.

Normally the surgeon performs the operation in ten to fifteen minutes, maybe twenty. The doctor predicted "menos trente minutos" as he began. I figured he gave himself 30 minutes since I harbored a dense cataract. It lasted 45 minutes and I felt pain that required two shots for it before I left the clinic.

Prior to the operation, a nurse took my blood pressure that surprisingly tested normal. She put drops in both eyes because the intense light might bother the other eye and one needs to lie very still. Then she dilated my left eye. I had to sit outside for about 20 minutes while it happened. Finally, she directed me to a dressing room and told to remove my outer clothing and put on a gown that one pulls over one's head, a cap like food preparers wear to keep the hair out of the way, and covers over my shoes.

More drops, again in both eyes and then twice more in the left eye. She swabbed the area around the eye with a sponge soaked in iodine. Slowly I felt my cheek numb similar to the way it feels when the dentist shoots a deadener into a gum.

For some reason a man who came into the dressing room area after me went first. His operation took a long time. According to reports, he also suffered pain and my friend said his wife swabbed blood from his eye. Eyes rarely bleed and I saw no blood after my surgery. Later my cousin told me about her friend who had the surgery done in Charleston, North Carolina six years ago. When her cataract shattered during surgery like mine the doctor stopped her procedure and she had to wear a patch until the second surgery. All ended well.

Finally after surgery and I could dress, more drops were applied and a patch. A nurse instructed me to buy two types of eye drops to bring back the next day. The doctor said that when he sucked out the pieces of cataract, some pieces floated back toward the retina. His letter later indicated 45% of the cataract stayed in the eye. His probe from the incision closer to the front of the eye on the outside lacked enough length to reach the pieces. He said I needed a specialist that deals with retinas. When I asked what the cost of a second procedure would be, he assured me that the fee at the clinic covered the cost due to the unexpected rare occurrence. The next day my friend verified the fact with the specialist. In the States, doctors charge for each operation regardless of complications.

Obviously, I received anesthesia for a far shorter surgery and it had worn thin especially since I require more drugs to keep me from feeling pain. In retrospect, a referral to a specialist made sense due to the dense cataract but doctor did not anticipate the rare complication. Let me reiterate that all the staff was very concerned and caring.

I rejoice that I did not go through the CAJA even though it cost nothing more than the monthly fee because the cataract might have become even denser. The CAJA doctor would not consider the procedure an emergency and would not have acted immediately. A Tica friend told me she needed a hysterectomy, considered an elective. Finally, after several postponements by the CAJA she gave up pursuing it.

Years ago, I had an impacted tooth in the left sinus and since then the area reacts easily so it ached. My friend gave me Ibuprofen because I could not take enough Aleve due to other medications even though it works best. Sleeping challenged because I strived not to roll over on the eye.

Here's what I recall of the operation. I sat in a reclining chair (like in the dentist office) in the operating room. The nurse attached a blood pressure machine and a heart monitor. She laid a cloth with a hole in it over my face after another iodine swab and drops. The doctor warned the light shone very intensely. An understatement! He set a plastic clamp in place so I couldn't blink followed by a metal clamp. Repeatedly he told me sometimes in English and sometimes in Spanish to look at the light because the eye tried to avoid it.

The center of what I saw reminded me of the very bright light like you see in movies when someone has an out of body experience. Patches of colors -- blue, yellow and red – circled around in circles or blobs. Another woman said she saw the colors in circles around the center light.

Then I saw floaters. They reminded me of the amoebae grown in Petrie dishes. I conjectured that these must have begun when the cataract pieces started floating to the back of the eye. Or, possibly I could see them as the doctor sucked the pieces out of my eye.

The next day we all went back to the clinic Asembis. Everyone treated me with deference and the doctor made an appointment with a specialist after applying drops. After his exam, a nurse applied cream around the eye and taped a new patch very tightly because of the inflamed cornea. When I blinked, it felt like a badly fitting contact lens. The irritation continued until a few days after the second operation.

Due to the situation, the retina specialist Dr. Carlos Cabezas Charpentier (2440-8537, 2208-8412, or email calcabe@racsa.co.cr), who offices in Alajuela and Escazú wedged me in between his appointments. He removed the patch and examined both eyes; then again after dilating the left one, he took photos. He showed my friend and me some photos on the computer and reiterated how he performed such an operation. He confirmed he would administer a larger dose of anesthesia. He did not charge me and told me not to worry that Asembis covered his fees at Clinica Biblica. (He subsequently moved to CIMA hospital.) Then he said not to use the about $25 worth of drops that I only had opened that morning and instead prescribed steroids, three other types of drops and a saline solution all totaling about $110.

I wore only dark glasses (wrap around style that my neighbor lent me). Bending over or lifting heavy objects (no more than 21 lbs.) were not an option, just rest. No attending meetings either but I could drink one vodka a day.

Two steroids a day; the saline drops every 12 hours, other drops every two and four hours formed my medical routine. My friend and I made a schedule and spread the medicines on a counter.

He prescribed taking two Ibuprofen pills every eight hours. A friend teased that I might grow hair on my face from the steroids; I said no, larger muscles. I told the doctor he needed to do a good job because I expected to live 37 more years!

While the scratchy feeling persisted on and off, minimal pain occurred by the second day. On the following Monday he checked the eye to see if the swelling had subsided any although the surgery to remove the debris had to proceed regardless. My vision remained cloudy and I could see little black pieces floating around. I gave him my patient number at Clinica Biblica so he could check my records about my heart and lungs because every four months I visited my stroke doctor that treated me about a year before.

While waiting for the follow-up exam at Asembis, my friend and I talked to several other patients, none of whom had pain. So count me as unique. My experience doesn't change my concept that Costa Rica has good medical services. It remains a good place for me to live.

I rested a lot the weekend spent at home. Some vision returned. Dr. Cabezas gave me good news on Monday morning. He could see the retina and the cornea inflammation had decreased.

He arranged for me to see my primary at Clinica to get a letter giving permission and stating that my heart and lungs, etc. functioned well. Told to get to his office by 11:30 a.m. we waited and waited, arriving home at 4 p.m. We needed to return to the hospital by 4PM the next day for the surgery at 5 or 6 depending on the availability of the operating room.

The doctor couldn't predict how good the vision would be afterward until he assessed the amount of scar tissue. He confirmed the right eye tested essentially 20/20. During the operation, he made three incisions and sutured behind the lens. He said Restor, his favorite lens, would remain. He reassured me that the first doctor ranked at the top of his skills and that my experience rarely happened.

It wasn't until after 7 p.m. that Dr. Cabezas began the operation after seeing a number of patients including one woman, at least 70 years old, with no vision in her right eye and a loose retina in the left. My neighbor and I visited with another patient who waited for my doctor. He said that he had two loose retinas, one for seven years, and the other for three years, thanks to botched surgery in the States at a reputable retina clinic. He had found his way to Columbia where they have a renowned eye clinic. His doctor there, Doctora B. Carmen Barraguer referred him to Dr. Cabezas because due to the altitude she couldn't operate on him.

The second time I had anesthesia via an IV. I didn't realize that I went to sleep because I heard at some point singing, talking and laughing. I believe I felt the prick of the last stitch but had no other pain until the middle of the night when my sinus kicked in big time. The doctor said that the pain resulted from the pressure in the eye.

The next day, five days later, another five days later, then 11 days later I saw the doctor for follow-up exams, meanwhile following the regime of Ibuprofen, steroids (that I weaned off) and a variety of eye drops. By the third visit my eyesight had improved to 20/50.

Over time, the blood red whites of the eye recovered, first to a stage that looked like I had a hangover. No makeup so you can imagine what my new photo for my permanent residency looked like. No Glamour Shot there. When my neighbors couldn't take me to the doctor, another friend did. I truly felt blessed by friendship and support during my ordeal.

When it came time for the cataract operation on the right eye it was an entirely different experience. My friends picked me up at 9 a.m. and I was home before 1 p.m. This included driving into San Jose, locating the clinic, pre-opt procedures (a series of drops), changing, waiting my turn, and the short procedure. I had intravenous anesthesia and the doctor instructed me to hold my head in a certain position while looking at the ceiling light fixture. I don't recall the procedure; afterward the nurse gave me a bag with more patches, tape, sun glasses, and drops, and explained what to do. I could see right away even through wearing a clear plastic patch which I had to wear for 24 hours.

At home, I napped several times. I was careful to wash my hands often, not pick up heavy objects and to refrain from looking down for long periods.

The next day I went for my checkup and was in and out in ten minutes. The only time I had to wear reading glasses was just after applying drops. Once again I highly recommend Dr. Carlos Cabezas Charpentier who offices in Alajuela and CIMA hospital in Escazú. He speaks English although his assistants do not.

Unlike me, you may prefer not to know all of the details but I find the more I know, the more prepared I am for complications. What

215

happened to me, even though rare, could happen to anyone anywhere in the world. So if you don't choose Costa Rica for eye surgery you still need to do due diligence. My good fortune was having caring, competent surgeons that focused on getting the job done right regardless.

From all the recommendations for the Asembis clinic, I still feel it has adequate facilities and medical staff, and offers a good choice for people that require simple basic cataract surgery. Had I known more about the rare problem in advance, I may have sought a second opinion or asked for a specialist before undergoing surgery. My recommendation remains to review all possible complications and credentials before making your final decision for any medical procedure.

CHAPTER Thirty-five

Giving birth in Costa Rica

An Option

At my age no way can I claim a personal experience. If you are of retirement age this chapter may not be of interest unless you are bringing relatives of childbearing age.

Therefore, without permission to name names, I paraphrase one woman's reported experience about having a baby in Costa Rica that I recall reading. As a R.N. from the States, she appeared more qualified than most to assess the process. Her evaluation concluded the system outshines U.S. procedures. She gave birth at CIMA hospital. If you get pregnant, check out the other private hospitals as well. Also, talk to people who have opted to have children in Costa Rica.

Another thing on your list, verify that the child will have dual citizenship. My understanding has been that those who meet the criteria can apply for Costa Rican citizenship without losing U.S. citizenship. **http://travel.state.gov/travel/cis_pa_tw/cis_1753.html**

For a second pregnancy, the same nurse had pre-registered at the hospital to speed up the check-in process. Costa Rica INS insurance covered $2,500 in expenses with the first night in the hospital room as the deductible. According to her report, the costs totaled the following and are listed as a guide to what you might expect but double check with the Hospital or clinic of your choice.

These are the fees she listed:

- $1,350 OB/GYN fees.

- $300 Anesthesiologist fees.

- $1,000 for two nights at hospital, food, and miscellaneous expenses.

- A complimentary dinner for both Mom & Dad with wine and free parking after the birth.

In view of her amusement at what people unfamiliar with Costa Rica think about its medical care, she pointed out she had no qualms about having a child in the country. Of course, before the birth of her first child, she had no expectations. She emphasized that the attention from the medical staff rated a top-notch score. She felt the friendly staff appeared truly to have her best interests at heart.

Again, according to her report, her day before the birth of her first baby went something like this:

At 7 a.m. she checked in and made a deposit of $1500 (paid with cash or a credit card), having not availed herself of pre-registration. (If your bills are less than the deposit, you receive a credit for that amount when you check out of the hospital, or additional fees are charged.)

At 8 a.m., a nurse escorted her to a room in the maternity ward and gave her a tour of the area and room instructions. An hour later on her doctor's advice, a medicated drip began that a nurse monitored every hour until 5 PM. When nothing happened, they broke her water.

Pain relief happened she reported about 10 pm in the operating room when the staff administered a spinal block after first trying to insert an epidural catheter in her back. In the wee hours, she gave birth to her first baby.

Obviously because she felt her first birth went well, she went back to CIMA for the second. Look for information about CIMA at **http://www.cimahospital.com/start.html**.

Although this next experience by another woman occurred in the late nineties, it pinpoints the need for investigating current options. She explained when she gave me permission to relate her story that the in-laws of a friend touted having her first and only baby at Hospital Mexico, one of the CAJA (socialized medicine) facilities. After 28 hours in natural labor, while help watched the World Soccer game on TV, the staff performed an emergency C-section. Because the mother lacked breast milk, she found another woman in the eight-patient room who had too much. The hospital offered no formula or allowed it. When it came time to go home, the hungry child had a fever and had to stay several more days.

During the stay, a nurse asked the mother, "Do you want your baby?"

She later found out that many women give up their children at birth before filling out the birth certificate.

A family that wants a child comes in, takes over as though having given birth, and avoids adoption procedures. My friend also told me that if the parent makes a mistake on the form, the child lives with it because the birth certificate remains as originally written.

In addition, please note that as of 2011 a mother with U. S. citizenship may pass on her citizenship automatically when she gives birth overseas. However, the father from the States of a child birthed by a foreigner has to fulfill legal requirements for the child to obtain U.S. citizenship. The U. S. Supreme Court upheld the law as of 2010 but it could change when reviewed again. In addition getting a passport for a child born in Costa Rica of two U.S. Citizens is more complex, apparently in an effort to crack down on child trafficking. Once again, it behooves double-checking the law and proceeding accordingly.

To learn more about costs for medical or dental procedures, go to **http://qualityinternationalmedicalcare.com/ and click on Pricing**.

CHAPTER Thirty-six

Long Term Care Facilities Sprouting

Or Hiring Home Care

Long term care facilities, especially reasonably priced retirement villages, are far fewer than needed. Since I have lived in Costa Rica, several planned facilities like seedlings showed promised then withered.

It's important that a developer have the capital to build at least a portion of a facility properly permitted and not sell from the pie in the sky renderings. As I will discuss, several developments that looked like promising residences fell by the wayside, not only for lack of permits, but because the investors foolishly assumed they could sell shell units and use the funds to build more.

AM Costa Rica Columnist Jo Stuart lived for a period of time in a long ago developed assisted living residence called the Jose Pujo Marti located in Ribera de Belen (the outskirts of San Antonio de Belen), phone number 2239-0295. The secretary does not speak English. The cost per month included TV, access to the Spanish Country Club, broad band access, light, water, and laundry and cleaning of the unfurnished apartment; although an option included renting furniture,

Jo wrote the following about moving in. "Tuesday was moving day. With the help of three masochistic friends, two strong movers, a small truck and SUV, we managed to bring most of the things I need to my new digs

My disorganized approach to moving (after about 59 moves in my life) can drive my dearest friends to thoughts of murder.

"My apartment is small but ample, and right now rather cluttered because I have not found a home for everything. My biggest challenge will be the bathroom, which is very small and where there is practically no storage. I do not understand how anyone can install a sink without a cabinet. The shower was a pleasant surprise."

She noted that her former apartment offered scalding hot water that took time to adjust properly. The hot water in the new shower sprayed just warm and eliminated the danger of anyone hurting himself or herself.

"My first morning, shortly after seven, and after making myself a pot of espresso, I took a walk along the walkways . . . (and then) through the grounds of the Country Club that is attached to the Residencia ... The Country Club, which contains two pools, a sauna, a Jacuzzi, tennis and squash courts, ping pong and pool (tables), and a restaurant and bar, to list a few of the accruements, seemed huge to me the first time I visited it. .. Subsequently my walk(s) entirely around it took less than fifteen minutes.

"My first morning was busy. Dixie, the nurse, came to take my blood pressure and explain the rules and tramites. Karen stopped by to ask if I wanted breakfast in my apartment or in the dining room and what would I like? (Scrambled eggs, well-done toast, corn flakes and orange juice in my apartment.) My laundry...would be picked up in the morning and delivered in the afternoon.

Dixie took me to the laundry area to meet the laundress and learn that they actually dry clothes on a line in the sunshine, which made me very happy.

"I will have to get used to informing both the nurse and the front office when I leave. And to inform the kitchen if I will not be here for meals and whether they should save them for me. No one should go hungry here since besides the three meals a day, there is a morning snack, an afternoon snack and a snack after cena. I seldom eat after my midday meal, but my first night I was brought a tray with fried chicken breast, rice, French fries and black bean soup with a hard-boiled egg and two large chunks of plantain in it. I made a gallant effort to eat but failed. I explained that I preferred fruits and vegetables. I have a feeling I will be buying and preparing my own fruits and vegetables. . .However, the president of the organization was visiting and told me that all I had to do was make a list of the foods that I liked and those I didn't and give it to the cook."

Note: Jo later moved back to an apartment in San Jose where she could take up her old habits and enjoy city life again.

The Tico Times reported in February 2009 about three facilities under way. However, since then Pura Vida Life Care wasn't able to get its permits. Finca Futuro Verde has a few rooms and offers the opportunity to live as one big family. Verdeza, set for completion in 2010 as a 125-unit facility, decided to change properties and seek more investors. Wall Street legend Henry Kaufman allegedly decided to develop a 500-unit facility in Santa Ana not far from the Cruz Rojo building. However, after initial reports, I have heard nothing further about the alleged fully permitted complex.

Justifiably, retirees refuse to plunk down money on future promises. Perhaps, by the time you visit Costa Rica to investigate options at least one development will exist. Search "retirement centers in Costa Rica" in Google to find out!

Bibi's Bed and Breakfast -- http://costaricanbandb.com/ -- still functions as a small family style operation run by Bibi and Jim Twomey where people can stay by the week or month and have some care if needed. It's located in Santo Domino de Heredia 600 meters north of the Basilica and 400 meters east of the super market Mega Más y Más. The house has a number: 27K. Call for availability. Home 2244-7324 E-mail: jptwomey@foxinternet.com. The phone number from the USA or Canada is: (011) 506-2244-7324. The rates (in 2011) ran $25 for a single, $35 for a double room with breakfast and a shared bath. Or $35 for a single and $50 for a double room with a private bath and breakfast.

Bibi has a lovely garden. Jim has a sense of humor. For example, he observed, "machismo is a virus that makes many Costa Rican men think that they are NASCAR drivers." Or, "The difference between Gringo time and Tico time is about an hour and a half." Finally, "The howler monkeys resemble those televangelists in the United States. They're small, make a lot of noise, and try to scare the hell out of you."

One of the reasons Costa Rica appealed to me was the ability to hire someone to care for me if that becomes necessary. Without immediate family, I don't feel I can count on friends or distant relatives to take care of me. I can hire a person to assist with day-to-day chores. If the need is greater, I could make space for a live-in whether as a companion, housekeeper, or a medical practitioner. Several expats have expressed the concern that the person might take things. My answer is, "So what?' I would weigh priorities and put my health needs first.

In conclusion, your best bet if interested in continuing care facilities in Costa Rica remains to Google them when you are ready to make the move.

CHAPTER Thirty-seven

What if I die in Costa Rica?

Seek Guidance in Advance

Most of us prefer not to face death so I will tread lightly.

It might be more complicated for friends and relatives to handle the death of a love one living in a foreign country with different rules and customs. Not touting myself as an expert about procedures in such an event, and knowing rules may change, I suggest investigating dying in Costa Rica.

One of the sources to check for information is **http://www.top10costarica.com/dying-in-costa-rica/.** The site also informs you about writing wills and testaments in Costa Rica. FYI, my attorney told me that my U.S. will was not legal here. A will written in Costa Rica must follow local requirements and be ratified by a court. The ARCR highly recommends having a valid Costarican will in place as the alternative (via court) is cumbersome, slow, and costly for the legal fees according to the standard rates. Another website to check about matters concerning death is: **http://costarica.usembassy.gov/emergency_death_estates.html**.

I donated my remains to a program administered by the Universidad de Ciencia Medicas (UCIMED). As a single person, I feel it takes the burden off friends and distant relatives not living in Costa Rica. As a result, if I die in Costa Rica, a person need only obtain a death certificate and call the number on the card 2548-0000, x1119 or 1125 (with area code 506 if out of the country).

Someone will fetch my corpse and handle all government paperwork WITHOUT charging the estate. After preserving my body, doctors will use it for teaching purposes for five (5) years. If I die in a hospital, any useable organs will be harvested

A friend died and her husband rated the service as excellent. He also donated his body. The Tico Times ran my article in its May 25-31, 2012 issue on page Weekend – W3. Look for Medical Donor Program Eases Burden of Death.

Learn more about the program from the attorney Ana Isabel Borbón at 2549-0000 x 1170 or email her at **borbonma@ucimed.com**. She has been with the medical school for eight years (2013) and does not practice elsewhere. FYI: Now you also can donate organs on your Costa Rica driver's license.

CHAPTER Thirty-eight

To Own a Pet or Not

Rescue a Four-legged Friend

"You don't have to buy a dog," a friend told me before I moved to Costa Rica, "because so many strays roam the byways". And I didn't. My neighbor's dog had puppies and he wanted me to take the last two. I had a vision of owning a medium sized dog, not two little ones. I finally said okay as long as he babysat the girls when I traveled.

Hence, Davida and Leda, part Chihuahua and part Heinz 57, came into my life. Both sweet loving almost black dogs, a friend dubbed them the "black girls." Later another friend called them cat-dogs. They grew up with a mother cat and her kitten that I named Oracita, playing and sleeping with them. They learned to wash themselves by licking a paw and to lick each other. They don't understand why cats aren't friendly. They also learned some things from the stray male dog I called Boots because his paws had white fur but the rest of him was black. Sometimes Leda raises a leg.

Often Davida will curl up on my lap without asking permission as I watch TV. Further expanding the concept that they behave like cats in some ways includes Leda's ability to survive serious bites. The first time dogs attacked her occurred in January 2009

The Guachipelin house swayed and I clung to my laptop on the desk. Somehow, a worker outside perched on a ladder three stories above ground made it to safety. Gates in the area popped open.

Amazingly, nothing suffered damage in the house although the 5.8 earthquake on January 8, 2009 hit areas of Costa Rica hard. After the tremors ceased the girls went out for their afternoon run and Leda as usual slipped under the main gate. A neighbor's two former street dogs freed by the jolt stalked and attacked her.

Alerted by the shriek, I ran to find Leda suffered bites in four places, the largest area stripped to the muscle required 14 stitches. For a few hours, I couldn't call the Vet because the phone wasn't functioning. I had no car. My neighbor, who didn't arrive until after her usual time, drove us down the hill to the Vet.

Somehow, Leda didn't bleed and finally let me comfort her during the wait. She spent a night with the Vet after surgery but soon slipped under the gate again if with a little more caution. Davida seemed to have learned from the event and carefully slithered out thereafter after surveying the land. The neighbor paid the Vet's bill.

Fast forward to Sunday January 31, 2010! About 5 p.m., I walked my dogs on leashes down my road past the large rotunda to the other end of the street where a large lot stands empty behind a guard house. We stood in the road at the end of a friend's house on the right and just as I started to return home a man living in the then last house on the right, two houses past where we stood, opened the garage door without warning and without first checking who lurked outside. Two large brown German Sheppards and a medium size Poodle ran out directly for me. I thought they might attack me.

Instead, one German Sheppard grabbed Gordita Leda, and bit her as she appeared to defend me. The man did not stop the dogs sans leashes from charging.

Leda screamed. Davida fortunately stayed closed to me. If one dog had grabbed her, she probably would have died because of her small size. She trembled. The man's third dog, a fluffy white medium sized poodle chased Leda as she took off for our front gate.

Leda's leash caught my ring finger on the left hand. The joint swelled. Months later, it still ached occasionally and many rings couldn't go over the knuckle for most of a year.

Leda had a wound about four inches in diameter, all hair and skin gone in the area, muscle exposed, blood oozing. I asked the man in Spanish to come help me but instead he called his dogs as he should have done immediately, went back in his house, and closed the garage door. The neighbors, a young couple living between the man's house and my friend's house opened their door, holding their dog, and saw and heard me screaming. They did nothing.

Unfortunately, no vet was available on Sunday. As I hadn't need one since I moved, I hadn't established a relationship with one in my new area. I sprayed the wound with a medicine geared to prevent infection and wrapped it with a gauze bandage with a neighbor's help. The dog remained untreated for nearly 20 hours but came through the operation. The vet said it was the largest wound she ever stitched and kept her two nights. Requiring 34 stitches, the vet feared the center might pop open. Leda wore a collar and it healed magnificently, although the center portion no longer grows hair.

Subsequently I saw the man walking past my house, his three dogs without leases as Costa Rica and the development's rules require. I made a report to the administration of the development in which I live and to the police. The Administration could do nothing I learned when I met with a board member. The police officer said I needed to prepare a Denuncia in San Joaquin but before I did that, I prepared a smaller report in Spanish for the dog owner and he reimbursed the medical expenses. He wrote a note stating he kept the dogs as protection from the "bad men" who work in the adjacent coffee fields. He continued to stroll standing tall like a General in front of my house with his dogs roaming freely. My dogs went ballistic when they saw them through the window. One day I threatened to call the police and he didn't come down to my rotunda as often.

Weeks later my neighbor warned, "Be careful," afraid for my dogs. "A brown dog is wandering around the house and he looks ill."

When a friend came by and saw the dog, part chocolate lab, she immediately fetched regular dog food from her house since I fed my little dogs light food. It ate heartily and drank water. It looked like it had fought because of an infected wound. I telephoned people for help, finally calling my vet who treated the dog without a charge. I made a pallet outside the fence as the property owner didn't want him on the premises and I could not take him in. Having just had two cataract operations in one eye I had to avoid getting an infection. I didn't want my dogs to get ill either.

Attempting to find some place for him, I called a shelter in Heredia. She charges because she neuters, feeds, treats injuries, and gets animals back to health to place them. On her website: she had a notice about two stolen chocolate Labs. I called and the owner said they had found Coco but were still looking for Bailey. Therefore, when I went looking for the stray afterward I called Bailey and he came. *It could have been the tone of my voice.*

At first, the couple wanted to rush over, and then decided to look at the photos I emailed them. They had found Coco in a bad part of San Jose and ransomed her. You rarely see such dogs wandering the streets; however, sometime later friends found a Pomeranian, a darling dog roaming near their house. They would discover that Miel couldn't bark, her vocal cords having been severed.

I spent two weeks feeding and giving water to the dog that I called Bailey with some neighbors' help. One couple in the neighborhood wanted to take him but decided he was too ill. Then another neighbor took him to one of the veterinarians she works with through her foundation for animals. He cured Bailey, neutered him, and found him a home. I backed out when he took over because I was still recovering from my operations, suffered fatigue, ran behind on writing deadlines, and had no safe place for him to stay after he recovered. The two German Sheppards who ran without leashes posed a possible problem.

Twice I have rescued dogs, one I named Boots in Puriscal, and Bailey in Cariari. When Boots joined my two small dogs I assumed someone had left him on the roadside because he seemed trained except he could jump over the fence or dig holes under it. My "adopted Tico son" Felipe and I forever devised ways to keep all the dogs in the garden and on the sheltered patio where they lived.

One of the discussions on Costa Rica Living (CRL) suggested that if you take care of a stray, it joins your family. One person wrote that his attorney said he was accountable for the dog's action because he fed the dog. He warned that when you adopt a street dog bad habits come with it.

However, I've seen dogs that feared people become gentle animals due to subsequent loving treatment. An example is the part German Sheppard seen on the cover of this book.

Walk around any small town in Costa Rica and the number of strays overwhelms. Rumor has it that the stray population exceeds the two-legged group. One woman who has a foundation to aid animals estimated 500,000 live on the streets in Costa Rica. Many hang around restaurants and meat markets seeking and getting handouts.

While I lived in Puriscal, I learned about Lisa Schaefer who rescues dogs and cats (up to 30 at a time) and places them into good homes, 2416-2422. She operates on donations to Amigos de Zaguates (friends of mixed breeds). Very knowledgeable, she may assist in finding the pet of your choice if you live near her

Another group called Stop Animal Suffering – Yes! (SASY!) -- may be a good source of information. http://www.sasycostarica.com/. Another option might be to Google for pure breeds. Look for Costa Rica Asociacion Canofila Costarricense. Visit the website in Spanish: http://www.costarica-acc.com/

A group called Coco Animal Rescue & Education (C.A.R.E) is run by a small group of likeminded volunteers that try to make a difference for dogs and cats in Playas del Coco and surrounding communities in northwest province of Guanacaste. It commits to helping sick and abandoned animals by conducting spay/neuter clinics and running educational programs about the health and proper care of pets in local schools. CA.R.E. sponsors fundraisers throughout the year and operates solely on donations from people in Costa Rica, the U.S. and Canada.

Through the generosity of donors they have garnered enough funds to hold a spay/neuter clinic every second Saturday of the month when surgeries on at least 30 animals are performed each time by Veterinarian Dr. Francesco Arroyo from San Jose. He has been going to Coco for over two years and has never missed a clinic according to the volunteers.

C.A.R.E. pays him $18 per surgery but charges the pet owner $10. If an animal has no owner, the organization pays the full amount. If the owner truly cannot afford to pay then C.A.R.E also picks up the tab. In addition it helps sick and injured street dogs by providing medications and transporting them to a veterinarian for treatment.

Owners Frances and Bruce of the Lighthouse Animal Rescue in Atenas have an array of animals. They board pets when people travel and work with a vet to treat rescued animals. www.mrbudbud.blogspot.com. Phone: 506 2446-0434. They also have a guest room: www.airbnb.com/rooms/37923.

If you opt to bring a family pet from the States research the latest import requirements. Contact the Embassy. Also, check with your airline about its policy because some destinations are not serviced year round by all airlines. Remember to Google to get answers to the current importation questions. Visit

http://www.therealcostarica.com/moving_to_costa_rica/moving_pets.html

Keep in mind that not all property owners allow animals. Real estate agents lament that it makes their job more difficult. Possibly true but one can find a rental that welcomes pets.

Just like elsewhere in the world, not all veterinarians are equal. Some specialize in large farm animals; others focus on household pets. What's the best way to find a good one? Ask for recommendations from friends who live in your area. With a car, you have more options although some vets make house calls. When I lived in Puriscal, I used to rent a car to go to a great vet in Cuidad Colon. When I moved, I changed vets, especially since she offered Express (home delivery) service. Overall, lower fees prevail in Costa Rica but check costs with the doctor you select before taking your pets to him or her.

Should your pet need grooming (peluqueria canina), find them on website: http://costarica.anunciosdiarios.com/20699/grooming-peluqueria-canina/. A member of a club I belong to, Laurie Sklar, trained in the US, lists many members as clients. At club bazaars, she gives away home baked doggie treats or candy when a visitor to her booth votes for the cutest animal on her poster, all pets she has groomed. (She provided a selection of photos so I could choose several for my cover.) She treats all dogs on a one on one basis with products imported from the US. Contact Doggi Divino at 2289-2162, FAX 2228-4384 or Doggidivino@yahoo.com

Note that Costa Rica has an Asociación de Animales en Costa Rica (ANPA). that can be investigated online at Facebook. http://www.facebook.com/pages/ANPA-Costa-Rica/101774234247

Finally, while grocery stores sell animal supplies, one specialized place in central Santa Ana Agroservios El Salitre, S.A. features a wide variety of items from a pet pharmacy to a veterinarian. Call: 2282-6858, 2257, 1771 or 7910 for directions. Check http://agrosalitre.com/ A post on *Costa Rica Living* in December 2011 noted "I've been using Dr. Edgardo Herrera Zuniga out of El Salitre in Santa Ana Centro for about 6 years: he's excellent w/ animals and fair w/ prices."

Questions to ask yourself follow.

Will you bring a pet to CR and have you considered how to do it?
Will your living facilities allow animals?
What veterinary requirements exist regarding importing animals into Costa Rica?
Does the airline of your choice ship year-round?

CHAPTER Thirty-nine

Domestic Help.

Pros and Cons

An unattainable luxury back home could be an affordable benefit here! Many foreign residents employ a house cleaner, either full or part time depending on their lifestyle. One reason I chose Costa Rica included the fact that one may hire a nurse, daily or live-in, if ever needed.

Expats might have gardeners and nannies too. However, exercise care about the people you let into your home. A reliable recommendation ranks a top priority and even then, you need to check references, copy both sides of their cédulas, and visit their homes. People have experienced petty and not so petty theft who failed to exercise care. Luckily, people only pinched unimportant items from me. Speaking Spanish rates an A+ when instructing help about your requirements. Also, secure important items to cut down temptation. Stay home with them until confident they are trustworthy. Isn't this a good idea no matter where you live?

Currently the labor law has two categories of holidays called *pago obligatorio,* and pago *no obligatorio.* The only dias feriados in the second category are the Dia Virgen de los Angeles on August 2 and the Dia de la Cultura on Oct 12. In Costa Rica Mother's Day, celebrated August 15th, is a legal holiday. You can't assume holidays here are the same as in the United States.

Upon checking the website of the Ministerio de Trabajo y Seguridad

Social one finds that there really is little difference for an employer. Unless a worker is on a weekly schedule, the employer pays him or her for every holiday and double pay if the employee works that day.

So far, I've limited hiring help to independent entrepreneurs, for example a person to clean the house every four or five weeks. When I had a garden, I occasionally hired a local to cut the grass, or to cut down heavy growth. I teased my Tico son that all Ticos love cortar, cortar, cortar – to cut, cut, and cut. However, plants grow back rapidly, especially in the rainy season.

Keep in mind that employees have many benefits in Costa Rica except if they quit or commit a crime. If employees are injured on the job all the benefits must be paid to them and they must file with INS/CCSS (insurance and CAJA) for a pension.

My understanding, keeping in mind I'm not an attorney and the laws change, is benefits include the 13th month Aguinaldo (usually paid in December), vacation pay, Cesantia or separation pay (one month for every year worked up to a maximum of eight years) and the Preaviso (notice in advance). By current law, you do not pay the latter two if an employee committed a crime. Keep an account in which you put one month's pay to prepare for paying the Cesantia when a person quits. Remember to save each year and include any increases granted in pay. Sometimes an employee will ask for advance against Cesantia but lawyers advise against it. My friend's attorney said that if the employer advances it and the help leaves the next day, the employer still has to pay the full amount of benefits and count the advance as lost.

When asked why she didn't tell my friend up front, the attorney said employees don't usually last eight years at one job. If the reason the employee requests the advance is for something serious, like a broken front tooth, and the employer wants to help, the attorney suggested lending the person the money with a payment plan. Have a lawyer draw up the papers to keep everything Kosher.

Note if an injury occurs outside the work place but during work hours, employees are entitled to the benefits as long as they worked that day. If it happens outside the work hours and away from the business location, they only get CCSS. If an employee gets injured outside labor hours, he/she must quit. If the employee refuses to quit, the employer must prove the disability prevents them from performing required duties.

The employer needs to check out the requirements in the Código de Trabajo (labor code) with the Ministerio de Trabajar or a knowledgeable attorney, and abide by them to avoid unpleasant occurrences. Sometimes the employee will hire a lawyer and a fight ensues. Take the precaution of consulting with a lawyer at the sign of any problem and follow the letter of the current law. Along these lines a post on Costa Rica Living in January 2012 stated the following:

My Costa Rican accountant said, "The law makes no distinction between part/full time or minimum monthly earnings. Everyone working a full year gets two weeks (14 days) vacation in time off or pay. For someone working less than a year they get one day per month. For the person who worked the full year, figure out how much was earned in the period and then figure out the average pay per calendar day in the period, and multiply by 14 (2 weeks).

Let's say the person worked a year for a fixed ¢15,000 per week, and did not take any vacation days off. 15,000 x 4.33 (number of weeks in a month) = 64,950 per month (this is also the aguinaldo amount, if they worked the full year), 64,950/30 = 2,165 per day, 2,165 x 14 = 30,310 vacation pay for the year. Be sure to get a signed receipt with the cédula number, and keep it in a safe place." This website appears to have up-to-date information about firing an employee:

http://costaricalaw.com/index.php?option=com_content&task=view&id=95&Itemid=44.

Another source of information appeared in the July/August 2011 edition of El Residente, the magazine for members of ARCR. Check out the Legal Update by Allan Garron, Attorney at law on page 12. Attorneys at ARCR also can help you to calculate the 'liquidacion' for an employee who quits or is terminated. Don't even think about firing someone who is pregnant as you will pay dearly.

If you choose carefully and follow caution, you will enjoy the services of help at a good price. One friend has employed the same person for seven years; others boast long-term help too.

CHAPTER Forty

Changing Ownership from Rich Expats to Ticos

Crime in Costa Rica

The tour guide said that local thieves think they are merely switching ownership when they steal stuff from people that appear to have more wealth than they do. It appears that petty crime in Costa Rica has increased as well as more major violent acts but isn't that the case worldwide?

Just like in Dallas, Texas when I lived there, groups here have speakers who tell people how to protect themselves from theft or burglary. One firm specializes in self-defence methods as well as advising about precautions one can take to avoid an incident. Few people feel the law enforcement groups will do something even if a crime is reported. Thieves sometimes break car windows to snatch a purse from the passenger's seat. Apply a film to keep windows from breaking. Put handbags and wallets out of sight. In other words, the name of the game is precaution while avoiding becoming paranoid. Simply stay aware of crime's existence and take care.

A friend said she saw a man throw a rug over the razor wire curled on top of a fence in order to enter a property. She thought about calling 911 but then reflected she couldn't tell them where to find the alleged thief due to the lack of addresses here.

Just about everyone knows a victim of crime, whether of an insignificant item or at gunpoint. The word on the street states that the police lack motivation to catch a perpetrator because the courts will only issue a slap on the wrist, if that. Witnesses fear retaliation especially if they know the thief lives nearby.

Some crime may be prevented by locking the gate to your house so someone can't enter the door unannounced. This is especially necessary if the house you live in is at the rear of a property with a back entrance. If a workman asks for a drink, you can pass a plastic glass through the bars.

While it might be a bit inconvenient, separate ID and credit cards, passport, cell, extra money, and hide them in different places. You can gather in a few minutes what you need before going somewhere. Keep only a little money in your wallet. Put your handbag out of sight in your house too. Thieves like easy targets and pickings. If you make their job a little more complex, they'll go to another place.

Reports noting tourists as prime targets for crime indicate it often starts at the airport. Rental car trunks open easily. Ask the car rental place about how secure the trunk is. Sometime the target has a flat tire; the thief who caused it offers to change the tire and then helps himself to whatever. Tourists like residents need to watch their luggage and avoid distractions. Drive on the rim to a filling station if you must without accepting a stranger's offer to help. Store valuables in hotel safes and don't carry all of them in one place. Wearing some of them – credit cards, passport, and money -- in a flat pouch under one's clothes can prevent heartache. If you put purchases in a cab's trunk, knot the plastic handles and count the number of bags. Usually taxi trunks contain very few items at most. I also carry a cooler bag with a zipper that not only keeps cold items chilled, but also what's inside remains a mystery. Years ago a driver in Puriscal put my packages behind the seat and I sat up front. I missed one bottle of vodka when I unpacked my groceries. Since then I sit in the back with the bags or store them in the trunk.

Many times burglaries result from inside jobs. If you hire household help or guards make sure you can trust them. Get recommendations from friends, copy their cédulas, and know where they live which I mentioned in a previous chapter.

Just like travelers, residents need to take precautions. Use the local currency, don't flash dollars. Avoid accepting help. Carry copies of your passport and cédula. If you are traveling with a companion, exchange copies of your documents. Stay alert. In other words, use common sense.

As I have written, my personal experience with crime remains minimal. Currently I live in a secure compound without bars on windows and take naps with doors open. Probably my lack of problems is due in part because I follow advice given years ago by Dallas police. Of course, I can't say it will never happen but I don't live in fear as I didn't in Dallas. Crime, which has been a fact of life worldwide for years, is one more factor that requires consideration when choosing where to live in Costa Rica or anywhere.

CHAPTER Forty-one

Finding familiar foods

Dealing with Cravings

"I have actually found a meat market that keeps EVERYTHING in refrigeration, is clean and the service is very courteous . . . no sausages and such hanging from unrefrigerated poles, . . . no tortillas or anything else on the counter tops except the pricing electronic scales and the "money dishes" to make your payment into. In addition, best of all, their prices are very reasonable, even lower than most in the area. You can point out and select the pieces you want to buy and they are not discourteous if you reject an offering. Your carefully wrapped purchase is ice cold. I have bought from them almost exclusively since I discovered them and so far (disclaimer) have never been disappointed. Fresh and clean is always the rule. They sell eggs, chicken, beef, pork and sausages which include cold cuts," one man wrote in a chat group post.

While I have never shopped there, the name of the market is Carniceria La Malacrianza, phone 2257-3798. It's located just north of the south-east corner of the Coca-Cola market. If you crossed in front of the north entrance to Hospital San Juan de Dios on Paseo Colon in San Jose, walk one block, and cross the first east-west avenue, Avenida 1. It's located a few meters north of the corner. If you have trouble finding it, call.

Is your tongue still hanging out?

Finding edible, clean, and refrigerated meat and fish plus other reasonably priced items challenges some people. Why? Very often beef is not tender because of different processing or lack of aging. While veal may taste good, any resemblance to a veal chop found on a U.S. meat counter generally is purely coincidental. Often people change their diets because they can't easily purchase good beef or specialty meats where they live.

In the Central Valley, for example, Don Fernando's meat markets stock products from the farm the man owns. When you walk into a shop it feels like you stepped into a fine meat market in the States. Some clients fly into town from Guanacaste and stock up. For a higher price the products are tasty and edible, not chewy and tough. They now have restaurants associated with the markets so one can get a good steak fix now and again. Call 2289-9165 to find out locations. I'm considered rich because I can indulge myself by buying better quality cuts. People forget I have only one mouth to feed. Due to the fresher diet, eating my main meal midday, and walking in due course, my body reduced its weight to nearly that when I was 30 years old. Can't complain!

The grocery chain Auto Mercado has a good selection of meats, chicken and fish but I usually don't buy beef there, just veal, lamb, and ground beef with a very little fat in it. In fact it is difficult to find ground beef with a high fat content. Sometimes I add some fat to the meat to make it moister. The club big box Price Smart carries meat but beef in both places requires marinating to come close to melting in your mouth.

At Fresh Market I have found a vacuumed meat product that I marinate for maybe an hour with complete seasoning, garlic power, pepper, and light soy sauce that usually is tender. The brand is Elarreo Cusa, available in other places. I like the Rib Eye best. These stores also carry many foods that foreigners crave for a higher price. However, I ignore the price per kilo of the steaks I buy but rather look at the size and how many servings I can get by cutting two steaks into 3 or 4 pieces. I judge by the portion cost.

If you live in towns like Santiago de Puriscal, your choice of food of necessity is more native. I found a meat store across from the main Super Mora with good quality products but a bit higher priced. They cut pork chops to my order, nice and thick. The owner liked the quantity I bought. I won a contest for $50 worth of free meat and chicken.

As some meat counters in various stores aren't good places to shop for such items, ask for recommendations from your friends or on chat sites like *Costa Rica Living*. Ticos often have stomach problems. Maybe they buy at shops without proper refrigeration and cleanliness that they shouldn't custom?

In San Antonio de Belen, the Centro de Carnes ALCHA has quality meats, honey from Guanacaste, and some good-looking vegetables and limes. It's located across from Banco National near a major bus stop. The telephone number is 2293-0164.

A Tica friend who was born in San Joaquin de Flores, Heredia introduced me to Carniceria Muñoz owned by Hansel Muñoz. The butcher cut meat and chicken to my order and tenderized Lomita in a machine for a beef dish I make. He sawed through the bone on the thick pork chops I bought cut to order so that I could split the bone for my two little dogs. Hansel speaks only Spanish so I learned the meat cuts in Spanish or pointed. The phone number is 2265-6207. It's located on the same side of the main street between the CAJA clinic and Banco Nacional across from the bakery Mus Manni which was recently bought by the Cerveceria (beer factory). Pali is around the corner at the nearby street before the bank.

My landlord in Santa Ana introduced me to Aldofo in the Carnicería Obando, a family run business that also has its own farm. It's located on the old road heading toward Escazú across from the Servicentro Hemanos Montes 2282-9557. A soda on the corner has a wrap-around counter with stools. The butcher cuts pork chops to order, tenderizes beef in a machine for a special dish, and gives me bones cut in small portions for my dogs, and a bag of tortillas as I spend from ¢6-12,000 at a pop.

One day in Cariari I walked to an AMPM store, a large convenience store that is owned by the same company that owns Fresh Market. They both have a limited supply of items, AMPM with fewer items, with prices higher than larger grocery stores depending on the product. That particular day I had selected items that should have totaled about ¢18000. The total came to well over a million colones. The culprit was muslo entero (long and short legs). The clerk deleted the chicken from my bill and I wasn't charged for it so it came to ¢16500.

Some expats in order to cut grocery costs opt to eat Tico foods. Good grocery store choices for local products include Pali, MasXMenos (referred to as Mas por Menos), Mega Super and Perimercados. A good place to sample some favorite dishes at low prices is at a Soda, a small hold-in-wall often family owned restaurant that usually accepts only cash.

You can try empanadas, a pastry stuffed with meat, chicken, beans, potatoes and/or cheese. Ask for filled peppers called Chile rellenos, tortas de huevos con cebollines (omelet with onions) or one with beans (frijoles); stuffed pasta called cannellone ticos rellenos de carne, or an enyucada, a combination of beef and cheese wrapped in yucca and deep fried. In Puriscal go to Hugo's near the bus station where you can get an omelet American style because he spent 12 years working on a cruise boat. He speaks English and caters to expats. His name isn't on the wall of the Soda but it is next to a parking lot on the same side as the bus terminal before the road takes a sharp climb uphill.

Many food items, like mayonnaise, jam, tomato paste, come in various sizes of squeezable bags, making it very useful. (Keep them upside-down to avoid "water" escaping first.) Many crackers come in single servings within a larger bag although the extra packaging adds cost. When one opens a large bag, if it's not sealed properly the crackers suck in water until becoming soggy. The fruits and vegetables taste so much better. In Puriscal, I cut flowers from my garden. If I bought cut flowers for the house in town that I almost rented I expected to pay about $3 a week but undoubtedly, the cost is higher now.

As an aside, foreigners dress very casually. They shop at Ropa Americana stores or on trips to the States or Canada.

Most days I'm in shorts (slacks if it's cool) and a T-shirt, plain or advertising something. When I go to San Jose and environs or church I dress up but not like I did in Dallas. Nobody does.

The local females tend to dress better than the males. The young women follow the latest style, pants low on the hips, midriff showing unless they wear school uniforms. Like the world over, even those overweight follow the trend. Jeans appear painted on and look uncomfortable.

Feasting and Foraging in Costa Rica is a great reference book for finding restaurants that author Lenny Karpman keeps updated at www.lennykarpman.com. He points out the restaurant landscape keeps changing. The book also contains handy culinary words in Spanish. He has written a new book *The Food Bridge to Everywhere, Confessions of an Old Foodphile*. Check out his blog at http://zt.typepad.com/lenny_eng/

Another source for checking out restaurants in Costa Rica is online at Costa Rica Eateries (CRE).- http://eating.therealcostarica.com/cgi-bin/yabb2/YaBB.pl. (Note: I have written several reviews for CRE.) The moderator created the website as a central location where people may find a good place to eat, or to perhaps to avoid a restaurant. Use it as a guide, or write a review yourself. Registration is not required to read the reviews, only if you wish to post. No need to sport credentials as a food critic or a gourmet, you simply must enjoy dining out and sharing that experience with others.

A non-commercial entity, CRE permits no reviews or promotions from restaurant owners or members of their own businesses. The site keeps members' contact information strictly private and does not shared it with anyone. According to a moderator, you may rest assured that you will not be spammed by signing up.

If you opt to post, please try to make sure each review includes the exact name of the restaurant, its location plus phone numbers, reservation information, type of food, the approximate cost per person, and most importantly of course, your objective opinion! If posting a negative comment or review, it is best that you have visited the place at least two times to remain fair to the owner. If the restaurant has a web site, list it. These requirements are not necessary to add a comment to an existing review.

If you still have cravings, you can learn to make the items yourself like I did with sweet pickles when I can find small or at least skinny cucumbers. Auto Mercado carries them again for about $5 a jar. It's not an item I try to bring back in a suitcase due to weight and fear of breakage even if sealed well. Or you pig out when you make a run to the States or Canada.

Progress marches forward. The Tico Times on August 12, 2011 featured an article about imported gourmet foods, beginning on p W4. The variety of foodstuffs now available is growing. More shops compete to sell delicacies. No longer are we faced with filling suitcases with items we miss when we visit our home country and hoping customs doesn't confiscate them. Now we may crave only the rare item.

CHAPTER Forty-two

A Glimpse at Yesteryear's costs

Sit Down First

Jo Stuart who writes online for AM Costa Rica included in one of her columns a letter she had written friends shortly after she moved to Costa Rica. She explained that when she came here in the 90s, she sought an older woman-friendly destination.

"After spending the first month studying Spanish and living with a Costa Rican family, I moved into a small townhouse-style apartment in Sabanilla, a 20-minute bus ride from the center of town. I'm paying $360 a month, which is a lot for the space, but it is a closed compound and the bus stop is just across the road. . . (And unlike most of the apartments and houses here, it doesn't have bars on the windows.) I decided I wanted to live in the Central Valley, near San José rather than by the beach. Aside from swimming, horseback riding and sunning, there's not much to do, and it's usually a long trip to the market. I prefer living near good markets and entertainment.

"I have everything here. . .I can check out books and read American newspapers in The Mark Twain Library in the Costa Rican/North American Cultural Center. There are several movie theaters within a short bus ride. They show movies in their original languages with Spanish subtitles. There is also an art movie house. I went to see a French movie one afternoon and found it a bit embarrassing because the line waiting to get in was made up mostly of single men (as in alone), all unsavory types, and older foreign women, like myself. However, all was decorum inside during a rather boring movie.

"A wonderful national symphony gives concerts Sunday mornings. Seats in the first balcony are only $4.50. There is a Little Theatre Group here and I went to see 'The Mousetrap,' which was much better than the Albee play we saw in Chapala, but the 70-year-old actress who was my favorite, got killed in the first act.

"On weekends there are ferias (farmers' markets) in and around town. Last Saturday I bought 10 oranges, a cauliflower, 5 tomatoes, onions, potatoes, chayotes and carrots, and it came to under $2.50.

"Seafood and fish are expensive at the 'foreigners' fish market in Los Yoses. I think it's because they have begun to export them. The fish in the Central Market looks good, but I won't buy it until I have something to keep it cold in on the bus ride home. I bought three completely boned and skinless chicken breasts for $2.

"Restaurants seem expensive to me, mainly because they include 12 percent tax (now 13%) and 10% service on the bill. But I have found a nice little second floor restaurant with a large window overlooking the street where I can get the 'plato del dia' for about $2.30. I like to write there since my word processor broke down. I can sit as long as I like; the waiters don't bring you your check until you ask for it. I am happiest writing in sidewalk cafes, but they are almost non-existent here. "What else can I tell you? It's the rainy season now so it rains almost every day, usually after noon. Sometimes umbrellas don't work because of the wind but when it stops raining, everything dries up."

For her single woman's view of life in Costa Rica, check out Jo Stuart's book "Butterfly in the City, A Good Life in Costa Rica" ISBN 9977-47-357-9. Arden Brink wrote, *"Unravelling the Mysteries of Moving to Costa Rica"*, available on Amazon.com.

Another book that details a couple's adventure in moving to Costa Rica from Zimbabwe is *Beside the Mango Tree by Celia Coleman,* also available on Amazon.*com.*

CHAPTER Forty-three

Cost of Living Increases

Where Can You Escape Higher Prices?

Bursting your dream bubble of living like a millionaire on a beer budget, Costa Rica has not escaped upward spiralling costs. However, the strength of the dollar benefitted foreigners by remaining well over 500 colons until 2010. After hovering around 500 mas o menos later in 2011 it crept up just over 500 again. Bottom line, if you try to live as if you are back home you will spend more money in Costa Rica but maybe less than in your home town especially if you hail from New York City.

When I investigated moving here, the exchange rate was far lower. As an indicator of what it cost to live, I checked out food prices. Of course, lists online probably remained behind the times but they gave me a starting point. Then during the few weeks I visited CR and lived in a small casita, I wrote down what I spent to compare with what I found online. Basically the cost of produce especially in ferias remains low enough that if a head of lettuce spoils you don't feel wasteful tossing it.

You also have ways to keep grocery prices in check. You can shop at stores like Mega Super, MasXMenos, Pali, Perimercados, and Price Smart, where one buys in bulk although not guaranteed to be the least expensive. You can eat more like the natives and limit the specialty items you buy from upper end stores like Auto Mercado. However, to insist that one store charges much more than another across the board is not true. If you price certain items at different mercados, you might be surprised to find that the higher end store has lower costs for some items, perhaps because they sell more. Or another store manager in an area where many Gringos live may perceive foreigners willingly pay more for a taste of home. As in your hometown, it pays to know costs especially because no coupons are available. However, some stores offer discounts for cash or to seniors on certain days of the week.

The majority of expatriates that I spoke to on a random basis agreed up until 2010 that the cost of living remained lower in Costa Rica than in most comparable situations in the US, Canada or Europe. The boom in shopping malls and American-style commercial centers means that many of the same products found back home await purchase at higher prices allegedly due to import taxes. One also has to consider the 13% sales tax; in restaurants, an automatically added 10% service charge brings the total on the bill to 23%.

Utilities compare favorably although the cost per kWh is higher and real estate varies tremendously but seems lower than in major cities in the States and Canada. Certainly, property taxes are a bargain.

Vehicles, more expensive to buy, have traditionally had lower running costs and insurance. Now taxes, inspections, and the ever-rising gasoline costs make it necessary to really budget for a vehicle especially when a person has a modest income. Rough roads may cause damage that requires more repairs. More and more friends with cars moan about the cost of maintaining them but the convenience outweighs the whines.

A new company handling only auto insurance for now is Mapfre. Recommended by a Canadian friend, reach agent Andrés de Carrino Beck at 506-87018209 or 8000-6277373 or drop him an email: scaminob@gmail.com. More choices of insurance companies with more types of coverage are expected to enter the marketplace.

Have you thought about what sort of lifestyle you hope to carve out for yourself in Costa Rica?

Running a current year 4x4, and renting a four-bedroom house with pool in Escazú, will absorb many of your dollars. Weekly splurges for imported goods at a quality supermarket, and a country club membership keeps the monthly budget high. Honestly, evaluate your income, whether it comes from Social Security, investments, pension funds or savings, to ascertain it will support expected living standards.

Currently a single may live on an estimated $1200 a month without a car. A couple needs a minimum of $2000 if owning a home. Add rent if the budget doesn't include funds for buying. One person suggested if you lack these minimums to consider Panama. Remember there air conditioning will add to utility costs whereas in Costa Rica in many more areas people live comfortably without AC or heat. Due diligence makes all the difference.

Restaurants of all types charge more as costs rise. Eating out less keeps your entertainment budget at a manageable level. Many menus quote a charge for the item, followed by the total that takes into account the 13% tax and 10 per cent service. Who's to say that these won't increase? If service is good, I always hand the waiter some extra colons because he undoubtedly shares the tip with cooks, bus boys and other help. Some people, locals and foreigners, debate giving extra. However, I know the wait person has gotten something. Of course, lousy service doesn't rate any additional money.

Discussing tipping can result in arguments among locals and foreigners. Many locals feel that the percentage added to restaurant bills is sufficient and that when foreigners add money they do everyone a disservice. I for one like the idea of the automatic charge, except when service is bad.

The Tico Times on July 11, 2008 carried an article entitled "Lawmakers Serve up a Slice of Tipping Bills" that described the controversy about the laws surrounding the percentage. It disclosed how at that time the servers received a daily wage of less than $11. Restaurant owners pay two-thirds of an employee's cost for the Social Security System known as the CAJA. The employees pay the balance.

However, the Editor of AM Costa Rica wrote as a note to one of Jo Stuart's columns explaining her CAJA experience that employees pay 9 per cent of their salaries to the system and on top of that, employers have to pay an additional 23% of that salary to the CAJA. On the down side, if the service charge, which apparently no proof existed that the servers received all of, were added to the salary, it could result in putting some restaurants out of business.

Maybe by the time you read this the matter will be resolved or maybe not. Make it a habit to check your bill to confirm the establishment added a service charge automatically before leaving a tip and add some *colones* only if inclined.

Everyone seems in agreement that the people who guard your car deserve some coins although once again people dispute the amount. Generally, 2-300 *colones* is welcome; however, outside the Teatro Naciónal during a symphony performance guards charge 2-4000 colones for watching cars. Usually the guard hands you a tiny piece of paper indicating the amount so you will know what to pay. I have noticed that symphony regulars rate the lower rate and tourists the higher rate. However, a friend of mine tipped the guard extra money even though she lives here in return for the guard saving her place very close to the entrance of the theater as it's difficult for her to walk.

To view the money, go to this website: **http://www.bccr.fi.cr**

Another friend promotes tipping even taxi cab drivers who normally don't expect one. I tip if the driver carries my groceries up the steps to my front door or by rounding up to the next hundred *colones*. I explained to her that I tip according my financial ability. Note that some people who have substantial incomes choose not to tip.

CHAPTER Forty-four

How to Live on a Limited Budget

Like it or Not

It's easy to live large on a substantial income but if you have an essentially fixed income to retire on, you may need to adjust your lifestyle to live comfortably within your means and avoid running up credit card bills. These ideas apply more to those whose budget is limited.

With your abode near a bus line, you can eliminate owning a vehicle. If you must have a car, buy the most economical one that you can find. Plan your outings so you make a big circle and accomplish several things in one trip. Avoid running into town just for one or two items. Using your car frugally saves on gas and possibly on repairs caused by bad roads.

Look for local stores that sell fruits and vegetables nearby and each week shop for fresh produce at a feria (farmers' market). Walk to them if possible. Check out if vendors sell in your area. For example, I bought fish some Fridays from a man who came by my house. In the same area, a man sells veggies from his truck on Mondays and Fridays unless his ancient truck breaks down or something else happens. He has been making the rounds for twenty years but reportedly less often in the last year.

Some expats grow fruits and veggies in their gardens. They also buy produce in season. They don't indulge in imported items, or perhaps only on a limited basis. Check out Fred Holmes book,

"How to Live in Costa Rica on $1500 a Month" at http://www.costaricaholmes.com/ https://www.smashwords.com/books/view/120623 His information supplements what you are reading here.

Buy basics from stores like Pali; chicken at the counter tastes good. Buy bulk at Price Smart and split with friends. Some people share the $30 membership that covers two people. Check out prices elsewhere to determine what items are more economical and that the product will keep if not used up immediately, like laundry soap or nuts (stored in freezer).

Drink beer; shop for wine and liquor specials. Even the AMPM during certain holiday periods will carry expensive vodka; two bottles for just a bit more than the normal price for one. Buy from the duty free shop at the airport when you travel. Learn about other bargain establishments from friends.

Occasionally I ride with a friend to a liquor store where prices on many items are half that at a grocery store. I make the trip count and stock up. Then if necessary, I shop at Magu in Santa Ana because the prices are lower than the grocery or other private liquor stores but not as low as the one out of town. Limit travel; have people visit and ask for help with food costs. After all, the guests benefit from a free room.

Joining the CAJA is required in order to obtain a cédula, get regular check-ups and all the medicine you can from your local clinic.

If you look for a place to live, search until you find the most reasonably priced rental or house for sale. Think about the amenities you don't need. Remember that a smaller place requires less of everything from furniture to maintenance. If you lease, do it for three years in dollars to keep your rent the same. Consider having a roommate to share the rent.

One of the electricity providers, Compañia Nacional de Fueza y Luz, S.A. (CNFL), a subsidiary of ICE, offers meters that have different rates for use depending on the time of day. For example, running the washer and dryer at off peak times saves moola. The company provides a list of rates when you sign up for the service. Choose compact fluorescent bulbs, although more expensive to buy, they usually last longer and use less electricity than standard bulbs which I have heard are being phased out. Of course, electrical surges can shorten any bulb's life. On-demand water tanks only provide hot water as needed and don't keep water hot in a tank between uses. Save up laundry so you run full loads. Use a dryer sparingly.

Get basic cable and Internet or make due with local channels if you're not a big TV fan. Limit your landline and cell phone use to keep costs down. Get a water meter from AYA if you don't have one so you can save on the water bill.

At the east end of Paseo Colon in San Jose a number of Ropa Americana stores sell good used clothes often a better investment than cheap new ones. Sometimes they have new clothes. Limit meals out; eat local food at sodas or a restaurant with more economical menus, saving the expensive restaurants for special occasions.

Use ceiling, table, or floor fans instead of air conditioning; or use air conditioning prudently. Turn off equipment where possible in rooms not in use. Leave windows open; invest in screens so bugs remain less prevalent.

Do your own housekeeping and gardening; have family members share in the upkeep rather than hire a house cleaner on a regular basis. From time-to-time, you can employ help as an independent entrepreneur to do a deep cleaning without all the government-required expenses that come with full-time help.

Repair anything you can. In San Antonio de Belen, around the corner from the park in front of the church, you will find an electronics repair store. He doesn't charge for an item he can't repair. The shop is called Punto Electrónico; phone 8369-1573 and some help speak English. Check for parts online; friends may bring in parts for you if you don't have a mailing service. Do preventative maintenance on larger items. Have Tico friends help with getting prices from repairmen to ensure fair prices.

Finally pay with cash, using credit cards only when you can pay them off entirely. If you have debt, work out a plan (at least on your own) to pay it off. Check out Oprah's Debt Diet for one or Suzy Orman's recommendations on their respective websites. Plan to pay more than minimums on cards if possible. Pay cards with the lowest balance first so you feel like you are making progress. Reward yourself for each accomplishment. Call the credit card companies and negotiate lower interest rates. Keep a minimum number of cards.

Creativity can make "retirement" the stress free life style you envisioned while enjoying your adventure.

CHAPTER Forty-five

Legal stuff

More or Less Information

Should you incorporate? Aside from putting it on cool business cards, the principle reason for incorporating permits one to transfer property by the sale of shares. Corporations have additional protection under the law, and it separates personal assets from litigation. If you're planning on owning a car and real estate, plan to have separate corporations for each. Keep in mind that taxes apply even for a dormant corporation.

However Ryan Piercy, General Manager, Association of Residents (ARCR) warns that a corporation like any good tool can 'cut you' if you don't know how to use it properly. Members can see him to learn the guidelines of a corporation or have him check over already created ones. He can help you avoid potentially costly problems. Ask yourself: Who exactly has power over my assets?

Some residents who own just a car often elect to put it in their own name. Make the decision with the help of an attorney, taking it with a grain of salt because he or she will make money forming one. Also, as a non-resident, another advantage of having a corporation is a cell phone may be put in its name. Unless you have a cédula, you can't get one in your name. If you select a S.A. with all its requirements – three officers and three directors—investigate the requirements with an attorney referred to you. Alternatively, choose a less complicated Limited Liability Company (Sociedad de

Responsabilidad Limitada or LTDA). Doing due diligence before making a decision about which one remains especially critical.

A corporation or residency has been necessary to obtain any kind of phone or even power service in one's name: Before paying for a corporation in order to get a phone line, investigate other options. A friend with a cédula got me a cell that I used for more than two years until I received my cédula. I told him that as a woman alone I could not live phoneless. My house phone was never in my name, as the line was included in the rental, until I moved to Los Arcos and had to get one.

The United States Embassy has guidelines for Retaining an Attorney in Costa Rica and may provide a List of Bilingual Attorneys. (Refer to Appendix E.) It is my understanding that attorneys request a listing and remain there until someone complains. So ask a friend for a reference. Look for more legal information in the book "The Legal Guide to Costa Rica. The author Roger A. Petersen updates the manual regularly so it's only about a year behind when published. However, much remains valid and it's a starting point for obtaining helpful data.

As requirements for the different types of residency keep changing, begin with Petersen's book and then contact ARCR to determine the current procedures. You will undoubtedly require an attorney. Be sure to get a recommendation.

CHAPTER Forty-six

Immigration Requirements

Remain Less Complicated than for Ticos Immigrating North.

Bottom line, every couple of years legislators propose changing the rules regarding residency. Usually new laws take time while rumors fly, and expats fret. Ask a Consulate what laws are valid before proceeding to obtain papers. As daunting as it may seem, the procedure compares favorably to the requirements for Ticos who want a U.S. Green card. Expect anything to happen.

ARCR provides members free guidance in understanding which type of residency to select. Staff will explain all the necessary documents and how to legalize them. Sometimes even the Consulate gives incorrect information on these issues. **www.arcr.net**

If you receive a pension or Social Security, find out how to get it transferred to a preferred Costa Rican bank if you will apply for a pensionado status. Keep in mind persons receiving Social Security payments abroad in recent years were not eligible for several special assessments. On the other hand, Costa Rica officials want to be sure you have a regular income in the country. Check with your attorney about current laws.

Therefore, you might want to have SS payments deposited in a U.S. bank and arrange for transferring money as needed to Costa Rica provided the type of residency you apply for allows it. Learn what fees are charged.

If you write a check to deposit in a CR bank, it could take up to 30 days before funds appear in the local account although the money has exited the U.S. bank weeks before. Currently, no Costa Rican taxation applies to funds coming in from outside the country although a change also is under review. I pay a small fee ($6.00) for transferring the Social Security benefit to Costa Rica. Regarding information about Social Security, go to http://www.socialsecurity.gov/pubs/10137.html#what

Compared to gas driven autos, immigration often appears stuck in the wagon and oxen age. While progress included computerizing some parts, the need for multiple copies, some handwritten documents, and stamps (rubber and paper stamps) to attest its authenticity keep the wheels of residency turning laboriously slow. While fingerprints in San Jose are free, you will need two passport photos and your passport (plus notarized copies of all the pages).

Go to the 3rd Police Station (Terceira Comisaria) in front of the South Commercial Center on the road to Desamparados. Tell the taxi driver: "Llevama a la tercera comiseria frente al Centro Comercial del Sur." If taking a bus ask the driver to leave you at the Centro Comercial del Sur. It's a two-story blue and white building near the center of San Jose across from McDonalds. If driving, you will need to get directions from your location.

A new twist in 2010 added the requirement of submitting your local Hoja de delincuencia (Costa Rican police letter). No longer necessary but Embassy Registration is required for new cédulas and renewals. Ryan Piercy wrote an Immigration Update in El Residente (p.10 July/August 2010), the magazine published for members of Association of Residents of Costa Rica (ARCR) Another article was published in July/August 2012. (See information in Appendix B for this and other handy numbers.)

The year 2010 marked yet a new immigration law (#8764) that upgraded the requirements for income. By the time you decide to immigrate another law could have taken its place. That's why guidelines for obtaining residency and eventually citizenship form a void in this book. Note US citizens as of 2010 could have dual citizenships. So check out the latest law before deciding to apply when you qualify. Stories of renouncing U.S. citizenship circulated.

The new law set up a Junta (board) with three members, each with a substitute. All the members must have a degree and a certain level of experience; two along with their substitutes must be lawyers. Put on your "To Do List" to check the Tribunal Administrative Migratorio because the board will have the final word in appeals of those denied residency by Migración.

Computer generated Digital Entry Stamps rate as the latest development in the war to prevent undesirables from entering Costa Rica. When they ask you at the airport how long you plan to stay, say 90 days in order to get a visa with the maximum time. Make sure you get it before leaving the passport station. Before departing Costa Rica pay a $28 tax (as of 2013) at the airport. If you pay with a credit card, be aware that it costs an extra $10.

A deceased friend of mine who had lived in Costa Rica for about 50 years obtained his cédula 47 years ago within two weeks. He said he procrastinated about going to get it. A few years ago he lost his ID card. When he went to replace it, the computer contained no record of his number and his hard copy record had disappeared among thousands of old paper copies. It meant he had to hire an attorney to help him secure a replacement and it took months to obtain a new one. Fortunately, he had a photocopy of the old one.

When you need to go to the American Embassy check out these tips (and refer to information about it at the end of the chapter). They deal with proof in providing information to the Embassy but help with other things like renewing your passport, replacing a lost or stolen one or getting extra pages for your passport. Note that in 2010 fees for passports and renewals increased. So check for current rates.

At the Embassy, present your US passport to the guard at the door so you can enter without waiting in the long line of visa applicant hopefuls. You should also have a copy of your passport, maybe more than one. You could send a copy to your email account so you can access it at an Internet café. Flashlights, cell phones and garage door openers are among the items taken by security. They are put in a bag with a lock and you are given the key. You present the key when leaving and receive your belongings.

After you get past security, go to the desk in the middle of the courtyard and select a fiche from the kiosk ticket machine. Go inside the doors up the steps to the right and the guard will direct you to the correct set of chairs to wait in.

The computer will call your number and direct you to a ventanilla where you tell the funcionario you need official proof of having your whereabouts registered with the Consulate.

Bring a copy of your printout and passport and you get a form to fill out to give the cashier along with a U.S. dollar fee for the notary. (Be sure to ask what the current fee is because it changes.)

A few minutes later the same funcionario will call your name to return to the ventanilla where he will ask you to swear all the data is correct and sign the form that he witnesses. Then he'll notarize the papers, officially stamp it and add a grommet.

If you get done early enough and you need to accomplish something else at immigration, you may have time to make it to the Dirección General de Migración y Extranjería, located directly across the highway from Hospital México. Remember they quit passing out fichas (numbered papers) at noon although the agent will help you after that time as long as you have a number. The easiest way to get there is to head up the access road toward Heredia from the same intersection as the Pavas exit. Stay on the access road for a kilometer or so until you see the ADOC Shoes sign (yellow y black) right before an entrance ramp. Turn right on the street by the sign and go 100 meters or so before turning left. Go a few hundred meters and park. Follow the crowd through the gates at the end of the street and ask which door you should go to.

One person reported in a chat group what transpired as a result of meeting immigration requirements about leaving the country every 90 days since he didn't have a cédula. "We went to the Nica border today. (We) asked for the jefe of immigration to clarify whether or not we needed to be out of Costa Rica for 72 hours to renew our tourist visas. We were all prepared to spend 3 days in San Juan del

Sur. He just laughed (as if he had been asked a million times before) and motioned us towards the Nica border, suggested we pay them the $7.00 fee, get the receipt and stamp into Nicaragua and return."

Ryan noted that depending on who is on duty at the border, officer deny some individuals re-entry or a new stamp for not remaining out of the country for 72 hours. Although a misapplication of another law (regarding duty free allotments) may occur, he warns it is unwise to argue with any immigration officials in any country.

"All seven of us returned to Costa Rica without (our passports) being stamped as exiting Nicaragua as the border clerk said we must spend 3 hours in Nica. Of course, a helpful soul expedited our exit for US$10.00 each. We walked back over to the Costa Rica side and presented our passports. We all got the official digital 90 day stamp."

An interesting tale, but check out the new laws and consider computerization that may thwart such possibilities.

Why renounce U.S. Citizenship? (This isn't what I would do; I would only apply for Costa Rican citizenship if I were permitted dual citizenship.) Consider these reasons against it.

A. You may forfeit your Social Security and 100% of your other rights in the US.
B. You stop 7/11 year rule for how long you need to keep your tax documentation. Instead, it's indefinite and may entail an audit at any place in the future (although it may be unimportant if you have

no assets in the U.S.).

C. It is permanent. You will not get it back.

D. You'll need a VISA from the US embassy on your CR passport to travel to the US.

For more information, check page 8 in The Tico Times for July 30, 2010. Chrissie Long wrote an article entitled "Turning Tico: On the Path to Citizenship. The sub heading cautioned about the twists, turns, and perils of applying for Costa Rican citizenship.

Once you decide to follow the renunciation path, you must go to the Embassy and try to take an oath. However, since it is a monumental decision, you will not complete the process that day. You must sleep on it for a day or longer. After you sign the oath, you have to wait to see if the US accepts it. Figure approximately 30 days before you get a "Loss of Nationality Letter".

American Embassy - American Citizen Services Section
Embassy Hours: Monday 8:00-11:30 a.m. -- 1:00-3:00 p.m.
Tuesday - Friday 8:00-11:30 a.m.
Web:: http://costarica.usembassy.gov
Email: consularsanjose@state.gov

Location: At the intersection of Avenida Central and Calle 120 in the Pavas Section of San José, Costa Rica.

Street Address: Calle 120 Avenida 0, Pavas, San José, Costa Rica
Local Mailing Address: 920-1200 San José, Costa Rica
U.S. Mailing Address: US Embassy San Jose, APO AA 34020

Telephone: [506] 2519-2000 From the U.S.: 011-506-2519-2000
Embassy Fax: [506] 2519-2305 From the U.S.:011-506-2519-2305

Consular Fax: [506] 2220-2455 From the U.S.: 011-506-2519-2455

No information about visas is available at that number.

Fax: (202) 234-6950 Email: consulate@costarica-mbassy.org

Attention to the public: Hours are Monday to Friday from 9 a.m.until 2 p.m. **by appointment only.** Phone Service is available Monday to Friday from 9 a.m. until 2 p.m.

http://www.costarica-embassy.org/index.php?q=node/81

For a current list of consulates in the United States link to: http://www.aneki.com/consulate/costa_rica_consulates.html

Costa Rica expected as of 2011 to maintain embassies in 35 nations, 10 consular offices and 5 international missions.

CHAPTER Forty-seven

Could Immigration Dedicate a Special Window to Baby Boomers?

Remember Wheels of Progress Turn Very Slowly

Around the first of March, 2010 Attorney at Law Roger A. Petersen, author of 'The Legal Guide to Costa Rica, wrote that "The President of Costa Rica Oscar Arias was expected to sign an Executive Decree which will make the attraction of foreign retirees to CR a National Priority. www.costaricalaw.com/legalnet/residency.html By implementing this policy the government possibly may provide incentives to Baby Boomers, at least 70 million strong in the United States, seeking retirement in Costa Rica. The government may provide incentives and streamline the permitting process for companies that build retirement communities for Baby Boomers.

In 1971 Costa Rica ranked at the forefront in legislation attracting foreign retirees. The program provided several tax incentives to those that settled in Costa Rica including duty free importation of an automobile and tax exemption on household furnishings brought into the country. These incentives remained to at least some degree into the nineties. I recall the situation because about that time I first looked into living in Costa Rica.

While Costa Rica minimized the incentive package in recent years other countries in Latin America including Belize, Ecuador, Mexico, Nicaragua, Panama, and Uruguay implemented and strengthened their programs. Signing this decree may indicate that Costa Rica wants to once again take the lead in attracting retirees. It suggests that Baby Boomers may receive tax breaks and incentives for settling in Costa Rica. The full extent of the program has to wait until the signed Executive Decree has been published in La Gaceta, the country's official newspaper. Now on the web, having died in print as of February 2013, access *Las Gaceta Digital* at www.gaceta.go.cr.

No law or project can pass, change or cancel, unless published in the Spanish language paper La Gaceta first. The publication includes sections listing Executive power decrees, agreements and resolutions, changes in public transportation and services, public education, and justice as well as environment and energy.

It will be interesting how those without the Internet will access this information. The Tico Times also died in print last year. I have not gotten used to reading it online.

CHAPTER Forty-eight

Applying for Residency

Prepare Yourself for an Experience

Months before I moved to Costa Rica I began assembling all the paperwork required to get my pensionada residency. A huge loose leaf filled with printouts of information confirmed the hours spent. Based on a recommendation made during the tour I took the summer before, I contacted a recommended attorney. I learned after the fact I should have contacted his brother (we'll call him Eduardo) directly because he handled my application. The first attorney claimed a 50% referral fee that had to increase my costs.

Amazed, I blurted out, "50%. Ten or even 20% is reasonable but not half the fee Eduardo."

"Well, he has a wife and children."

Shaking my head at the response, I remembered no one ever paid me based on raising my son alone. When it came to paying the bill, the first attorney and I argued over the price. Fortunately, he had agreed to deduct the fees I had paid up to a certain point from the $1250 he claimed. The lawyers deducted no additional fees after that. Unfortunately when changing Internet providers I lost the original email that spelled out the costs in 2004. I avoided interest payments for paying it out over a few months after I begged for the bill for several previous months. The attorney never provided an itemized bill. Since he angrily pointed out that oral agreements are valid in Costa Rica, when I reached the amount we had agreed on, I gave him the day, time, month and year of a phone call when we made an oral agreement. He never contested it.

In January 2005, I shipped all the paperwork to Eduardo; I received my cédula in October 2006! Depending on whom others hired, the person handling the application completed the process in four months to three years or more. Part of the problem allegedly included that my file disappeared more than once. The way the clerks handled files at immigration made such excuses feasible. Basically having patience and keeping one's cool make it possible to go with the flow even it's not rushing forward like a river fed by a severe storm.

Since I first applied, and became grandfathered with the then current laws, some requirements have changed. At the time I had to start the procedure in the States, now one can handle it in Costa Rica from what I've heard. Therefore, when you decide what type of residency you want, as there are several, check out the laws. Google, attend an ARCR seminar, and ask, ask, ask questions. Make sure you understand all the rules and get costs in writing. Unless you are fluent in Spanish and have some legal background, hire help. In one of the chat groups, a participant recommended a group **http://www.residencyincostarica.com/**

According to the Dirección General de Migración y Extranjería (DIMEX) the end of August 2011 legal foreign workers, students and volunteers will receive a cédula instead of just an imprint in their passport. For about $98 a year after the first year when it costs $123 (double-check costs), they will have a secure plastic card similar to those carried by permanent residents with a unique number identifying the holder. Scanning the information encoded in it facilitates verification.

About 20,000 legal workers have the right to stay in the country. These include domestic employees, construction workers and those with special skills, students, researchers, volunteers, teachers and even victims of human trafficking.

CHAPTER Forty-nine

Renewing a Cédula

Becoming Easier – Well, Maybe!

When Pablo who hailed from Cuba went for his cédula renewal, an ID card similar to a Green Card in the U.S., he had an old paper type of ID. He had escaped paying the $300 in case Costa Rica officials decided to send him back to the U.S. where he had citizenship. Somewhere I read that 80,000 people had missed depositing the fee in Immigration's bank account so he wasn't the Lone Ranger.

Pablo appeared for his appointment set for five months after his cédula expired, but the clerks couldn't locate his file. When finally found, it lacked the $300 receipt. Despite this, the clerk took his record of exchanging dollars into colones to a supervisor who approved the evidence including paying bills with a Costa Rica bank credit card. I had heard that one had to have made the exchanges in cash at a bank.

Bottom line Pablo had to wait to deposit the $300 the next day and return. He processed the renewal and had his photo taken for the card. He received a paper to take to his post office where he paid ¢2300 (less than $5) to have his card mailed to him about three weeks later. Surprisingly he found it at the post office as scheduled but over 65 he should have received it the day he processed.

The $300 is only returned if you 1. Become a citizen of CR.
2. Cancel your residency (usually costs more than the deposit) or

3. Pass away (your beneficiaries can get it after a court process)

Every two years I need to renew my cédula. If you ask an attorney to help, or an organization, you will pay a fee for as much as $600. Because I had the help of someone fluent in Spanish and who had renewed his card, I decided to try it on my own.

Learning from Pablo's experience, I went into overkill, even bringing my U.S. passport. Basically one needs to have written a letter certifying one's address, pay a designated fee into an Immigration account provided when one makes the appointment, bring the expired card and arrive 15 minutes before the appointment . It also had been made five months after the card expired.

Pablo went directly to the man at the door to "sign" us in and we went to the end of a short line. However, the gatekeeper found my name and told us to go inside, perhaps because we arrived right at the appointment time. He had us sit in some seats where we played musical chairs as clerks called people.

However, Pablo decided we should move to the anteroom closer to the place where cédulas are processed and we sat there waiting for a summons. It didn't take long. The young man, who wouldn't give me his name because Pablo threatened to write La Nación about his experience, was very helpful. He corrected the gender from M to F, checked that I had paid the fee, and took my photo. I wound up with a $10 credit because I deposited too much but I didn't want to get my money back, and have to go to the bank again. Not worth the effort! We had to remind the clerk to take my letter stating my address; he never asked for my conversion proof!

The first year I hadn't exchanged dollars according to the rule and worried until a bank officer wrote me a letter. The second year, I had all my receipts. I waited about an hour but received my cédula without having it sent to a post office. Overall, it took about two hours, a record for bureaucracy.

Pablo said next time he would request this type of service since he was old enough. However, the clerk accepted his letter requesting permanent residency but I have to turn it in at another location. Fiches (numbers taken for service) weren't issued past noon. It meant I had to arrive one morning after 8:30 a.m. and possibly wait all day. Pablo felt suspicious that his letter hadn't been turned in and decided to check it out one day. I wrote a note giving him permission to turn mine in, which a guard said was okay, so he would try to save me a trip.

Pablo subsequently wrote letters requesting permanent residency for the both of us and we went back to turn them in the week before Thanksgiving. As I limped from a fall that happened on the way to meet Pablo, we went to the head of the line. Pablo ran to get the required stamps to authenticate the letters while the clerk started processing the paperwork. He noted on each file to fax acceptance to Pablo.

"If you don't hear by the end of February, come back to inquire," the clerk told us. Early in January, Pablo received an acceptance letter for me written in such a convoluted fashion that I asked a friend who works in a city law department to verify what it said.

However, Pablo received nothing. Knowing the letter was valid for only a month, we toddled back to immigration and made an appointment for a month later for me.

Pablo learned when he called that he could request a search for his file and come back in a few days to get the answer. The clerk who by now knew us told him to wait, found his file, and announced he had received approval.

Back to the information window where miracle of miracles he got an appointment 15 minutes earlier than mine. Normally the computer randomly selects a date but after we explained my carless situation, the clerk found a canceled appointment.

Once again, I met Pablo, cane in hand, and we showed up for our appointments. Only Pablo had left his papers at home and couldn't get duplicates at immigration. I stayed and sat inside the door to proceed while Pablo returned home.

One of the guards motioned me to the section where it is easier to hear one's name. When the clerk called me, she made some men give me a seat. I communicated in Spanish with her. She told me to wait in the outside room for my new card. As I verified the facts on the card after getting it Pablo returned.

He started getting upset that another clerk wouldn't help him until I explained that the woman only processed passports. I asked the woman who helped me if she had called his name. We realized he hadn't given in his paper so no. She made a note on the form and told Pablo to return on the following Friday.

As he arrived for the new appointment, the clerk left. He talked his way into getting someone else to process his application but he had to wait a month for the new card because the card machine only spewed out cédulas at whim that day!

Next time we renewed separately at one of 32 branches of Banco Costa Rica that handles licenses, passports and cédulas. Only foreigners cannot renew licenses or passports, only cédulas, a very easy process. This time the fee was $123 in colones plus ₡3200 for sending the new card to the nearest post office. No matter one's age, the bank doesn't create the cédula. A Tica that I spoke to had to pay $240 for five years as opposed to the two years I obtained. The new card was at the post office the day it was due to arrive.

Friends recently renewed their cédulas at the local post office. It will be interesting to learn where I can renew mine later in 2013. Will I get one for five years now?

CHAPTER Fifty

Banking Experiences

Sometimes easy, Sometimes an inconvenience; Try Online

Whenever I hear a certain ad on US TV, I smile. It's promoting getting postal equipment for one's office. One actor, who undoubtedly has never banked in Costa Rica, says, "There's nothing worse than standing in line at a post office."

A grocery store ad reports that a person spends two and one-half days standing in line. In Costa Rica, queuing seems inevitable. I suspect we spend much more time than that estimate waiting on lines here.

What a shock! The other day I walked into two different banks and neither of them had a line. No tarjeta de oro, a gold colored card that gives "mature" people certain benefits like bypassing the line, required. It simply meant that I avoided going on a Monday or Friday or on a payday, the first day after a three-day weekend, or even the day after a holiday.

Yet tales of terrible banking experiences among foreigners living in Costa Rica abound. Ranking high among complaints includes standing in lines for long periods of time, slow help, and much paper work!! Despite having a Ciudadano De Oro, sometimes going to the special window resulted in a longer sojourn than standing in the general line.

On these occasions, it seemed like the person in front of me had saved up a month's worth of banking to make the visit count. Sometimes another patron noticed my predicament and waved me to a place in front of him or her.

When I investigated banks here in 2004, several people recommended only opening accounts with national banks. In the U.S. we have deposit insurance but it's not available everywhere here. Since a number of private banks have gone under, check benefits offered by the bank of your choice. Two banks I've used without major problems are Banco Nacional and Scotia Bank (not associated with Scotia Bank of Canada). Other people have had major incidences perhaps because they didn't understand how procedures varied in the Costa Rican culture. Friends have used HSBC and BAC. Some people have had difficulty opening an account. Besides keeping a stateside address, it also behooves you to keep a stateside bank account and a U.S. credit card billed to an address there. You can bank online. Granted some procedures in CR annoy until you learn to live with them.

Here's an example of an incident. One day as a friend and I went to Santa Ana for another reason, I had researched the locations of a branch of Banco Nacional and the Post Office to make the trip do double duty! Little did we know every Carlos and his family had selected the same time and day to do business at the same branch creating a crowd larger than one usually found in Grand Central Station in New York City. Banks in small towns have these gizmos, a glass security box that one enters to get into the branch. You slide your finger over a reader to open the door on the outside. After you enter the small space, the glass door closes behind you.

If you have too much metal on you, it won't open the glass doors on the bank side. The computer voice spoke to me, probably suggesting I check something in the security boxes provided outside the entry box, but I kept turning with my hand covering a pocket until it finally let me in. I can never understand what I have that the voice doesn't like.

When my friend wearing a heavy gold necklace tried to enter, sesame didn't part. She didn't know that she could have asked a security guard to check her bag and override the system to give her access, something I learned in Puriscal when I lived there. She returned to sit in her black car and got sunburned on one arm. She tried to call me on my cell but recalled the use of cells isn't permitted inside banks because it might interfere with its electronic systems.

That particular day the gold card proved of no benefit in the area of the bank where I had to go for service. Seats stuffed with patrons that slowly moved from one seat to the next made me believe everyone ahead of me had saved up several years' worth of banking transactions or had problems handling their business.

Giving up didn't seem an option because I had important business to transact immediately. In addition, my friend expected to turn her car over to the mechanic with an unknown completion date (another long story).

After waiting for my turn for some time, I sent out a bank manager to tell my friend the problem. The manager didn't find her but returned carrying take-out.

Finally, at a desk or platform as called here, the clerk told me that the bank system had my old expired passport number. I showed her a copy of the new passport even though she had my cédula ID. She didn't input the new passport number. She printed two copies of receipts for taking out the money. They look like narrow sales receipts from a cash register. The bank keeps the white copy often difficult to read and gives the client a yellow copy. How dark the ink appears on the receipt seems a function of the age of the carbonless paper tapes.

Next the clerk fetched (very slowly because she had a sore foot) a huge multi-part international check form. She fed the form into a behemoth electric typewriter, and with two fingers hunted and pecked the name of recipient and all the data, part in English and part in Spanish. After I signed it, she scribbled her initials in a box before toddling off to get an officer's signature. I hoped the recipient company had employees that could read Spanish!

As I waited for my signed international check, another bank manager approached me on a mission for my friend. Her patience had worn thin. He went out and told her my mission was nearly accomplished. An hour and half after I first entered the bank I completed my business but the job wasn't finished until I mailed the check.

The clerk in the Post Office was training a new person. He didn't like it because I used the envelope the bank clerk had given me with its return address so I had to put mine on the envelope too. He scratched out the bank information, muttering in Spanish that if the letter came back, it had to be to me not the bank.

Both of my letters contained checks so I sent them "certificado," similar to certified mail but more labor intensive. First, the clerk pulled out bar code labels, removed two from the sheet and attached them. The small envelope took a bit of ingenuity to get the code on the front without covering my return address or the recipient's information. Then he filled the certified forms in by hand. Next he printed out self-stick stamps, putting one on each envelope, and obtained a receipt for the charges. In a ledger book, he handwrote the numbers and other info and then made change. He then cancelled the stamps and shoved them into a slot.

(When I moved to Santa Ana years later, I got a PO Box for mail. David, the new clerk, let me pick a number. He is very helpful every time I go to the facility when he is working.)

The icing on the frustrating day happened when we returned to the Toshiba service center to fetch my computer that we had left earlier. Another dealership in San Pedro on the east side of San Jose provided the missing tiny screw (lost when taking the computer apart to clean it). The tech estimated another two hours. Fortunately, the next day when I picked it up, I owed nothing.

It's easy to understand why a teensy screw could disappear because when the laptop is dismantled for cleaning, it seems like a million pieces are piled up. It is definitely not a do-it-yourself project for the average Joe or Jane. The branch, no longer there, that worked on my laptop didn't stock screws just in case.

Most people living in Costa Rica can relate a bank saga. The first time I encountered a problem happened at the Popular Bank in Puriscal when my ability to speak Spanish measured nil to none.

I went there to cash travelers' checks during my exploratory trip. Somehow, I didn't sign a check to the teller's satisfaction – exactly as my other signature -- so she wouldn't cash it. Then she charged me a double conversion rate for a second check. Luckily I hadn't signed any more checks and went elsewhere for more money. While I seldom use Travelers' checks any more, I've heard they have become very difficult to cash in Costa Rica. Years later I went to a different branch of the Popular Bank to buy a tax form and received excellent service.

After my move to Puriscal from Dallas, I opened an account at the Banco Nacional;. My travelers' checks were cashed and deposited. I could keep cash from one of them. A friend who had a business account with the bank introduced me. Eventually bank personnel greeted me outside the bank on the street or in a grocery store.

For safety sake, if you want to open an account in Costa Rica, bring a notarized letter from your bank stating your banking history and noting how you earn your money – have you worked for a company for a number of years or owned your own business? If you have other accounts, bring letters from them too. Bringing evidence of other financial documentation may help even if not required.

Over the two years I lived in the area of Puriscal, and my Spanish speaking ability improved, I established friendships with tellers to a point that I didn't have to show identification. The procedures may have changed since I moved.

In the city branches, employees seem more security cautious and don't form relationships as easily. In addition, branches in populated areas often lack the security boxes at entrances and storage boxes.

but have guards with wands to "search" patrons. Later some employees I knew in Puriscal came to work in other branches I frequented. Every so often, the bank transfers personnel. I don't know if it entails a promotion.

In Puriscal, I soon learned to avoid banking on the day pensioners arrived at the bank for their monthly monies. The line spilled out the door and down the block. Although non-pensioners could bypass the line, the bank simply lacked sufficient personnel and space. That problem doesn't seem as horrendous in the city branches. Although one day I saw a line at Banco Nacional and the guard said it was for pension checks. Regardless, payday isn't a good time to visit any bank. Unless you have an urgent reason to stand in line, and the patience, choose another time or use an ATM. Some expats have Spanish speaking help handle their transactions.

As recounted before at times it's a pleasure to walk right up to a window. Banks serve bottled water and coffee at many locations. ATM's abound and it's possible to withdraw money from a foreign bank as well as a local one, most recently for a fee if it's not the same bank's machine. Check what the daily limit is at your financial institution in your home country and its fees. I find it best only to take money from an ATM in a safe area.

Flip the coin a moment and consider needing an international ATM card issued by a Costa Rican bank. The original card at Banco Nacional allowed use only in country.

When I asked for one I could use in the U.S., a clerk informed me that I had to maintain a $1000 balance for 12 months. While I generally maintained that balance, I believed for some reason I had dipped a bit one month. Finally, I convinced a bank officer I knew to help me get one, questioning the logic when one couldn't remove more money than the account contained. She actually went into the main office in San Jose after I spoke to her because we knew each other. Later, I had to have the card replaced and received a non-international one. However, when I questioned the change, I received another international card within a few days.

To find out about the banks in Costa Rica check with Superintendencia General De Entidades Financieras (SUGEF) the regulatory body that oversees them. Banks include BAC Credomatic, Banco de Costa Rica, Banco Nacional, Banco Popular, BCT, Cafsa, Caja Ande, Groupo Mutual, and Promerica. Many people feel that one cannot assume that information about a Costa Rican bank account is private and not shared with U.S. authorities.

Depending on your wealth, perhaps keeping say six months of expenses in the account here and the rest of your funds safely elsewhere might be the answer. Those who practically live from one retirement check to the next probably have fewer concerns about shared information.

With transparency a buzzword of the Obama administration, and the realization it hasn't hurt the banking system in the United States, the Costa Rican government broadened the Superintendencia General de Entidades Financieras.

It's an organization designed now to ensure Costa Rica's transparency while strengthening and promoting Costa Rica's financial development. The Superintencencia that many people felt a new entity actually operated since 1995 but only for workers covered by the CAJA (socialized medicine).

With the "new" law, banks bombarded people with bank accounts with requests to update banking information, thus reducing the privacy clients have experience for years. The old laws made it easier for U.S. companies and their employees to avoid U.S. taxes. While I heard complaints, the change in procedures didn't really affect me until months later when I had to update my information. Due to my financial circumstances, I have filed U.S. taxes since I moved to Costa Rica. I encourage others to do so unless told by the proper authority they don't need to file. Full access granted to local and foreign tax agencies will allow them to allegedly ferret out unreported rental activities, off-the-books jobs, sports book and gambling operations as well as Internet businesses. People applying for bank accounts may expect financial institutions to improve due diligence.

When I went to Banco Nacional to update my data in 2010, I brought copies of an electrical bill that showed my new address even though it'was not in my name. I also carried copies of a phone bill with my name on it, of my lease, of my passport (though not needed), and a copy of both sides of the cédula. I also had the originals with me. A bank representative had emailed a form in advance that I had filled out to the best of my ability. It took about half an hour once I got to the platform desk.

Rather than make me return because I don't have a car, the helpful clerk also made some changes in how I access my account online.

The first time I tried to use the new method, I couldn't access it but the representative helped me do it over the phone, something not usually done. I didn't realize immediately that the change dropped the link to an account in another bank. Impatient to re-establish the link, I persevered and reinserted the link before the same helpful person had time to call me back to assist me. It did not affect the links to other accounts in Banco Nacional that I use to pay bills online. When I couldn't change the password that the rep had entered, he told me I could change it when the bank requested it online in 30 days.

Due to some security issues, Banco Nacional added a string of security devices. One I used was called the "Token," a word which for the longest time I couldn't understand. The virtual identity card with a window displayed an eight-digit number used only once after you press a button on the card. The banker who gave me mine said it could display numbers a million times.

It worked well but since I got the card, the system changed and a devise similar to a car door opener replaced it. I read that other services include a digital keyboard and cell phone software but I haven't investigated these.

When I accessed my account number, I had to put a three-number code that indicated I'm a foreigner followed by my cédula number. Currently I only enter my ID number. (A different code worked with a passport number.) Then the system directs me to a virtual keypad where the numbers appear, arranged differently each time accessed. Letters in the password are typed in but numbers are inserted using the keypad followed by clicking on the enter arrow.

Then a window appears where you enter the Token number that you just punched up. According to a bank official, the procedure thwarts hackers who use key logger, virus, and Trojan systems to steal information from personal computers.

One time I had a problem accessing my account online; one day it worked, the next not. I had discovered that two transactions to pay bills that I had confirmations for had not posted a week earlier. After verifying the recipients had not gotten the payments, I wasn't able to access the account. Again, the rep at the bank tried to help me over the phone to no avail. It required a trip to the bank, a chore because sans a car I could access no branch in the area easily. Later a friend provided a phone number to the Internet help desk where people speak English because explaining problems in Spanish without the ability to demonstrate the frustrating inability to get into the account offered some difficulty.

Online AM Costa Rica Columnist Jo Stuart wrote about her experience when two banks informed her that two accounts had been *congelados* (frozen). Panic set in as she feared a raid. After questioning bank employees, she learned that everyone who banked, at least with national banks, had to update their data every two years. It meant returning home to gather her information and waiting in a long line to comply.

When I worked as an editor of a real estate magazine published in Costa Rica, I applied for and received a business cédula without any problem. That enabled me to work legally as an independent contractor without permanent residency.

Of course, I filed Costa Rican taxes too because I understood that like the U.S. IRS of old, you don't want to mess with the Costa Rican tax office. The rule applies to natives as well as expats. Tax evaders face hefty fines I've heard. My intuition suggested that Costa Rica no longer offered the tax haven it did years ago, even though old timers espoused differently, and I wanted to function legally.

After earning money for two years, the third year I had no income in Costa Rica. Sensing I should still file, I tried to buy, yes, buy, the form I needed at the bank where I had bought it before. Not available, the clerk said. The guard explained I needed to go to the government office for the less than ¢200 (40¢) form.

Instead, I called the office to verify I needed to file and to see if I could download the form. When I wasn't sure I understood everything in Spanish, I asked if someone who spoke English could call me.

Fifteen minutes later he did. He told me I could pick up the form at Banco Popular, the principal bank for tax forms now He called back a second time to tell me that the mall near me had a branch, open 1-7 p.m., and that I could obtain the form there. When I went, I bought two copies because the form isn't dated and I'd have one for next year. I had to show my cédula and pay ¢240 for both. The following year it was necessary to fill out forms online, print three copies and take them to the bank.

One of the things I urge, check out from authorities what you need to know and not to rely on what others say. Now that I'm a permanent resident, I can legally work but who knows if the law will change. If you want to work or own a business, do your due diligence and then double-check your findings. At my age, my bucket list does not include going to prison anywhere.

SINPE stands for Sistema Nacional de Pagos Electricos that means and translates into the national electronic payment system. It allows you to transfer money from one bank to another. BAC San Jose only allows up to 1000 USD at a time, some banks limit it to $400 a day. In order to transfer dollars or colones, gather the 17-digit account number, and the name and cédula of the receiving party. In BAC San Jose at the time, a person could a transfer without a charge for transfers set if the payment was for the next day. (That means the bank kept the money on hold for a day.) To have same day service, the request needed to process prior to 3 pm and required a fee.

BAC issues a Credomatic credit card that enables a cardholder to get a discount when using it at various places turned down a friend who's over 65 despite her excellent financial situation.

She offered to open an account and explored other avenues to no avail. Finally, the representative said she could have one if a Costa Rican who had a salary equal to her income would co-sign with her. Her Tica friend that was with her wasn't eligible because her income came from rentals. Now an attorney will get her one.

From what I've heard, getting a bank loan in order to buy property in a foreign country is fraught with more requirements than in the United States. The owner of the row house I rented in Germany in the late sixties told me that the loan covered only 50% of the purchase price and the term lasted a maximum of ten years.

An article in The Tico Times on March 6, 2009 "Tough Times Make Home Loans Harder to Get." appeared in the Real Estate & Construction Special Section on page S11.

It spelled out the required documents and listed the banks offering loans. Actually bringing cash to the closing remains more prudent. While the article provides a jumping off point, plan further investigation, especially to obtain current rates at the time you apply.

To view Costa Rican money (new bills have been issued), go to this website: **http://www.bccr.fi.cr** and click on Billetes en circulación.

What contributed to the changes in banking laws, you may ask? Part of the reason came after the terrorist attacks on September 11, 2001, the reason given for so many changes in lives worldwide. Stack onto that base an increase in money laundering, drug trafficking, and tax fraud.

To me it all boils down to what I touted at Neiman Marcus in the 1970s. If we do what we are supposed to do, like giving personal information to a bank to prove we are upstanding citizens in Costa Rica, we don't have to worry when the Stanley Marcus types of the world walk into our spaces.

CHAPTER Fifty-one

Real Estate Market

Hard to Evaluate but Definitely Evolving

"We're back Baby," an article in the Tico Times touted cautiously after nearly two years of worldwide economic recession. The article quoted area agents as optimistic. Without a MLS system in Costa Rica, gauging the market loomed difficult especially for someone not actively trying to sell or rent properties. Later in 2010, the paper noted that those selling real estate reported more interest in properties but suggested not to pop the cork yet. How many times have you heard someone say, "I sold the house," only to find out later the deal never closed?

So how can you tell if you are getting a fair deal? Start surfing real estate websites long before you want to explore the market in person. Investigate real estate agents and get recommendations of people who have worked with them. Remember no entity licenses agents here so dealing with a well-known company makes sense. Never, ever, buy a property sight unseen! Once you have found a house, visit it at different times of the day. If you don't speak Spanish, ask someone you know to go with you to knock on neighbors' doors to inquire about the neighborhood. Ask questions like, "If you could, would you move?" "Why?"

If you know someone who has sold a property where you have one for sale, ask him or her for the price it sold. Perhaps you will get an answer to use as a guideline.

Often you will hear, "no zoning laws exist in Costa Rica". However, if you decide to build, you will need to check the laws for the particular town and surrounding area, including required permits, where you want to acquire property. While zoning in the traditional sense found in the States is unheard of here, you can avoid costly mistakes by doing your due diligence before you buy the land and begin construction.

Doing due diligence also applies to rentals, vacation homes, and houses you might like to live in as a retiree. Never give real estate agents money; hire a recommended attorney and get receipts. Like location, location, location, document, document, document. Rent first to make sure you really like an area. If hubby envisions himself a dairy farmer, and has no experience, make sure living in an area away from the action appeals to you. Bottom line; it's never wise to start a business anywhere in the world without prior experience in the industry.

Fascinating to me is that many of the people I know moved to Costa Rica from Florida. Living there never interested me. Ending up in Dallas Texas happened by default when the company of an ex-husband transferred us there. The exodus to CR caused the Tico Times (Feb. 26, 2010) to ask the question, "Could Costa Rica Be the next Florida for Baby Boomers?"

During my time in Costa Rica, I've visited expensive and humble homes. One house where an orchid devotee lives, sprawled from a rancho to a house with very formal and expensive furnishings. It sort of reminded me of castles in Europe but brighter. Another friend owns a new house built on multiple levels on a golf course.

It's well-appointed with a pool and guest house.

A house that belongs to a couple where the wife buys and renovates properties has a lovely garden with a rancho in the back for entertaining. If you can get a copy of Vista Magazine for June 2008, the last one published by Coldwell Banker, you will find descriptions of houses costing up to several million. Or you can check out the website: www.coldwellbankercr.com

Keep in mind when choosing a location that if you travel often, or leave your home unattended for days, weeks or months at a time, you may want to live in a gated community with a guard. Home and personal security needs vary with lifestyles and where you live.

The best advice, find a rental in an area you believe you want to live. Make friends and learn the language if you don't already speak Spanish. Never ask immediately, "Do you know of a property I might buy?" Eventually the topic will come up and someone will offer to show you a property. If it is right for you, proceed. Otherwise, thank the person and say you will keep it in mind as you continue to investigate places.

CHAPTER Fifty-two

Expat Caveat Emptor or Rentor

Expats may be an Expat's Worse Enemy

"Your friend is gone," the email from Elena, her Tica (affectionate name for Costa Rican females) landlady in Costa Rica wrote.

"It can't be," Dawn said aloud, glad she sat firmly in her chair. A mutual friend she trusted introduced Marilyn to her three years earlier.

"She apparently took all the things she sold you and left while I shopped today," the email continued. "I only went to check the apartment because no lights glowed after dark."

The email ended, "Please send me a letter authorizing me to investigate what has happened with OIJ (Organismo de Investigación Judicial) officers and a police attorney."

Dawn leaned back in the executive chair she used in front of her computer. She still couldn't believe that Marilyn had behaved in this fashion. Originally, Marilyn had rented the small apartment tucked behind some businesses in the center of Alajuela. When she decided to return to Alabama, she let Dawn obtain a new lease for the apartment from Elena and sold her household stuff and appliances because she couldn't afford to ship them to the U.S.

After a few months "back home", Marilyn realized she could not live on her Social Security even in a small town in the south and decided to return to Costa Rica.

Dawn, feeling sorry for her, let her stay with her "until she could find another place to live." Then the problems began. Marilyn begged Dawn daily to give the apartment back to her. Finally settled in after many months of looking for a secure location Dawn stood her ground and said, "No. It's my place now."

In the midst of all the discontent, Dawn had to return to Texas because she needed to sell her home and dispose of unwanted items, leaving Marilyn in the apartment. Naturally, following Murphy's Law, the trip had taken longer than initially anticipated.

Dawn heard herself ask out loud, "How could Marilyn do this after all the assistance I gave her in getting her paperwork done for her cédula (green card equivalent), introducing her to people who assisted her in settling in the country, and saving her hotel expenses?" She immediately sent back authorization.

When the landlady and her entourage confronted Marilyn, she refused to return the items even though informed that in the eyes of the law she had stolen them. She agreed, however, to reimburse the money paid for them. Fortunately, when Dawn presented the check at the bank for cash the account had money. However, she had to use additional money from the Texas sale to refurnish the apartment and once again felt unsettled for several months.

Count one tale among many of how some expats, not all, may behave toward other foreigners. Just like anywhere in the world, one has to choose friends carefully and build trust over time. If something appears to be too good to be true, such as the infamous Brothers' scam that many consider a Ponzi scheme, shove greed back and run in the other direction.

A Ponzi scheme results when the scammer gets money from investors by promising big returns. The creator lures new word-of-mouth investors. Happy investors roll over the interest. Early investors received their promised returns with money from later investors and sung the Brothers' praise. Amazingly a number of investors defended the program even though no portion of their funds was refunded.

Brothers Luis Enrique and Osvaldo Villalobos operated an alleged Ponzi swindle in Costa Rica from the late 1980s until 2002. Many of their clients have said the operation failed the Ponzi scheme test because it lasted so long. Others suggested it could last for years if investors rolled over their interest. The fund netted an alleged $400 million. American and Canadian retirees plus some Costa Ricans invested the minimum $10,000. In all about 6,300 individuals received interest rates of 3% per month, allegedly paid in cash.

Supposedly, Luis Enrique Villalobos received sufficient funds to maintain the scheme from an existing agricultural aviation business, investment in unspecified European high yield funds, and loans to such firms as Coca Cola. Osvaldo Villalobos' role primarily consisted of moving money around a large number of shell companies and paying investors.

Funds eventually ran out for whatever reasons. In May 2007 Villalobos received a sentence of 18 years in prison for fraud and illegal banking while Luis Enrique Villalobos remained a fugitive. When I took the tour of the Central Valley the guide also warned me about unethical real estate agents, one in particular that operated big time in the area around Puriscal. He wasn't the only one to tell me about the man.

A friend that shared vital information that I needed to make the move experienced another deception. He made the mistake of giving a particular real estate operator $35,000 that he never saw again. Other acquaintances admitted to handing him money. Learn from their experiences and hire a well-recommended attorney for all your real estate transactions.

The incidence of fraud in relation to land sales, building contracts, and legal services is quite prevalent in Costa Rica. Often the problem stems from the lawyer you hire to defend your interest. More often than not, he or she willingly makes a deal with the other side for a commission, and the penalty for his doing so is almost non-existent and nearly impossible to prove. The attorney chooses the more profitable side resulting in ill-spent attorney fees and loss of the case. Hire legal representatives with proven track records on a contingency so you pay a percentage only if you win.

CHAPTER Fifty-three

Book Lovers Don't Despair

Obtaining Books to Read Still Possible

"Do they have any bookcases for sale," my friend asks every time I tell her about a moving or garage sale. She brought several thousand books with her, sends back a slew of books duty free every time she visits the U.S., and receives book care packages periodically. Even though she has a Nook, she still likes to attend book sales. However, most people like me, only shipped their favorite books, collectibles, or reference books (less used with online search services). Harking from the days before Google, I still check a hardbound copy of a dictionary or Thesaurus on occasion, old habits ingrained.

Bookstore chains like Librería Internacional, scattered throughout the country, sell new books and CDs at a higher cost than the same books sell for in the States. The store offers a Libro Club membership for discounts on certain purchases and during the month of your birthday. The main office number is 800-542-7374. Check out the website: **http://LibreriaInternacional.com**. A branch of Lehman´s is located behind the Grand Hotel (near the National Theater) on a pedestrian street in San Jose. It sells all kinds of books, both in Spanish and English.

Each year the Women's Club of Costa Rica and the Newcomers' Club feature book sales traditionally as part of their annual bazaars, occasionally as a separate event. Members of the Bridge Club bring books they have read and donate them to a box. Other members pay ¢500 (about a dollar at 2011 exchange rates) for a book. The money goes to support an animal shelter. People often swap books. Some lending libraries exist.

Here is a list of bookstores and libraries found in Costa Rica. Hopefully they still exist despite Kindle and Nook. For current information about hours, and location because some stores move, call first. In most cases, someone speaks English. If not, ask a bilingual friend to call for you. Included are known web addresses or other references.

Driftwood Bookstore

Escazú Centro, Northwest corner of the park

Phone 2288-0142

Goodlight Books Alajuela Centro: 100 N. and 300 W. of La Agonia Church, or 100 meters south and 70 meters east of the Alajuela Post Office (just north of the cathedral). The bookstore is on the north side of the street. Download a great map of Alajuela from the website. **www.goodlightbooks.com** Owner Larry buys books. It features a substantial selection of English-language used books on all topics and a very large VCR rental section. Enjoy espresso & pastry on a nice patio in the front.

Mora books

calle 5, avenida 5/7, and 75 meters behind/North of the hotel Holiday Inn Aurola in San Jose. Owner: Darren Mora (506) 8383 8385. Used Books in English (some in Spanish), some CDs & DVDs, will trade. **http://www.morabooks.com/**

New Day Cafe and Bookstore

Ciudad Colon phone 2249-5627

It's located at the first right about 25 yards from the corner on the left after the second blinking light about two kilometers before you reach the town of Ciudad Colon. Look for a sign. No website found.

Lexicon Library

(506) 2291-4383 -- lexiconlibrary.wordpress.com.

Open limited hours so check the website for details and obtain a map. It's located in a house behind the Italian Center close to UCIMED, the medical university, on the old Escazú road going west from Sabana Sur toward Anonos Bridge, membership is required; then you can borrow two books for two weeks. If you return them on time, thereafter you can then borrow up to 10 books for 30 days.

7th Street Books

(Noted for having hard to find books, have some used books.) 2256-8251 Barrio La Soledad San Jose 10101. 50 m Norte del Hotel Balmoral (between Avenidas Central and One on Calle 7) See review on fodors.com

Solo Bueno Internet Café

1 block north of the gas station entering San Ramon. As you come into downtown San Ramon from the Autopista, it's on the right side of the street. Over 3,000 books in English are stocked, ranging from paperback novels to lengthy hardbound tomes having to do with the Civil War, and a lot of stuff in between. Drink free coffee in a

very pleasant, non-crowded venue.   8340-8853

Mark Twain Library

This is an English-language library located near San Pedro. It's a part of the Centro Cultural Costarricense Nortamericano, the same place that houses the Eugene O'Neil Theater. It's on Calle 37 north of Ave. Central (Paseo Rubin Dario) in Bario Escalante. 2207-7575, Fax: 2224-1480 and email: bibmarktwain@cccncr.com. Membership. For more information, phone 2232-2731 any weekday. FREE loan of unabridged recorded books, no strings attached. It is completely FREE.

A great restaurant with reasonable prices is in the facility. The staff serves a wonderful turkey dinner the day before Thanksgiving. Tell my friend Pat Miranda, the proprietor, that you read about it here!

ebooks

Emilia shared information. She downloads books from different sources and finds that if you shop around online you can get a better deal than buying the print copies. The Sony Reader Digital Book is quite easy to use and reads Adobe(R) PDF, RTF, TXT, BBeB and Microsoft Word formats so it's a lot less limited than other e-readers which include the Kindle and Nook. Places from which to download books: http://planetpdf.com/free_pdf_ebooks.asp http://witguides.com http://free-ebooks.net .

If you don't own a reader, Amazon offers a free download of its Kindle for PC. I have it on my computer and it works. Garage Sales traditionally few & far between are gaining popularity. Look for notices in La Nación, Tico Times (published on Fridays now only

online), and on Costa Rica Living
http://www.groups.yahoo.com/group/CostaRicaLiving

Many small restaurants and cafes like Bagelmen's have bookcases with books to read and exchanged. Some expats in Puriscal have arranged events to swap books.

CHAPTER Fifty-four

Climate is a-changing

Like the World Over

Most guidebooks will report that the climate is perpetual springtime in the Central Valley and a tropical paradise on the coast. Actually two seasons, wet and dry, exist throughout Costa Rica mas o menos. The dry or summer season runs from about mid-November to mid-April when winter storms the U.S. The wet or wintertime lasts the rest of the year. No spring. No fall. The Pacific Coast features more weather that is temperate year round.

Let's do a reality check here. The dry season in my area of Guachipelin felt like living in a wind tunnel as air currents whipped down through our valley, flattening plants and piling up dust throughout the house. The winds apparently originated in the Caribbean and gathered strength between volcanoes. It illustrates how important it is to choose your location carefully in this land of microclimates. In fact the hottest April in 17 years occurred in 2010! For a person that rarely works up a sweat, I perspired while sitting still in Cariari.

Continually I am moved by natives who whine, *Hay mucha lluvia* when it rains a lot during the winter or wet season that lasts from approximately May through November. When summer or the dry season starts and winds blow a chilly wind, they lament *Hay muy Frio. It gives strangers something to discuss at the very least.*

On January 8, 2009 the country literally shook as an earthquake that caused damages and deaths rocked the land. The strongest quake, 7.6, I ever felt occurred on September 5, 2012. It resulted in no reported deaths associated with it but some damage near the epicenter. These proved that Costa Rica remains geologically unstable. If you lived in San Francisco, you know about tremors. On the other hand, what do you know about earthquakes or hurricanes (not here) and how they affect your choice of location?

Questions:

Can you take the heat and exposure that comes with living on the coast?

Do you mind days of mist, chill and no views due to fog if you chose the hills above San José?

The Caribbean side has almost year-round rainfall and the Guanacaste peninsula with great beaches may turn into a dust bowl during the dry season. What is your preference?

CHAPTER Fifty-five

Moving on or back

*Avoid This by Doing Due Diligence Before Moving to
Costa Rica*

"Our furniture arrived safe and sound in the UK packed extremely
well in Costa Rica by InterMoves SG Global SA," friends wrote.
(The company boasts 30 years in the business of moving World
Wide.) "We dealt with José and found him very efficient and helpful,
giving us an excellent price too and enabling us to save our money
by sharing a container.

"Every bit of furniture was thickly wrapped with cling wrap. In fact I
wish they had not put quite so much on everything! Each leg of the
tables was individually wrapped then the top and the space
underneath made use of in the crate. All the ornaments I had
already packed in bubble wrap were further wrapped in paper and
cling wrap. I glass stem was broken but my fault not theirs"

Referring to someone else's experiences, my friend continued,"
Maybe he had bad packers and we had good (help). I agree about
the Jesus and God Bless you statements. He starts every email with
"Blessings" . . . (my husband) and I ended up calling him Blessings
instead of José!! (We) had to be careful when emailing him!

"We highly recommend the company to anyone looking for a
removal company in Costa Rica in the future; please pass this on to
your friends."

Jose Antonio Sueiras, General Manager, InterMoves SG Global SA www.InterMoves-SGCR.com   506) 2258 0018 Fax: (506) 2256 5705 US – Costa Rica Direct Line (305) 395 3230 or in North. America: 866 491 6816

The same friend wrote, "Regarding Charlie Zeller, we used him too as he persuaded us at the ARCR seminar that he was the best. We already had a mover from Zimbabwe, their representative in CR, and furniture on the way, but Charlie ... took over from Brussels. Our Zim mover told us it would cost more, but we believed Charlie and all the problems he forecast for people who did not know the situation in CR like he did. In the end it cost us $4000 more than quoted and we would have paid the previous movers."

Personally, I worked with Charles when I moved to Costa Rica in 2005 and had a fine experience like several others. (**http://www.solutionscostarica.com/relocating/**) He quoted a price in 2004 that only increased about $300 in 2005. This underscores the need to get a firm quote in writing up front as well as to get referrals from current customers Places to look for movers {no guarantees) but the links provide starting places: .**http://www.mudanzasmundiales.com**;   **http://www.winmovers.com.** To rent furniture go to **http://www.mudanzasmundiales.com/storage-furniture-rental.html**

CHAPTER Fifty-six

Leaving Costa Rica

Most Returnees Failed to Accomplish Due Diligence before Immigrating

Exodus from Costa Rica comes in spurts. You hear about the people who after some time find that living in Pura Vida wasn't for them. Some leave because their company sends them elsewhere even if they feel sad about departing. Some should have never migrated to Costa Rica in the first place.

What reasons cause people to flee? Some excuses appear to mask the real causes. Some say they can't stand the potholes, the apparent proliferation of guns and increased crime, and the alleged disrespect by natives. Increased traffic on the narrow streets as more families have two cars and soaring prices join complaints. (In Dallas a couple of years ago I found many drivers had discovered my shortcuts through upscale neighborhoods that once had light traffic.) Things change.

Regarding prices, have they priced milk in the U.S.? With the increased cost of living in Costa Rica, some claim they can live for less back home or elsewhere. Perhaps what people expected resulted from lack of a thorough investigation of the land and culture and what they actually experienced made them angry?

Could some of their problems resulted from the inability to communicate in Spanish? Perhaps you can come up with some generic statement to explain their feelings. Seldom do the people take responsibility for what happened to disenchant them.

These outbursts remind me of a discussion I had with an Episcopalian priest about my second husband and my feelings about an inevitable divorce. I explained I couldn't come up with one main reason to resolve the marriage but had many smaller concerns about our relationship. He responded, "Your life is like a pin cushion. With only a few pins in it, it doesn't hurt but when the cushion is full, it is unbearable."

One person I know lived in Costa Rica for about two years, constantly complaining about so many things during his sojourn. Finally, he sold most of his belongings, including items he had shipped here from the States. Fortunately, he had rented so he eliminated the need to sell a property before exiting.

Another couple, on the other hand, began immediately building an expensive house before determining if Costa Rica met the retirement paradise requirements they sought. Remember, any place you live will have its own set of problems. Add learning a foreign language, different customs, and adjusting to a new life style. It may all add up to the proverbial straw. In any case, the pair proved extremely lucky to retrieve their investment by selling their house without living in it and moved on to a place better suited for them.

Some people move back because they feel homesick for what they left behind. Did you consider before moving that missing your children and grandchildren or even great grandchildren as well as your friends would be bearable? Did you allow sufficient and increasing funds to visit them for those special occasions that you might otherwise miss? Does your need to live within a budget prevent unlimited visits home enable you to adjust to missing some events? Can you live without amenities you crave?

Moving to a foreign country is costly; moving back drains more funds needlessly. When you consider where to live, what to bring, trudging through data about immigration, also consider your mindset. If you have no or few close family relatives, and perhaps have lived abroad even as an Army brat, you may have a chance of acclimating to your new country better than some other people adjust. Remember it doesn't mean you give up on your homeland; you just enjoy your new adventure in life.

Why do so many people leave paradise? Some reasons may include unreasonable expectations (we're not in Kansas), insufficient funds relative to age as prices increase and no way to supplement income, investing savings in risky businesses, and being scammed whether in real estate or investment programs. For one reason or another, some don't feel safe. They may have been robbed or feel paranoid because of what they have read in the papers. Their experience, if any, with public medical care make them feel (and feelings are valid even if they don't reflect the actual situation) the treatment wasn't up to American standards. Some didn't plan to live here permanently, probably transferred for a specific time, and had no reason to make it home.

Boredom, not addressed often, offers a major threat to expats who seek a successful life in Costa Rica. How often can one rave about a successful foray to a local market, solving a problem, or viewing a sunset from one's finca (farm)? Bottom line, if these people suffered boredom in Dallas or Seattle, it makes sense for it to creep into their lives anywhere they live in the world.

Costa Rica laws prohibit most new arrivals from holding a regular job. That cuts off many expats from the daily routine of life that they grew accustomed to at home. Add to that the challenge of daily life routines and sometimes becoming fresh fodder for scam-artists, crooked lawyers and others.

One-stop shopping rarely happens in Costa Rica. Sales are only beginning to appear. Returns in some areas don't exist; at some stores a limited policy is now in effect. Having to keep boxes and receipts to prove purchase for returns annoys many expats. Sometimes one can only get a store credit but that's an improvement.

In the end, the individual has to adjust his or her life to create new options and experiences. For some, the answer lies in a Costa Rica-related discussion list such as Costa Rica Living on Yahoo that provides an electronic meeting ground for expats and expat wannabes. Topics sometimes repeat but a lot of information is doled out each day to the thousands who subscribe. Other groups include Costa Rica Central Valley Living, Escazú News, and AM Costa Rica. Some expats hang out at a local soda (hole in the wall restaurant), coffee shop or bar to fill a void. Others delve into joining clubs and organizations. Curing boredom is not an option for some.

Other reasons for exiting may include that people didn't do due diligence prior to living in Costa Rica. They believed promotions that the country offered a paradise for everyone. They sold everything and plunged into a new life, often buying a home or property without ever setting foot in the country. Everything changes once one must adjust to the real Costa Rica when daily tasks and chores loom largely different.

Some people believe that because Costa Rica offers a simpler life it will solve issues in the U.S. or Canada. Not! Couples with health issues believe they will discover cures. Often people don't visit their former country due to their financial situations probably made worse in recent years. Not speaking Spanish complicates things. Living away from the action makes expats, especially women, feel isolated and lonely.

Younger couples who have read that Costa Rica has a fine educational system and the highest standard of literacy in Central America, lack preparedness for the condition of public schools or the cost of private schools.

People who came and immediately bought a home, usually in the wrong place, again without shopping around, find themselves disillusioned. Often they overpaid and can't find a buyer. So they sell out at a loss and head elsewhere perhaps to make the same mistake. Immigrants, probably the very ones that complain when foreigners come to their country and don't learn English, get angry because not everyone in Costa Rica speaks English. They fail to realize that if they learned at least a little Spanish, their experiences might be far better.

For some immigrants dealing with inefficiency and the speed with which things get accomplished (the different concept of time) and differences in expressing language creates a huge hurdle. Bottom line, most people return to their original homeland due to some level of cultural shock. If honest with themselves, they would realize they didn't leave because they couldn't find an appliance, but because they couldn't adjust to the culture.

Many settlers lament that the cost of living has risen. If you live in a ghetto where other Americans congregate and prices inflate more because, "All Americans are rich," and you opt to buy foreign products, your cost of living climbs higher than expected. When they return to their hometown, price shock may really sink in. Despite the challenges and obstacles, expats who make Costa Rica their permanent home believe the benefits outweigh the drawbacks. They have taken their international move seriously and have prepared for culture shock.

For another point of view, check out:

http://www.therealcostarica.com/living_in_costa_rica/culture_shock_adjustment.html

In addition, George Lundquist commented about this topic on We Love Costa Rica, an online newsletter produced by Scott Oliver. http://www.welovecostarica.com/ George, who granted permission to quote him, pointed out that no more than 10% of the people who take his tour move back within five years. He wrote that one major moving company claims that 50 to 60 percent of the people they transport to Costa Rica return within the first year.

He wrote. "After 8 years of guiding people interested in

investigating the possibility of living full or part time in Costa Rica I have a lot of experience in seeing why some do not make it here" George feels the common theme of people who failed to take his tour is:

"A: They were unable or unwilling to get over their intense self-interest.

B: Their impatience and sense of urgency to have what they want, when they want it irritated them and led to huge frustration.

C: They blame Costa Rica for their inability to control how they deal with the differences in culture and values here. Most of us who remain are betting they will never quit blaming external causes for their internal torments."

The reasons for returning stated by people who took his tour include:

"A: Two couples from Arizona found that they could not adjust to the higher humidity.

B: (Another) couple had other family issues that required they return.

C: ... a few did not take to heart my emphasis on learning to adapt to the Zen of this culture."

George concluded, "The common theme among the most happy who stay is that they find a whole new life. They became completely involved in doing things that were hobbies, or found a business that is not only fun but also (one from which) they (can) make some extra money. . . They discover that, like me, their life is not one of survival and worry about how to eek by until they die. Instead, our health improves due to more activity that is physical, better fresh fruits and vegetables, and a sense of exhilaration at having so . . . (many) fun things to do when we get up before dawn each day. (Not everyone sleeps with the chickens. Some of us go dancing at local establishments so our fun begins and ends later in the day.) One could argue that those of us who 'get it' here in Costa Rica would probably 'get it' anywhere."

CHAPTER Fifty-seven

Epilogue and Final Thoughts

Did my Adventure Live up to Expectations?

A resounding "Yes!" I can still hear my deceased son, my best friend, saying, "Mom, go for it." I lack lots of time to assess my most interesting life stuffed with good, bad, ugly and great experiences thus far due to a long "Bucket List" yet to complete. Certainly, living in a culture with a Pura Vida attitude has affected me. It has given me an opportunity to help people but also to accept assistance from still others. I truly would have lacked a fulfilling experience had I decided not to move to Costa Rica. Even though we don't know that we are missing something until we experience it, I feel that at my gut level I would know I had thrown away a great opportunity if I hadn't embarked on my adventure.

When I first journeyed to Dallas, I had no idea that I would live there for 35 years. Somehow, the months turned into a year and the years into so many seemingly in a blink of an eye. Therefore, when people, mostly natives, ask me how long I plan to stay in Costa Rica, I can only say that I cannot predict the length of my sojourn because one never knows where life will lead. What I know as a certainty, I will follow where life leads as I have thus far, embracing whatever I encounter to the fullest ever grateful for the exceedingly positive adventure in Costa Rica.

APPENDIX A

DISCLAIMER

Don't kill the messenger if you abhor these references. The purpose of including them aims to help you learn all you can about Costa Rica to enable you to make an informed decision. No one described moving abroad as a simple procedure. No endorsement is implied or guaranteed regarding the facts deemed viable and correct. It's up to you to check and double check everything. In fact, during the time it took me to compose this tome, facts changed so expect information to evolve. At some point, I had to decide that the book was complete as it could be at this time. Within six months of publishing the book, it was evident a second edition was needed.

Question! Question! Question! I can't stress enough that living abroad is not for everyone. Living in Costa Rica isn't for everyone either. Just make sure it is right for you to avoid a costly mistake unless like me you feel it's an adventure you just have to take

Another book to read is Insight Guide Costa Rica by Paul Murphy (Google the name, author, and you'll find several places to purchase it.).

Check out **http://www.therealcostarica.com/**, a blog site written by Tim Lytle who aims to tell it like it is.

APPENDIX B

Handy numbers and Links:

Keep in mind most numbers have eight (8) digits unlike 7 worldwide. The numbers are subject to change. Please notify me at helen@helendunnframe.com so I can publish updates.

To dial direct internationally: 00+country code +area code+number

To dial with assistance: 09+country code +area code+number

Emergency and access telephone numbers:

911 – Emergency – Local Collect Calls

1112 – Time of Day confirmation

1113 – Directory Assistance

1115 – ICE Phone and Internet Services

1116 – International Operator (Collect Calls)

1117 – Non-Emergency Police

1118 – Fire Department and Paramedics

1124 – International Information

1126 – Electrical Power Interruption

128 – Ambulance

1192 – National Parks Information

800-343-6332 – Bilingual Tourist Information

Airlines:

(Note: type www. before website address if it isn't automatically inserted for you.)

Airport Arrival Information: -- 2437-2626 – alterra.co.cr/fiws

Air Canada – 2441-8025 -- aircanada.com

Air France/KLM – 2220-4111 – airfrance.com

Alitalia – 2295 6820 – alitalia.com

American – 2248-9010 – aa.com

Copa – 2223-2672 – 2672 copaaiar.com

Cubana – 2221-6918 - cubana.cu

Delta – 2256-7993 --delta.com

Groupo Taca – 2299-8222 – taca.com

Iberia – 2431-5633 – iberia.com

Jet Blue -- 2241-6853 -- jetblue.com

Lufthansa – 2243-1818 – lufthansa.com

Martinair –2232-3246 – http://www.trycostarica.com/i/martinair

Mexicana Airlines – 2295-6969 -- mexicana.com

Nature Air – 2220-3054 -- natureair.com

Sansa Airlines– 2290-4100 – flysansa.com

Spirit Airlines -- 2293-4133 -- spiritair.com

United Airlines – 2442-6997 -- united.com

US Airways – 2520-0507 -- usaiarways.com

Bus/Taxi Lines

Airport Taxi – 2441-1319

Escazú Taxi – 2228-8051

Five Star Taxi – 2228-3159

Los Arcos Taxi de Aurora 2260-3050

Interbus – 2283-5573

Fantasy Tours/Gray Line – 2220-2126

Clubs:

American Legion Post 10 - 2228-0454 (Mel Goldberg)

ARNB or Bridge Club – Club House 2231-1097   or contact the Director: canachilsa@racsa.co.cr

Association of Residents of Costa Rica (ARCR) - 2233-8068 or 2221-2053 www.arcr.net Note that in the monthly magazine El Residente clubs are listed under the heading Club Corner.

Birding Club – 2282-**5365** - costaricabirding@hotmail.com

Casa Canada www.casacanada.org

Chess Club - 2284-0936

Democrats Abroad – 2279-3553 democratsabroad.org

Lions Club - 2221-0636

Little Theatre Group (LTG) 8858-1446 - littletheatregroup.org

Museums -- http://www.scribd.com/doc/141923606/Directorio-Museos-Costa-Rica   39 are in the country.

Newcomers Club (for women only) newcomerscr.org

PC Club - pcclub.net

Republicans Abroad - 2239-2262

Rotary Club - 2222-0993

Veterans of Foreign Wars Post 11207   wfw112072003@yahoo.com

Wine Club of Costa Rica 2279-8927   2257-2223

Women's Club of Costa Rica   WCCR now has a men's group wccr.org

Women's International League for Peace and Freedom   2433-7078 peacewomen@gmail.com

Young Expats of Costa Rica (under 40)   youngexpatsofcostarica.org

Embassies:

Belgium – 2225-6633

Canada – 2242-4400

China – 2291-4811

Columbia – 2283-6861

France – 2234-4167

Germany – 2296-6790

Great Britain – 2258-2025

Holland – 2296-1490

Israel – 2221-6444

Italy – 2234-2326

Japan – 2232-1255

Panama – 2280-1570

Spain – 2221-7005

Switzerland – 2221-4829

USA – 2219-2000

Medical Services:

Burn Center – 2257-0180

Calderón Guardia – 2212-1000

Clinica Biblica – 2522-1000

Clinica Católica – 2246-3000

Hospital CIMA Escazú – 2208-1000   Emergency CIMA – 2208-1143; 2208-1144

Hospital México – 2242-6700

Hospital de Niños – 2222-0122, Emergency – 2222-9635

Hospital San Juan Dios – 2257-6282

Poison Control Center – 2223-1028

Other Handy Numbers:

Alcoholics Anonymous (San Jose) 2222-1889

AYA (water) 2257-8822   Pipe breaks 800-737-6783

Air Ambulance Services -- SARPA-CR   **www.sarpacr.com**

Drug Control Police – 800-376-4266

INS Medical (Instituto Naciónal de Sequros, 2287-6006, 800-2835-3467, **www.ins-cr.com**

INS Traffic Accident Report – 800-800-8000

Locksmith: Seguridad Total Pacifico, the first locksmith shop on the Pacific Coast opened in 1999. Operated by Lee Swidler who began learning the business as a kid, and previously owned Sopris Security Systems in Carbondale, CO. he was a member of the American Society of Industrial Security (ASIS) for over 30 years. Read, "Jacó's Mr. Lee' is a Godsend to Motorist" at http://www.ticotimes.net/Opinion/Letters-to-the-Editor/Previous-Letters/Jaco-s-Mr.-Lee-is-A-Godsend-to-Motorist Phone (506) 2643-1248 Cell: (506) 8889-8113

Ombudsman (abuse or corruption) – 800-258-7474

Transit Police – 800-872-6748

Handy Links

http://groups.yahoo.com/groups. You can find Costa Rica living, Central Valley Living and Escazú News.

CHECK: ttp:**//groups.yahoo.com** _If you are not a yahoo member,_
you will have to sign up to use the links to groups.

Holidays in Costa Rica

_2013_	_2014 (if different)_

January 1 New Year's Day*

March 19 Saint Joseph's Day

March 28 Maundy Thursday *	April 17
March 29 Good Friday	April 18
March 31 Easter Sunday	April 20

April 11 Juan Santamaria Day*

May 1 Labor Day*

June Father's Day (the third Sunday)

July 25 Annexation of Guanacaste Province*

August 2 Virgin of Los Angeles Day

August 15 Mother's Day*

September 9 Children's Day

September 15 Independence Day*

October 12 Columbus Day - Discovery of America
(this holiday will be held the next Monday)

October 12 Limón Carnival

October 31 Día Nacional de la Mascarada / Halloween

November 2 Day of the Dead

December 8 Immaculate Conception

December 25 Christmas*

December 26 Horse Parade – Paseo Colon, 2nd Avenue, San Jose

December 25 to January 1.. Feria de Zapote. Town fair features rides, bull
chases, food stands, concerts, etc.

*Asterisks indicate paid holidays and days off for workers.

APPENDIX C

WHAT TO SHIP TO COSTA RICA

And How to Describe Boxes and Items

What you ship will depend on your lifestyle. When I lived in the casita for two weeks or so during an exploratory trip to Costa Rica, I noticed the limited lighting. In the little house, many recessed lights in the ceiling provided room lighting but when night encroached, reading was out of the question. Therefore, I shipped all my long loved lamps since I realized choices here appeared more limited. It proved an uphill learning curve to find where things are sold. For stuff on consignment that might help you in deciding what to ship, check out **www.facebook.com/fleamarketcr.rohrmoser**

As I enjoy cooking, I shipped just about all my pots and pans, small appliances, cutting boards, cooking utensils and cook books. I've since bought a few pots but to get decent equipment costs more in Costa Rica. Tips offers a lot of kitchen and restaurant stuff: 506-2543-2100, Website: .**http://www.tipscr.com/esp/index.php**   Map: **http://www.tipscr.com/esp/contactenos.php**

Mostly I sold antiques that I feared the tropical weather might destroy; I also sold expensive breakables because the ceramic tile used here extensively does not forgive when an item falls. However, I elected to bring my white dishes collected over the years rather buy new ones. Observe what you really can't live without.

As I expected smaller rooms, I sent smaller furniture pieces. Unless you know where you will live before packing, wisely leave massive pieces behind. However, send linens. I sent area rugs to soften the tile. Of course, memorabilia, books, music, a music center, TV, cherished decorative pieces and mirrors (that help the spaces appear larger) make good choices. I sent my Queen Size bed and a number of storage items as well as bookcases, printers, laptop computer (hand carried), office supplies (paper is dear here), items more costly in Costa Rica, and more.

Pack supplies not readily available here if you prefer them. For example, non-rust, non-scratch steel wool pads if you can find them (which I haven't been able to do lately. Rust can be a problem), favorite sponges (real sponges cost a lot and they don't last long here as a rule), foods like grits, cream of wheat, and sweet pickles (suddenly in 2013 Mt. Olive sweet gherkins appeared on the shelves at Auto Mercado.)

Here's how I listed my items in part to give you an idea of how to pack. Keep in mind I am a certified packer because I received training when I wrote an article for American Mayflower when I handled Public Relations for 17 franchised locations so nothing broke in transit.

Item or box	Description
Queen size mattress, box spring, frames	No head or foot board
Credenza	2 hats, 3 pillows inside
Stuffed living room chair	White (w/plastic cover)
Drop leaf table	Stained Dark Walnut
File cabinet	drawers with pillows
Ironing board	

Bookcases, 3 small wooden	2w/ area rugs
Drying rack for clothes	Black
Stepladder	Black/rose seat
Curtain rods	Variety
Coffee Table	Glass and metal
Hanging (4) and duffle (7) bags	Clothes
Trunk	Ornaments
Sewing machine	Portable

Stuffed tightly numbered boxes had only one or two items identifying the contents. Here are examples so you will understand what to do.

Box   Description

#1   Books

#2   Tools (regular and gardening packed in separate boxes)

#3   Paperwork   (Titled to hide office supplies)

#4   Files.

#5   Framed photos and prints

#6   Flatware and kitchen utensils

#7   TV

#8   Sewing supplies

#9   2 fans

#10   Games

#11   Dishes

#12   Pots and Pans

APPENDIX D

Finding Current Information

Joining chat groups like Costa Rica Living and Costa Rica Central Valley Living provide a way to share Cultural Activities, recommendations, suggestions, Q & A, almost all you need to know to live in the Costa Rica. Members share information about the Central Valley in Costa Rica (San Jose, Sabana, Rohrmoser, Pavas, Escazú, Santa Ana, Ciudad Colon, Puriscal, San Antonio de Belen, Cariari, Heredia, Santo Domingo de Heredia, Alajuela, La Gatita, San Pedro, Curridabat, Cartago, Moravia, Guadalupe, Tibas, San Cayetano, Desamparados, Atenas, Grecia, Palmares, and Sarchi etc.), usually in a positive way!

You might also like to read "Beside the Mango Tree" by Celia Coleman available on Amazon.

Some topics to search online for current information:

Airport + Airlines + Hotels+ Travel + Taxis

Banks

Books plus Office Supplies

Blogs & Groups about Costa Rica

Buses + car rental+ chauffeurs + taxis

Cable TV, Satellite TV, Internet Cable service

Cars: shopping for one

Children Activities

Consul and Embassies in Costa Rica

Costa Rica Consul & Embassies Worldwide

Costa Rica Government links

Exchange rate

Gyms

Health: Hospitals, Laboratories, Medicines and Medical

Hostels & Backpackers

Hotels in Central Valley Maps also see Photos section

Links to culture + theater + movies

Private Clubs, Country Clubs

Restaurants by Location

Restaurants by style

Sports

Schools

Shopping Malls, Supermarkets, Furniture, and more

Universities & Colleges

Weather Costa Rica

APPENDIX E

Retaining an Attorney in Costa Rica

The following guidelines (provided by the U.S. Embassy in 2009) may assist you in protecting your interests when retaining the services of a Costa Rican attorney, with reference to a private party dispute, a domestic relations dispute, or a small commercial transaction. (Note: The Embassy maintains a list of bilingual attorneys but take them with several grains of salt because an attorney may request being on the list.)

Selecting an Attorney

Contact several attorneys, briefly describing the nature of the services you desire. Most Costa Rican attorneys do not charge for the initial consultation. The list of attorneys contains some guidance as to the specialties of each of the attorneys, which may allow you to narrow your choices. The Costa Rican Bar Association (Colegio de Abogados) publishes a schedule of Minimum Fees, which attorneys in Costa Rica can charge. Realize that depending on the complexities of the case, the expertise of the attorney, and other factors may result in substantially higher fees than the ones contained in the official schedule.

In any case, before you decide which attorney to retain, determine whether the attorney is fluent in English and ask for a written estimate of his fees, including a detailed description of the services. Do not pay until you are satisfied that your attorney understands your case and is willing to handle it. Always ask for a receipt signed by your attorney.

Notaries Public

In Costa Rica a Notary Public has to be an attorney. As a matter of fact, in many instances attorneys' and notaries' public functions intertwine. That means that your attorney can draft instruments, wills and conveyances, and later acknowledge the authenticity of those documents. He/she can also witness your identity and legal capacity to sign them.

Assistance of the Consular Section of the U.S. Embassy at San Jose

Should your association with a Costa Rican attorney prove unsatisfactory, a U.S. Consular Office may, if requested, contact the attorney to facilitate communication. In addition, repetitive complaints against an attorney who appears on the Consular Section's List of Attorneys may result in the removal of the name from the list. If you have a complaint against an attorney on the list, please notify the Consular Section immediately, at 2519-2000, extension 2453. The Consular Section can also advise you how to file a complaint with the local bar association, including complaints about fees.

American attorneys cannot represent your interests in Costa Rica except through local counsel. American attorneys experienced in international law may help in explaining the complex international issues involved in your case. Some American attorneys may have associates, partners, or correspondents in Costa Rica to whom they can refer you.

Free Legal Aid in Costa Rica

No free legal aid associations exist in Costa Rica. Most Costa Rican attorneys do little, if any, *pro-bono* work. However, the University of Costa Rica's law school (Facultad de Derecho) sponsors a program called Consultorios Jurídicos. Consultorios Juridícos are legal-aid offices staffed by law students and supervised by a resident attorney. These offices handle small labor disputes, certain domestic relations cases, and a few other civil cases. These offices do not handle commercial transactions, immigration, or criminal matters. Remember that if you decide to take your case to a Consultorio Jurídico, a law student, not an attorney, will handle your case and he/she may not speak English. For more information about Consultorios Jurídicos you may contact the University of Costa Rica's Law School at the following number during office hours: 2207-4114.

The Costa Rican Judiciary provides free defense counsel for criminal matters. These public defenders, typically young attorneys who carry heavy caseloads, rarely have the time to provide personal attention to any single case.

How to Deal with Your Costa Rican Attorney

Find out the attorney's qualifications and experience.

Find out how the attorney plans to represent you. Ask specific questions and expect the attorney to explain legal matters in a language that you can understand. Ask what fees the attorney charges, and in what manner he/she expects payment. Some attorneys expect advance payment, while others demand a deposit before taking action, and still others prefer installments tied to the actions taken. Some attorneys will take some cases on a percentage basis.

Ask your attorney to keep you informed of the progress of your case, preferably in writing, according to a pre-established schedule. Court cases in Costa Rican can take months, even years before resolution. Therefore, you may wish the attorney to send you monthly reports, even though no real developments have ensued, simply to satisfy your wish to track the progress of the case.

Have your attorney analyze your case, giving you the positive and negative aspects and both possible and probable outcomes.

Do not expect your attorney to give a simple answer to a complex legal problem. Be sure that you understand the technical language in any contract or other legal document prepared by your attorney before you sign it. If your attorney acts as a Notary Public, make sure that he/she states in whatever public instrument he/she drafts for you that he/she has translated the instrument into English because of your inability to understand Spanish. This statement may safeguard your interests in case your attorney commits an error in translation.

Keep your attorney fully informed of any new developments in the case.

If you need to provide complex or technical documents to your attorney, you may wish to consider having the documents translated into the native language. Remember, an elementary knowledge of English may not enable the attorney to understand the documents you provide. Be honest with your attorney. Tell the attorney every relevant fact in order to get the best representation for your interests.

Find out how much time the attorney estimates the case may take to complete.

NOTE: In Costa Rica, half the Judiciary recesses in January and the other half in February. Consider these recesses if you expect a case to begin or end at the beginning of the year. Currency control laws may delay or make it impossible to transfer funds back to the United States once the case is resolved. Discuss this issue with the attorney if it is relevant.

If you decide to change attorneys in the middle of a case, you must obtain a statement from your original attorney that no fees are owed and the date in which he/she separated from the case.

Request copies of all letters and documents prepared on your behalf. Should you decide to change attorneys, request your file before you make the final payment to your attorney.

Complaints against a Costa Rican Attorney

If the services of your Costa Rican attorney prove unsatisfactory, in addition to notifying the Consular Section of the U.S. Embassy at San Jose, you may address your complaints to the local bar association: Colegio de Abogados, Zapote, Costa Rica. Attn: Fiscalia, Telephone Number 2283-0920, 2283-0586 or 2253- 1947.

Attorneys do not have to be notaries to practice law in Costa Rica, but all notaries must be attorneys. All attorneys must belong to the

Colegio de Abogados, Costa Rica's bar association, and notaries must register with the Dirección Naciónal de Notariado that is part of the court system.

File complaints against lawyers with the Colegio de Abogados. File complaints against notaries with the Dirección Naciónal de Notariado.

To check whether a particular lawyer received discipline or suspension, go to http://www.abogados.or.cr. Under "Buscador" (Search box) write "Suspendidos" and at the new page you get, click on "Suspensiones disciplinarias" (disciplinary suspensions). You can now search by name (BUSQUEDA POR NOMBRE), by carné (BÚSQUEDA POR CARNE), or you can click on "Ver lista completa" to see the entire list.

INDEX

344

T

U

V

W

XYZ

Made in the USA
Middletown, DE
24 October 2016